LIVING THE DREAM

FROM COCKLES FIELD TO THE MILLENNIUM STADIUM

An official Bolton Wanderers Football Club publication

DEAN HAYES

Foreword by Sam Allardyce

LIVING THE DREAM -
FROM COCKLES FIELD TO THE MILLENNIUM STADIUM
by Dean Hayes
Published by 90 Minutes Publications, Darwen
Text copyright © Dean Hayes 2004
Designed & Printed in the UK by Mercer Print, Accrington.
Photographs by Action Images, Dean Hayes, Laurence Flanigan and Tom Hall.
(compiled by Mercer Print / 90 Minutes Publications).
ISBN 0-9546251-1-0

FOREWORD
by Sam Allardyce

I found this book utterly fascinating. Not just because it covers the Club right up until the Carling Cup Final - which of course we unfortunately lost - but because it includes tons and tons of information from the early days at Cockles Field to recent times in the Premiership here at the Reebok.

Dean Hayes is I know, a lifelong Bolton fan, and whilst he has written books about other clubs, his passion for his hometown club is all too apparent.

As you know I am a very busy man, and the best thing about this book for me, is that you can pick it up at any time and dip into it. It is a great read and very, very informative. I can thoroughly endorse it.

FA CUP FINAL 1958
Nat Lofthouse with the trophy after beating Manchester United.

JANUARY 1st

1891 In the friendly match against Nottingham Forest, when the Wanderers won 3-0, goal nets were used for the first time, albeit for one half. They had been invented by an engineer named Brodie, who later helped design and build the first dual carriageway in the country in his home town of Liverpool.

1895 Charlie Henderson scored four of Bolton's goals in a 6-0 demolition of Derby County.

1910 Bolton were 3-0 up after the half-hour mark in their home game with Notts County, but after injuries to Greenhalgh and Owen left them with nine men, the Meadow Lane club came from behind to win 4-3!

1926 Bolton beat Birmingham 5-3 with John Reid Smith netting a hat-trick. Wanderers' other scorers were David Jack and Ted Vizard.

1930 Huddersfield Town were beaten 7-1 in front of a Burnden Park crowd of 27,355 with winger Billy Butler scoring a hat-trick.

1938 Bolton goalkeeper Fred Swift received a £50 bribe to concede two goals at Brentford. He handed it straightaway to his manager Charlie Foweraker who advised the Football League, but no action was taken - the game ended all-square at 1-1.

1979 Peter Reid, who had only just recovered from a pre-season injury, damaged his knee ligaments in a collision with Everton and Scotland goalkeeper George Wood. The conditions at Burnden Park were atrocious with a layer of heavy snow covering the pitch. It came as no surprise when at half-time, the referee abandoned the game. Unfortunately, it came too late for Peter Reid who was forced to miss the rest of the season.

JANUARY 2nd

1900 Tom McAteer scored a hat-trick for the Wanderers in a 5-0 home win over Port Vale.

1904 Four years later and the same visitors were beaten by an identical scoreline but this time the Wanderers' scorers against a sorry Port Vale side were David Stokes, Billy Yenson, Sam Marsh, Sam Greenhalgh and Bob Taylor.

1922 David Jack scored a quickfire hat-trick in Bolton's 5-1 home defeat of local rivals Oldham Athletic.

1923 Bolton beat Nottingham Forest 4-2 with Joe Smith scoring all four of the Wanderers' goals,

1935 In a game postponed from New Year's Day, Jack Milsom scored four of Bolton's goals in a 7-0 victory over Burnley.

JANUARY 3rd

1914 The Wanderers easily beat Manchester United 6-1 with Joe Smith scoring four of the goals - his first hat-trick for the club.

1953 Because of injuries, John Wheeler was moved from his usual wing-half position to centre forward for the match against Blackpool. Wearing the No. 9 shirt for the first time, he netted a superb hat-trick for the Wanderers in a 4-0 win.

1957 Birth of Barry Cowdrill. He began his career as a winger with Sutton Coldfield Town before joining West Bromwich Albion where they converted him into a pacy full-back. During his early days at the Hawthorns, his first team appearances were restricted due to the form of England defender Derek Statham. After a loan spell with Rotherham United, he joined the Wanderers for the start of the 1988-89 season. His first campaign ended with a Wembley appearance in the 4-1 Sherpa Van Trophy Final victory over Torquay United. During the course of that season, Cowdrill, who was voted the club's 'Player of the Year' scored his first-ever league goal in a 3-1 home win over Leyton Orient. He went on to help the Wanderers reach the play-offs in both 1990 and 1991 before losing his place to David Burke. He had scored six goals in 160 League and Cup games before joining Rochdale where he ended his league career. He later rejoined his first club Sutton Coldfield and returned with them to Burnden for an FA Cup tie.

Though the Wanderers won 2-1, the biggest cheer of the day was reserved for the popular Cowdrill.

JANUARY 4th

1896   Billy Joyce became the first Bolton player to sustain a serious injury at Burnden Park when in scoring one of the goals in a 4-0 defeat of Wolves, he broke his right leg. Despite being out of the game for over a year, he still ended the 1895-96 season as the club's leading scorer with 12 goals.

1902   James McKie netted a treble in Bolton's 4-0 home victory over Small Heath.

1964   Bolton were drawn away to FA Cup giantkillers Bath City in the third round of the competition. The club's blushes were spared when after the Southern League side had taken the lead in the 78th minute, Francis Lee equalised from the spot. For the record, the Wanderers won the replay 3-0.

JANUARY 5th

1918   Tom Buchan, who wore eight different numbered shirts during this wartime season of 1917-18, including a game in goal as Bolton won 3-2 at

Stockport, netted a fine hat-trick in a 5-2 home win over Blackburn Rovers.

JANUARY 6th

1917   Bolton were beaten 7-0 at Stoke in the Lancashire Section Principal Competition.

1974   History was made when the Wanderers entertained Stoke City in the third round of the FA Cup on a Sunday. The club became one of the pioneers for Sunday football and in this game, the highest crowd of the season, 39,138 turned up to see John Byrom net a hat-trick in a 3-2 win.

JANUARY 7th

1928   David Jack, George Gibson and Joe Smith scored two goals apiece as the Wanderers beat neighbours Blackburn Rovers 6-1 at Ewood Park.

1961   In what was the Wanderers' first-ever Football League Cup game, Dennis Stevens scored the only goal as Bolton won 1-0 at Hull City.

JANUARY 8th

1927   John Reid Smith scored a quickfire treble as Bolton beat Blackpool 3-1 at Bloomfield Road in the third round of the FA Cup.

1960   Birth of Robbie Savage. The Liverpool-born midfielder went down in Wanderers' folklore when he scored the winning goal at Wrexham in May 1988 that took the club out of the League's basement at the first attempt. After beginning his career as an apprentice with Liverpool, he had a loan spell with Wrexham where he was not only voted their 'Player of the Year' but was also their top-scorer. He then had a spell with Stoke City but after just a handful of games for the Potters he moved to Bournemouth. A regular in the south coast club's side, he helped the Cherries beat

Manchester United in the FA Cup before winning an Associate Members Cup medal when Bournemouth beat Hull City in the final. His next port of call was Bradford City before he joined the Wanderers in September 1987. In his first season with the club, three of his five goals came in the final three games of that promotion winning season whilst in 1988-89 he was an integral member of the Bolton side that won the Sherpa Van Trophy at Wembley. Early the following season he tore groin and stomach muscles and though he fought his way back to full fitness, he broke a leg against Preston North End that was to end his career. Savage, who had scored 13 goals in 102 games for the Wanderers, was awarded a joint testimonial with Frank Worthington in November 1992.

JANUARY 9th

1902 Birth of Bob Jones. The Liverpool-born goalkeeper began his Football League career with Everton but being unable to win a regular place in the Goodison club's side, he joined Southport. He arrived at Burnden Park in March 1929 and after making his debut in a 3-1 defeat at Birmingham, went on to miss very few matches over the next few seasons. Ever-present in 1931- 32, he had appeared in 77 consecutive league games when he was laid low by appendicitis.
In 1934-35, Jones was in outstanding form as the Wanderers won promotion to the First Division and reached the FA Cup semi-finals where they lost 2-0 to West Bromwich Albion after a replay. Jones went on to appear in 244 games for Bolton before moving to Cardiff City. Just before the outbreak of the Second World War, he returned to Haig Avenue as Southport's assistant-trainer and after the hostilities spent eight seasons as the Sandgrounder's first team trainer.

1926 Wanderers' third round FA Cup tie at Accrington

Stanley was switched to Burnden Park in the interests of safety. Bolton had Ted Vizard sent off for dangerous play and only sneaked home, courtesy of a late goal by David Jack.

JANUARY 10th

1870 Birth of James Munro. The Scotsman who hailed from Dundee began his career with local club Dundee Strathmore before joining Bolton in the summer of 1890. He went straight into the Wanderers' side replacing fellow-Scotsman James McNee who moved to inside-right. Munro scored twice on his debut as the Wanderers beat Notts County 4-2 and at the age of 21 was the youngest member of the club's Lancashire Cup winning side of 1891. The following year he sustained an injury that forced him to miss much of the season and when he did return to the side, it was discovered that he had lost much of his old magic. Munro, who had scored 21 goals in 52 games joined Burton Swifts before moving on to Swindon Town. Immediately appointed captain of the Robins, he won representative honours with the Southern League XI but after contracting what was thought to be a cold, he died at the age of 28 with the cause of death being spiral meningitis.

JANUARY 11th

1908 Non-League Woking were beaten 5-0 at Burnden Park in the first round of the FA Cup. The Wanderers forwards - Kilty Cameron, David Stokes, Jackie Owen, Walter White and Marshall McEwan scored a goal each.

1941 George Hunt scored four of Bolton's goals in the 5-3 extra-time win at Oldham Athletic.

JANUARY 12th

1889 Alec Barbour scored twice for the Wanderers on

their visit to Aston Villa but the Whites lost 6-2 to a side who ended the season as runners-up to double winners Preston North End.

1951 Birth of Peter Nicholson *(left)*. One of Bolton Wanderers' greatest utility players, he began his career with Carlisle United before joining Blackpool. It was from the Bloomfield Road club that the popular player made the move to the Wanderers, making his debut in a 2-2 draw at Oldham Athletic on the opening day of the 1971-72 season.

Though he made the majority of his appearances at right-back, he went on to wear all the different numbered outfield shirts in 11 seasons at Burnden Park. He won a Third Division Championship medal in 1972-73 when he scored in each of the last three games of the season and a Second Division Championship medal in 1977-78. Nicholson more than held his own in the top flight and went on to score 14 goals in 370 League and Cup games before leaving the Wanderers in May 1982 to join Rochdale. He later ended his career with Carlisle United before returning to Burnden Park to help out with commercial activities.

2000 Bolton entertained Tranmere Rovers at the Reebok Stadium in the League Cup semi-final first-leg and though they dominated the game for much of the 90 minutes, it was the Wirral based club who scored the only goal of the game in front of a crowd of 13,303.

JANUARY 13th

1968 Birth of Mike Whitlow. Rejected by the Wanderers without making a League appearance, he drifted into non-League football and was working as a labourer whist playing for Witton Albion when Leeds United signed him in November 1988. At Elland Road, he was treated as something of a utility player before settling into the No.3 berth and just failed to make sufficient appearances in their 1993 Championship side to gain a medal. In March 1993 he moved to Leicester City for a fee of £250,000 and was the only ever-present in the Foxes' three-year nine-game series of play-off ties. Settling in well in the Premiership, he won a League Cup winners' medal with the then Filbert Street club before joining the Wanderers for £500,000 in September 1997. A solid and dependable defender, he played most of his early games for the club at left-back despite the presence of Robbie Elliott and Jimmy Phillips but also played at centre-back when required. Injuries disrupted his progress at the Reebok until in 2001-02 he formed a most effective central defensive pairing with Gudni Bergsson that frustrated some of the finest strikers in the Premiership. Despite a persistent groin injury, Mike Whitlow, who was one of the club's most committed contributors to off-field activities, went on to play in 163 games for the club. His contract was not renewed last summer. He later signed for Sheffield United.

JANUARY 14th

1882 Bolton Wanderers recorded one of their pre-League highest scores when beating Great Lever 11-1.

1895 James Cassidy and Arthur Spence scored two goals apiece as the Wanderers beat Sheffield United 6-2. Bolton's other scorers were Alex Paton and Robert Tannahill.

1933 The Wanderers recorded their best away victory in the FA Cup when they beat Charlton Athletic 5-1 at The Valley. The Wanderers' scorers were Cook (2), T.Griffiths, Milsom and Gibson.

1978 During the club's promotion-winning season of 1977-78, the Wanderers travelled to Bramall Lane to play Sheffield United. In a superb display of attacking football, the Whites came away with a 5-1 victory. The pick of the goals was a superb strike by Peter Nicholson - the other scorers were Reid, Worthington, Greaves (penalty) and Whatmore.

JANUARY 15th

1895 The Limited Liability Company was incorporated and registered as Bolton Wanderers Football and Athletic Company Limited under company registration number 43026.

1938 Ray Westwood hit all Bolton's goals in a 3-1 home defeat of Grimsby Town.

1970 Birth of Scott Green. Although he arrived at Burnden Park as a midfielder, he became something of a versatile player in his seven seasons with the club. He started out with Derby County but on being unable to win a place in the Rams' League side he went on loan to Finnish side Auran Pallo where he scored 24 goals in 16 games. Bolton manager Phil Neal paid the Rams £50,000 for Green's services in March 1990 and has it was subsequently proved, the Walsall-born player was a bargain buy. He made a Wembley appearance in the 1991 play-off final against Tranmere Rovers whilst in February 1992 he came off the bench to score an equalising goal four minutes from time in the Wanderers fifth round FA Cup tie against Southampton. After playing a number of games up front he switched to full-back, helping the club to promotion in 1994-95 and playing in the Coca Cola Cup Final defeat by Liverpool. Green went on to score 31 goals in 286 games for the Wanderers - 65 of those appearances were as a substitute - a club record. In June 1997 he joined Wigan Athletic for a fee of £300,000 and became an important member of the Latics' side. He helped them win the Autowindscreen Shield at Wembley in

1999 and the Second Division Championship in 2003. Having played in 249 games for Bolton, he joined Wrexham on a free transfer.

1983 Wanderers' goalkeeper Jim McDonagh's long clearance from his own penalty area, sailed over the head of Burnley's No.1 Billy O'Rourke during a 3-0 home win over the Clarets.

JANUARY 16th

1892 The Wanderers lost 2-1 at Sheffield Wednesday's Owlerton Ground in an FA Cup first round tie but then protested that the ground was unfit.
The FA ordered a replay but this time the Owls won 4-1!

1924 David Jack and John Reid Smith scored two goals apiece in Bolton's 4-0 FA Cup first round replay win over Hull City.

1943 George Hunt scored four of Bolton's goals including two from the penalty spot in a 5-0 win over Oldham Athletic in a wartime league game.

1967 Birth of Stuart Storer. After just one appearance for Mansfield Town, the pacy winger drifted into non-League football with VS Rugby before Birmingham City gave him the chance to resurrect his League career. After just a handful of appearances for the St Andrew's club, he joined Everton but after being unable to break into the Merseyside club's first team, he joined Wigan Athletic on loan before moving to the Wanderers in December 1987. After playing in a goalless draw at Hartlepool United, he scored on his home debut as the Wanderers beat Stockport County 2-1. He made an appearance in the Sherpa Van Trophy Final win over Torquay United when he came on as a substitute for Jeff Chandler in the 4-1 win. However, it was the following season before he won a regular place in the Bolton side and in 1991 made another

Wembley appearance in the play-off final defeat by Tranmere Rovers. He went on to score 15 goals in 165 League and Cup games before joining Exeter City. He later ended his first-class career with Brighton and Hove Albion and in the last game of the 1996-97 season, he scored the vital winner against Doncaster Rovers, thus preventing the Seagulls' losing their Football League status. He then underwent a hernia operation but on his return, he found his pace reduced and so after appearing in 161 games for the south coast club, he moved into non-League football with Atherstone United.

1971 Under the managership of Nat Lofthouse, the Wanderers fielded their youngest-ever side for the home game against Sheffield United. The average age of the side, which included seven teenagers, was 20 and though they fell behind to a first-minute goal by the Blades' John Tudor, they fought back to win 2-1 with goals from Ian Seddon and Paul Fletcher - it was the club's last win of the season!

JANUARY 17th

1884 Bolton's game against Blackpool at Raikes Hall was abandoned after just 15 minutes with the game goalless after Wanderers' player Tom Howarth broke a leg.

1903 During the Wanderers' relegation season of 1902-03, it took the club 23 matches to record their first victory - a 3-1 defeat of Notts County! They had drawn three and lost 19 of their opening 22 matches!

1940 Birth of Freddie Hill. The midfield maestro turned down an offer from his home-town club Sheffield Wednesday in the hope of first team football with the Wanderers.
He made his Bolton debut as a replacement for the prolific Dennis Stevens in a 1-1 home draw

against Newcastle United in April 1958.
When Nat Lofthouse retired, Stevens moved to centre-forward on a permanent basis to accommodate Freddie Hill at inside-left. Hill responded by scoring his first hat-trick for the club in a 6-0 mauling of Chelsea. Hill had only played in three seasons of League football when he was chosen for the England Under 23 side and in October 1962 he made the first of his two full international appearances against Northern Ireland in Belfast. Hill's second trick in Wanderers' colours came in March 1963 as Bolton beat Sheffield United 3-2 - the club's first home game for three months after one of the worst winters on record. He went on to score 79 goals in 412 League and Cup games for the club before leaving Burnden Park in the summer of 1969 to join Halifax Town. He had almost signed for Liverpool during the height of his career but failed a medical owing to high blood pressure. He later played for Manchester City before ending his career with Peterborough United.

JANUARY 18th

1890 Davie Weir scored four of Bolton's goals in a 10-2 FA Cup first round win over Belfast Distillery.

1902 Goalkeeper James Sutcliffe became the first Bolton player to be sent-off at Burnden Park as the Wanderers beat Sheffield Wednesday 3-1. He received his marching orders for bad language directed at the referee after he had allowed a goal he claimed did not cross the line.

1975 John Byrom and Stuart Lee scored two goals apiece in a 5-1 home win over Bristol Rovers. Wanderers other scorer was Scottish international Hugh Curran.

1977 A goal two minutes from time by Neil Whatmore gave Bolton a 1-1 draw at Everton in the League

Cup semi-final first leg. Confidence was high that the Wanderers would reach the Wembley final but a Bob Latchford goal gave the Toffees a 1-0 victory in the return leg.

JANUARY 19th

1936 Birth of Ray Parry *(below)*. When the Derby-born forward made his first team debut for Bolton against Wolves on 13 October 1951, he became the youngest player in First Division history at 15 years 267 days. He was only given two outings that season before settling into the side at inside-left. One of a famous footballing family, Ray Parry developed into a player who could pass the ball with great accuracy and yet could strike it with great power.

Parry was the scorer of some vital goals, perhaps none more so than the one against Wolves in the FA Cup sixth round tie of 1958. A member of that season's FA Cup winning side, he also won two full international caps for England, scoring in a 2-1 win over Northern Ireland on his international debut.

Ray Parry had scored 79 goals in 299 League and Cup games for the Wanderers when in October 1960 he was transferred to Blackpool for a fee of £25,000. After four years at Bloomfield Road where he scored 32 goals in 146 first team outings, he moved to Bury where he made his debut against Bolton. He remained with the Shakers until 1972 before ending his playing career with non-League New Brighton.

JANUARY 20th

1910 Will Settle was appointed manager of the club. He had replaced his father Miles Settle JP on the board of the Wanderers in 1899 and served in that capacity until his appointment as Bolton's manager in place of John Somerville. Settle was unable to prevent the Wanderers' relegation in his first season with the club but in 1910-11, with the help of trainers George Eccles and Peter Bullough, he steered the club to promotion back to the top flight at the first attempt.

It was Settle who developed the great left-wing pairing of Joe Smith and Ted Vizard and brought many other fine players to Burnden Park including Alf Bentley, Jimmy Fay, Alex Donaldson, Bob Glendenning and Jimmy Seddon. On Christmas Eve 1912 he sold Tom Barber to Aston Villa, the profits paying for the new roofing to the Great Lever Stand. In 1911-12, the Wanderers finished fourth in Division One, sixth in 1913-14 and in 1914-15, they reached the FA Cup semi-finals. Then wartime football replaced the League and Cup competitions and in 1915 after finding certain responsibilities had been taken away from

him, he left the club under something of a cloud after 17 years' service.

1934 Birth of Billy McAdams. His performances for Irish League side Distillery prompted Manchester City to sign him in December 1953 and he was a regular marksman for the Maine Road club - scoring a hat-trick against Bradford City on only his second appearance. Injuries hampered his early years with City and he failed to make the starting line-ups for both the 1955 and 1956 FA Cup Finals. His best season for City in terms of goals scored was 1959-60 when he found the net 21 times in 31 games. He had scored 65 goals in 134 games when in September 1960 he was transferred to the Wanderers. In his first season at Burnden Park, the Northern Ireland international, who scored twice on his debut in a 4-1 defeat of Chelsea, scored 18 goals in 27 games. He went on to score 29 goals in 52 games for the Wanderers before being sold to Leeds United. Whilst at Elland Road, McAdams, who once scored a hat-trick for Northern Ireland against West Germany in a World Cup qualifier, made the last of his 15 appearances for his country. He later won a Fourth Division Championship medal with Brentford before seeing out his career with spells at Queen's Park Rangers and Barrow where he continued to score goals.

1965 Birth of Warren Joyce. The son of Walter Joyce who played for Burnley, Blackburn Rovers and Oldham Athletic, he made his Bolton debut as a substitute at Carlisle United in April 1983 before establishing himself as a first team regular in 1983-84. He was a virtual ever-present in the Wanderers side until 1986 when injury kept him out of the Bolton side, forcing him to miss the Freight Rovers Trophy Final against Bristol City. After the Wanderers' relegation to the Fourth Division in 1987, Joyce, who had scored 21 goals in 221 League and Cup games, joined Preston North End for a fee of £35,000. He helped the

Deepdale club to the play-offs in 1989 but after scoring 44 goals in 210 games, left to sign for Plymouth Argyle for £160,000. Unable to settle on the south coast, he left Home Park and returned to the north-west and joined Burnley. The tenacious midfielder made 90 appearances for the Clarets before signing for Hull City where his wholehearted performances led to him sweeping the board with the club's Player of the Year awards. Later appointed the club's player-manager he was instrumental in the Tigers' retaining their Football League status.

JANUARY 21st

1899 Despite being relegated at the end of this season, the Wanderers beat high-flying Sunderland 6-1 with Archie Gilligan and Bob Brown scoring two goals apiece. Bolton's other scorers were Tom Barlow and George Barnes.

1922 Bolton, who were without six first team regulars including Dick Pym, David Jack, Joe Smith and Ted Vizard, lost 2-0 at home to Chelsea.
To make matters worse, Wanderers' Tom Buchan was sent-off!

1925 The Wanderers won the Lancashire Cup Final by beating Blackpool 2-1 at Burnden Park. The winning goal scored by Harry Nuttall came as the referee put his whistle to his lips to blow for full-time.

1957 Birth of Dave Sutton. Though he was born in Tarleton, Dave Sutton began his career with Plymouth Argyle but following the Pilgrims' relegation to the Third Division, he had a loan spell with Reading before joining Huddersfield Town. In 1979-80 he was ever-present as the Terriers won the Fourth Division Championship and though he was forced to miss the whole of his last season at Leeds Road after breaking his leg at Manchester City, he had scored 15 goals in 284 games for the Yorkshire club when he joined the Wanderers for £15,000 in the summer of 1985. Immediately appointed club captain, Sutton led the Wanderers to Wembley in the Freight Rover Trophy. After Bolton was relegated to the Fourth Division in 1987, the popular centre-half played his part in helping them win promotion a year later. In July 1988, after appearing in 119 first team games for the Wanderers, he was given a free transfer and joined Rochdale as player-coach, later becoming the Spotland club's caretaker manager.

2004 Sam Allardyce hailed Jay-Jay Okocha's wonder strike as the "goal of the season" after the Wanderers put themselves within 90 minutes of a place in the Carling Cup Final with a 5-2 semi final first-leg defeat of Aston Villa. Simply outstanding, the Nigerian did everything he could to ensure that his first date with Bolton when he returns from African Nations duty will be in Cardiff.
Okocha was magical and it was clear to see after just two minutes of play that he was ready to give the send-off his manager demanded when he curled a wonderful free-kick into the only place Sorensen and his defence could not protect. Moments later, Kevin Nolan bulldozed his way through a series of flimsy tackles before sweeping a shot across Sorensen. Only 16 minutes had been played when Stelios made it 3-0 with an acrobatic volley.
Within three minutes, Villa had reduced the arrears when Juan Pablo Angel hoisted a shot over Jussi Jaaskelainen from the touchline. Villa's second goal early after the restart was lucky to stand as Angel stood in an offside position when turning Vassell's toe-poke past Jaaskelainen. The Wanderers soaked up the Villa pressure before Bruno N'Gotty rose unchallenged to head Youri Djorkaeff's corner past Hendrie on the line. Then, with 10 minutes remaining Okocha scored his wonder goal, unleashing another free-kick

past a bewildered Sorensen. So powerfully was the ball struck, that it threatened to burst the net!

JANUARY 22nd

1936 George T Taylor scored all Bolton's goals in a 3-3 draw against Everton at Goodison Park - the Wanderers' winger was an ever-present but only scored a total of seven goals.

1968 Birth of Mark Winstanley. The defender was offered a YTS place at Burnden and was still a trainee when he made his first team debut at Bournemouth in March 1986. Following two seasons on the fringe of first team football, he claimed a regular place in the Wanderers' defence in 1988-89 and scored three goals in the club's run to the Sherpa Van Trophy Final. The most crucial of these was without doubt, the last-gasp equaliser in the second round tie against Wrexham which took the tie into extra-time. He then headed home a second to help win the match. The Wanderers reached the Third Division play-offs in 1990 where they were beaten by Notts County and though they went one better in the play-off finals of 1991, injury cost 'Beef' his place in the side. He was a regular in the Wanderers' side that achieved promotion from the new Second Division in 1992-93 as runners-up to Stoke City and was prominent in the club's run to the fifth round of the FA Cup. However, he was not an automatic choice in 1993-94 and at the end of that season in which he took his total of appearances for Bolton to 285, he joined Burnley for £150,000. His vast experience was a great help to a young Clarets' side and he went on to make 182 appearances before following a loan spell with Shrewsbury Town, he joined Preston North End. He left Deepdale without making a first team appearance to rejoin Shrewsbury before ending his league career with Carlisle United. Mark is now playing non-League football for Southport.

JANUARY 23rd

1892 Bolton's game against Sheffield Wednesday at Owlerton a week earlier, which they lost 2-1, was scratched from the records after the Wanderers appealed that the ground was unfit. In the replayed match, Wednesday won 4-1, this after the Wanderers had taken the lead.

1985 Rugby League came to Burnden Park when Swinton took on the Sheffield Eagles in a Second Division fixture. The game started twenty minutes late after Sheffield's coach had broken down crossing the Pennines. A blizzard shortly before kick-off kept the attendance to just 1,438 but they saw an open game of rugby with Swinton winning 14-8.

JANUARY 24th

1891 Alec Barbour became the first Bolton player to be sent-off in the FA Cup in a 5-1 defeat against Accrington. He was dismissed for 'wilfully kicking an opponent'.

1917 Birth of Lol Hamlett. Though he joined the Wanderers from non-League Congleton Town in the summer of 1938, it wasn't until January 1944 that he made his first appearance for the club. Originally signed as a full-back, he settled into the side at centre-half and ended his first season with an appearance in the Lancashire Cup Final, the Wanderers losing 6-3 on aggregate to Liverpool. In 1944-45 he was ever-present as Bolton won the Football League North War Cup and won the North v South Final against Chelsea. In that match, Hamlett scored one of Bolton's goals from the penalty-spot in the 2-1 win. He was a member of the Bolton side that finished third in the Football League North and reached the FA Cup semi-final in 1946 and was again ever-present when League football resumed in 1946-47.

score some vital goals to keep the Wanderers in Division Two but after scoring 20 goals in 81 games, he joined Lincoln City on loan prior to a permanent move to Blackburn Rovers. At Ewood Park, Thompson reverted to a striking role and in 1984-85 when the club just missed out on promotion, he was the leading scorer with 15 goals. After suffering a spate of niggling injuries, Thompson joined Wigan Athletic and in only his fourth game for the Latics, netted a hat trick in a 5-1 win over his home-town team Walsall. Again injuries hampered his progress and he was soon on the move again, this time to Blackpool. After just one season with the Seasiders, Thompson *(below)* had a brief spell with Cardiff City before ending his career with Walsall.

Following the emergence of Jack Atkinson at centre-half, Hamlett *(above)* reverted to his original position of full-back but then after scoring nine goals in 85 League and Cup games, plus appearing in 97 wartime games, he left to end his career with Port Vale, for whom he made a further 109 appearances.

1960 Birth of Chris Thompson. An England youth international, he made his Wanderers debut in a League Cup tie against Peterborough United before being blooded in the club's last season of First Division football in 1979-80. Switched from forward to midfield, Thompson continued to

1993   The first big screen telecast of a Bolton away game was transmitted to Burnden Park. A crowd of 5,000 saw pictures from the FA Cup fourth round tie at Molineux against Wolverhampton Wanderers which Bolton won 2-0 with goals from Scott Green and John McGinlay.

JANUARY 25th

1941   In the wartime fixture against Manchester United at Old Traffiord, the Wanderers had to take to the field with just 10 men after goalkeeper Ron Bolton had got lost on the way to the ground. Harry Goslin went in goal and United scored in under a minute! The errant keeper turned up shortly afterwards and went on to give an outstanding display in a 4-1 defeat.

1997   Welsh international centre-forward Nathan Blake scored twice in Bolton's 6-2 FA Cup third round replay win over Luton Town. The Whites' other scorers were McGinlay, Thompson, Pollock and Green.

JANUARY 26th

1946   The FA Cup competition was again played over two legs and after defeating Blackburn Rovers 4-2 on aggregate in the third round, Bolton faced Liverpool in fourth round. The Reds were beaten 5-0 at Burnden Park in the first leg with Ray Westwood netting a hat-trick and Nat Lofthouse the other two goals.

1974   In one of the club's most exciting comebacks, the Wanderers trailed Southampton 3-1 at The Dell with just minutes remaining. Two goals in as many minutes made the final score 3-3, though the Saints won the replay at Burnden Park 2-0 after extra-time.

2000   Having already lost the League Cup semi-final first leg at home to Tranmere Rovers, the Wanderers gave a disappointing display in the return and crashed 3-0 to the Wirral side.

JANUARY 27th

1894   James Cassidy and Jim Wilson netted two goals apiece in Bolton's 4-3 win over Small Heath in an FA Cup first round tie - the Wanderers going all the way to the final where they lost to Notts County.

1912   Jack Feebury scored twice from the penalty spot as the Wanderers beat local rivals Preston North End 3-0.

1938   Birth of Graham Stanley. The Rotherham-born wing-half was playing for Steel Peachey's prior to joining Bolton as an apprentice and signing professional forms in the October 1955. Stanley captained Bolton to the FA Youth Cup semi-finals in 1956 where they were beaten by Manchester United. After some impressive displays in the club's Central League side, he made his first team debut as a replacement for the injured Derek Hennin at West Bromwich Albion in April 1957. The following season he won a regular place in the Bolton side and went on to appear in 161 League and Cup games for the Wanderers before leaving to join Tranmere Rovers in the summer of 1965. He made just one substitute appearance for the Prenton Park club when he got his name on the scoresheet before deciding to hang up his boots.

1972   Birth of Nathan Blake. The Welsh international began his career with Newport County before being taken on as a trainee by Chelsea. Unable top break into the first team at Stamford Bridge, he returned to SouthWales and began his league career with his home-town team of Cardiff City. He soon established himself in the Bluebirds' side and in 1992-93 helped them win the Third Division Championship. He had scored

40 goals in 164 games when Sheffield United paid £300,000 to take him to Bramall Lane. In his first season with the Yorkshire club, he top scored with 17 goals and was leading the way again in 1994-95 when Bolton paid £1.35 million for his services in December 1995. After managing to score just one goal in the remainder of that campaign, Blake *(below)* came into his own in 1995-96, forming a prolific goalscoring partnership with John McGinlay and netting 24 League and Cup goals as the Wanderers returned

to the top flight. Despite the club being relegated for a second time in three years, Blake was Wanderers' top scorer but after having scored 47 goals in 127 games, he left the Reebok Stadium to join Blackburn Rovers for £4.25 million. Most of his time at Ewood Park was spent on the treatment table and in three years with the club he made just 65 League and Cup appearances.

In September 2001 he joined Wolverhampton Wanderers for £1.4 million and in his second season at Molineux, Blake, who has won 23 full international caps for Wales, helped the club win promotion to the Premiership via the play-offs.

2004   Jubilant Bolton players drenched manager Sam Allardyce in champagne in tribute to the manager who led the Wanderers to their first major cup final for nine years.

They managed it after surviving a nailbiting finale as 10-men Aston Villa won 2-0 on the night but lost 5-4 on aggregate. Villa pulled a goal back when Thomas Hitzlsperger curled in a 10th minute free-kick. Villa's Gavin McCann had been sent-off for striking his former Sunderland team-mate Emerson Thome following a flare-up after the midfielder had lunged dangerously at Jussi Jaaskelainen.

There followed a combination of determined defending, with Thome, N'Gotty and Campo all prominent and wayward finishing from the Villa strikers before Jlloyd Samuel netted a second Villa goal in the 88th minute - but by then it was too late!

Later the Bolton players emerged from the dressing-rooms to dedicate the triumph to their two absent team-mates, Okocha, who was on international duty with Nigeria and Nolan, who was suspended. It was their goals in the first leg that helped the Wanderers build the three-goal advantage that was to prove so crucial.

19

JANUARY 28th

2001   Dean Holdsworth netted a hat-trick and Kevin Nolan scored twice as the Wanderers beat Scunthorpe United 5-1 in an FA Cup fourth round tie at the Reebok.

JANUARY 29th

1883   Birth of Herbert Baverstock. Signed from non League Brierley Hill Alliance in the summer of 1905, Herbert Baverstock played in 79 consecutive league games for the Wanderers after making his debut in a 3-3 draw at Notts County. When the Wanderers won the Second Division Championship in 1908-09, Baverstock played in all but one game and scored his first goal for the club in a 4-0 home defeat of Gainsborough Trinity. Though the Wanderers were relegated after just one season of top flight football, Baverstock showed his versatility in 1910-11, when the club once again won promotion, by playing the majority of the season at left-back. Baverstock was the club's first choice right-back until November 1921, one of just a handful of players who turned out for the club either side of the hostilities. He had made 388 appearances before losing his place to Bob Howarth.

JANUARY 30th

1892   Dai Jones took and missed Bolton's first-ever penalty in the friendly match against Everton which ended all-square at 1-1.

1935   Wanderers' top-scorer Jack Milsom, who netted 31 goals in 40 league outings, scored a hat-trick in a 5-1 defeat of Notts County.

1982   Former Manchester City and England wing-half Mike Doyle was recruited from Stoke City but he had a disastrous debut for the Wanderers, putting through his own goal in a 1-1 draw at Oldham Athletic. In his next game against Newcastle United, he was sent-off.

1988   John Thomas netted Bolton's first hat-trick away from Burnden Park for 21 years as the Wanderers won 4-0 at Peterborough United, with two of his goals coming from the penalty-spot.

JANUARY 31st

1914   Joe Smith scored a hat-trick in a 4-2 FA Cup second round win over Swindon Town.

1932   Birth of Ralph Gubbins. He began his career with Shell Mex FC before joining his home-town club in October 1952, Ellesmere Port. On his return home from military service in Malaysia, Gubbins was snapped up by the Wanderers. Though he was initially an inside-left, he spent most of his time at Burnden Park on the left-wing and occasionally at centre-forward. His moment of glory came when he deputised for the injured Nat Lofthouse in the 1958 FA Cup semi-final against Blackburn Rovers at Maine Road. With Bolton a goal down, Gubbins scored twice in as many minutes to put the Whites into the final. However, on Cup Final day, he was the Wanderers' 12th man, sitting out the game on the bench, immediately below the Royal Box. Gubbins had scored 18 goals in 101 games when he left Burnden Park to join Hull City. He spent 18 months at Boothferry Park before returning to the north-west with Tranmere Rovers. He scored 37 goals in 107 appearances for the Prenton Park club before entering non-League football with Wigan Athletic, whom he helped win the Cheshire League Championship.

1934   Jack Milsom, who scored 27 League and Cup goals in this campaign, netted his third hat-trick of the season as Bolton beat Brighton and Hove Albion 6-1 in an FA Cup fourth round replay.

1959 Eventual FA Cup finalists Luton Town were beaten 4-2 at Burnden Park with Nat Lofthouse, who scored 33 goals in 43 games, scoring his only hat-trick of the campaign.

1994 During the Wanderers' FA Cup fourth round game against Arsenal at Burnden Park, which was televised live on Sky TV, play had to be suspended when the attention of the 18,891 crowd turned skywards.
Someone buzzed the top of the stadium from a fan-powered parachute. The 'birdman' then disappeared - the result, a 2-2 draw.

FEBRUARY 1st

1890 Bolton recorded their biggest-ever first-class win, 13-0 against Sheffield United in an FA Cup second round tie. James Cassidy netted five, Davie Weir four and James Brogan a hat-trick. Wanderers' other scorer was full-back Bethel Robinson.

1941 George Hunt netted three of Bolton's goals in their 6-0 Football League War Cup victory over Bradford City. The second leg was also played at Burnden Park at Bradford City's request, with the Wanderers winning 3-1.

FEBRUARY 2nd

1893 Birth of Dick Pym. Known as the 'Topsham Fisherman', Dick Pym was born in that Devon village and earned his living from the sea before joining Exeter City in 1911. The Grecians were then members of the Southern League and Pym made 186 consecutive appearances for them before breaking his collarbone in an FA Cup tie against Watford.
In July 1921 after weeks of negotiations, the Wanderers secured the goalkeeper's signature. Although the precise fee was never revealed, it was thought to be around the £5,000 mark, which

was a record for any goalkeeper. Pym made his League debut for the Wanderers in a 2-2 draw against Preston North End and quickly settled into the team that won the FA Cup in 1923. His qualities were soon recognised and he played for the Football League XI in Belfast, yet despite his seafaring background, he was seasick on the crossing from Liverpool!
In February 1925, he won the first of his three full international caps when he played against Wales at Swansea. He went on to win two more FA Cup winners' medals in 1926 and 1929, keeping a clean sheet in all three Wembley appearances. The last survivor of Bolton's 1923 FA Cup winning side, he appeared in 336 games for the Wanderers before returning to live in Topsham.

1957 There was a remarkable game at Molineux where Nat Lofthouse once again had to go in goal. Wolves were leading 3-0 when Eddie Hopkinson had to go off with a suspected broken finger. Not only did 10-men Bolton pull back two goals through Stevens and Webster but Lofthouse saved a penalty!

FEBRUARY 3rd

1926 The Smiths - Joe and John Reid both scored twice in Bolton's 6-2 FA Cup fourth round replay win over Bournemouth.

1945 Nat Lofthouse netted a hat-trick in Bolton's 4-1 win over Tranmere Rovers at Prenton Park in the wartime Northern Section match.

1947 Only 4,280 saw the Wanderers beat Leeds United 2-0 in a First Division match. This remained as the lowest post-war League attendance on the Burnden Park ground until November 1985.

1967 Birth of Mixu Paatelainen. The Finn began his career as a youngster with FC Haka

Valkeakosken and began playing League football at the age of 15 for PS44. It was whilst he was playing for the Finland Olympic team that he was spotted by Dundee and ended his first season at Tannadice with an FA Cup runners-up medal after Dundee had lost 2-1 in the final.

During the course of that season, Paatelainen *(below)* scored all four goals for Dundee in a win over Morton. He continued to score goals for United until in March 1992 he joined Aberdeen. The Dons were runners-up to Rangers in every competition - League, League Cup and Cup - the Finn appearing in both finals and scoring 20 goals for the season.

In July 1994, Bolton paid £350,000 for his services and he scored twice on his debut in a 3-3 draw at Grimsby. He celebrated his first season by helping the club win promotion to the Premier League. Nicknamed 'The Moose' he then began to suffer with a spate of niggling injuries but returned to score one of the goals at Manchester City that saw the Wanderers return to the top fight. Paatelainen went on to score 18 goals in 83 games for Bolton before leaving to play for Wolves in the summer of 1997. He spent just one season at Molineux before returning north of the border to join Hibernian.

1967 Birth of Bob Taylor. After beginning his career with Leeds United, Bob Taylor joined Bristol City where he was an instant success. His first season at Ashton Gate ended in the Robins winning promotion and he was the Third Division's leading scorer. In January 1992, Taylor joined West Bromwich Albion and the following season, scored 30 goals as the Baggies swept into Division One via a Wembley play-off appearance. He continued to score goals for the Albion over the next few seasons until in January 1998 he joined the Wanderers on loan.

He proved to be so popular and successful that he was signed for a second loan period in March as cover until the end of the season. Though he lacked pace, he made up for it with great strength on the ball, a very high work-rate and scored some vital goals.

In the close season he joined the club on a permanent basis and in 1998-99 he found the net with some regularity regardless of who his strike partner happened to be! He scored two of Bolton's goals in the First Division play-off semi-final second leg defeat at Ipswich that sent the club to Wembley for the final against Watford. He had scored 27 goals in 96 games for the Wanderers when Sam Allardyce allowed him to rejoin the Baggies in March 2000. Since then injuries have hampered his return to the

Hawthorns, where his goal tally of 131 in 377 games places him eighth in Albion's all-time list of goalscorers.

1968 Two goals from Gareth Williams gave Bolton a 2-1 win over local rivals Blackburn Rovers. The match was significant in that referee Maurice Fussey - both by name and nature - blew for full time after 85 minutes. His mistake was pointed out to him by a linesman and the Wanderers then had to hang on for a further five minutes as Rovers pressed for an equaliser.

FEBRUARY 4th

1882 In their pre-League days, the Wanderers won and lost matches by fairly large margins. Their biggest win during this time was a 15-0 rout of Manchester Wanderers.

FEBRUARY 5th

1899 A crowd of over 5,000 were already inside Burnden Park in readiness for the match against Everton but it was announced that the visitors were refusing to play on the hard lumpy ground and so the game was postponed.

1955 League Champions the previous season and the current League leaders, Wolverhampton Wanderers were humbled 6-1 at Burnden Park with 19-year-old inside-forward Ray Parry hitting a hat-trick.

1997 Chesterfield became the last team to win at Burnden Park when they beat the Wanderers 3-2 in an FA Cup fourth round tie. Kevin Davies, now featuring in the Wanderers' side, scored a hat-trick for the Saltergate club.

FEBRUARY 6th

1943 George Hunt, who was a prolific wartime scorer

for the Wanderers, netted a hat-trick including a penalty as Blackburn Rovers were beaten 3-1.

1945 Birth of John Hulme *(below)*. The centre-half was aged just 17 when he made his Bolton debut as a replacement for the injured Bryan Edwards in a 1-0 defeat of Nottingham Forest in October 1962. He continued to deputise for the injured Edwards until the regular Bolton pivot returned to first team action. Then when Edwards hung up his boots. Hulme found the No.5 shirt taken by Irish defender John Napier.

It was only when Napier left for Brighton that Hulme won a regular place in the Bolton side. He held off a challenge from Charlie Hurley but following the club's relegation to the Third Division, he lost his place to the defensive formation of Paul Jones and Warwick Rimmer. After a loan spell with Notts County, he returned to Burnden Park and took his total of first team appearances to 215 before joining Reading. He later played for Bury before becoming player-manager of Swiss club Chaux-de-Fonds.

1970 Birth of Per Frandsen. The Danish international joined the Wanderers from FC Copenhagen in a double deal with Michael Johnasen in the summer of 1996. An energetic and powerful midfielder, Frandsen made his League debut in a 1-1 draw at Port Vale on the opening day of the 1996-97 season and then scored the only goal of the game on his home debut three days later as the Wanderers beat Manchester City. His displays during the club's Division One Championship-winning season made him one of the campaign's best buys and in 1997-98 he was voted the players' Player of the Year after proving himself very much at home in the Premiership. Despite the Wanderers' relegation, his form led to him making two appearances for Denmark in the 1998 World Cup Finals in France.
His form was quickly noticed by other clubs and in September 1999 he joined Blackburn Rovers for £1.75 million - a move which prompted Colin Todd to resign as the club's manager. However, whilst the Wanderers qualified for the play-offs, Rovers failed to return to the top flight at the first time of asking. Within nine months, he was back at the Reebok, the Wanderers paying £1.6 million for his return.
Since then, he has looked considerably fitter and has scored a number of important goals including a 30-yard pile-driver in last season's crucial clash with Middlesbrough. Still an important member of the Wanderers' squad, he has now scored 35

goals in 266 games in his two spells with the club.

FEBRUARY 7th

1927 Burnden Park hosted an England trial match. England were beaten 3-2 by The Rest with three of the Wanderers' players involved - Jimmy Seddon represented England whilst Dick Pym and Harry Nuttall played for The Rest before a crowd of 14,002.

FEBRUARY 8th

1890 James Cassidy netted a hat-trick for the Wanderers in a comfortable 5-0 home win over Stoke.

1958 Birth of Derek Scott. An England schoolboy international, he began his career with Burnley where he formed an impressive full-back pairing with Ian Brennan (another future Bolton player) in the Clarets' run to the final of the Anglo-Scottish Cup. Following the emergence of Brian Laws, Scott switched to midfield and was instrumental in Burnley winning the Third Division title in 1982. Though the club were immediately relegated, Scott's form in the Clarets' run to the League Cup semi-final was outstanding. Appointed club captain, he had scored 31 goals in 357 games when following Burnley's relegation to Division Four in 1985, he was transferred to Bolton Wanderers for £20,000. He made a Wembley appearance at the end of his first season with the Whites in the Freight Rover Trophy Final and missed very few games in the club's Fourth Division promotion-winning season of 1987-88. However in the close season, Scott, who had made 147 appearances for the Wanderers, was allowed to leave on a free and joined Northern Premier League first division Colne Dynamos before later joining the police force.

1966 Birth of Jimmy Phillips. After working his way up through the ranks, Jimmy Phillips made his Wanderers' debut in April 1984 as a substitute against Gillingham. Following Ray Deakin's departure to Burnley, Phillips established himself as the club's first choice left-back and appeared at Wembley when the Whites were beaten 3-0 by Bristol City in the 1986 final of the Freight Rover Trophy. In March 1987 however, Glasgow Rangers paid £75,000 to take the young Phillips to Ibrox Park and the following season he played in four European Cup ties for the Scottish giants. In the summer of 1988 he joined Oxford United for £110,000 before soon afterwards leaving to play for Middlesbrough.

While with the Teeside club, he helped them win promotion to the top flight as runners-up to Ipswich Town, but in the summer of 1993 he rejoined the Wanderers for a fee of £300,000. He was ever-present in 1994-95 when the club won promotion to the Premiership and reached the League Cup Final. He won a First Division Championship medal in 1996-97 and continued to be an important member of the Wanderers' squad until the end of the 1999-2000 season. Having scored eight goals in 411 games in his two spells with the Wanderers, Jimmy *(right)* is now the club's youth team coach.

FEBRUARY 9th

1994 The Wanderers travelled to Highbury for an FA Cup fourth round replay against mighty Arsenal. Ninety minutes failed to separate the teams but extra-time strikes from Jason McAteer and Andy Walker to go with an earlier goal by the prolific John McGinlay, gave Bolton a 3-1 win.

FEBRUARY 10th

1945 Nat Lofthouse scored four of Bolton's goals in a 6-1 home win over Tranmere Rovers, having netted a hat-trick in their earlier meeting the

previous week. Malcolm Barrass scored the Wanderers' two other goals.

1951 Birth of Ray Train *(right)*. The midfield dynamo played his early football for Walsall before joining Carlisle United in December 1971. He helped the Cumbrian club to the First Division for the first time in their history and was their only ever-present in that breakthrough season in the top flight.

In March 1976 he joined Sunderland and two months later he was the winner of a Second Division Championship medal. His stay at Roker Park lasted just a year for in March 1977, Bolton manager Ian Greaves paid £35,000 to bring him to Burnden Park. Though he went straight into the Bolton side, it wasn't until 1978 that he celebrated a hat-trick of promotions to Division One with three different clubs. He had appeared in 57 games for the Wanderers before joining Watford for a fee of £50,000 in November 1978. Whilst at Vicarage Road he won a Third Division Championship medal but after 110 appearances he was on the move again, this time to Oxford United. There then followed loan spells with Bournemouth and Northampton Town and a season with Tranmere Rovers, before he returned to his first club Walsall as the Saddlers' player-coach.

1965 Birth of Tony Philliskirk. A former England schoolboy international, he began his League career with Sheffield United and in 1983-84 his eight goals towards the end of the campaign helped the Blades win promotion to the Second Division. He had scored 20 goals in 80 games for the Yorkshire club before crossing the Pennines to sign for Oldham Athletic. His stay at Boundary Park was brief and in February 1989 he joined Preston North End, but four months later, he was on his way to Burnden Park for a fee of £50,000. He made his debut in a 2-0 win at Cardiff City on the opening day of the 1989-90

season, scoring the club's opening goal after just four minutes. He ended the season as the club's leading scorer with 25 goals and did so again in 1990-91 when two of his 28 strikes helped the Wanderers beat neighbours Bury in the play-off semi-finals. The club's regular penalty-taker, he continued to score goals with great regularity but after losing his place in the Bolton side to John McGinlay, the Sunderland-born striker, who had scored 75 goals in 182 games, joined Peterborough United for £80,000. He later returned to the north-west to play for Burnley and scored against the Wanderers in a 1-1 draw. In December 1995, he joined Cardiff City, where following loan spells with non-League Halifax and Macclesfield, he took refereeing examinations.

FEBRUARY 11th

1953 Birth of Stuart Lee *(below)*. He made his Wanderers' debut as a substitute in the match against York City on New Year's Day 1972. He played in two further games that season, scoring his first goal in Bolton's colours in a 3-0 win at Bradford City. After ousting Ralph Wright from the side during the early part of the 1972-73 season, Lee became a regular in the side and as the Wanderers won the Third Division Championship, he scored 15 goals including a hat-trick in a 3-0 home defeat of Halifax Town.

Top flight clubs began to show an interest in the 20-year-old striker but Lee, who found life in Division Two much harder then lost his place in the side to Neil Whatmore. He regained his place under Ian Greaves but in November 1975, after scoring 27 goals in 101 first team Outings, he joined Wrexham. He scored in each of his first four games for the Welsh club but the arrival of Dixie McNeil limited his appearances and he moved on to Stockport County. In his first season at Edgeley Park he scored 24 goals, prompting Manchester City to spend £60,000 on taking him to Maine Road. He scored twice in six First Division outings but after his contract was cancelled, he went to play in the NASL for Portland Timbers and Tampa Bay Rowdies.

1956 Joe Dean at 16 years 313 days old made his Bolton debut against Wolverhampton Wanderers at Molineux. Unfortunately he didn't finish the game, having to leave the field for stitches. He was replaced by Nat Lofthouse as the Wanderers went down 4-2.

FEBRUARY 12th

1910 Marshall McEwan and Billy Hunter scored two goals apiece as Bolton beat fellow First Division strugglers Chelsea at Burnden Park 5-2. Both clubs were relegated at the end of the season.

1927 Following Bolton's 2-0 defeat at Aston Villa, hundreds of angry supporters threatened to boycott the remaining League games, feeling that the club were more concerned in winning the FA Cup than the League title.

1933 Birth of Brian Pilkington. After beginning his career as a flying winger with Leyland Motors, he joined Burnley and following his debut against Spurs at White Hart Lane in September 1952, he replaced Billy Elliott on a permanent basis. He soon caught the eye of the international selectors and in March 1954 collected an England 'B' cap in a 1-1 draw against Scotland 'B' at Roker Park. In October of that year he played in his only full international replacing Tom Finney in a 2-0 win for England against Northern Ireland in Belfast. Pilkington won a League Championship medal in 1959-60, when in the last game of the season against Manchester City he scored the Clarets' opener in a 2-1 win.

The following season was to be his last at Turf Moor, for in March 1961 after scoring 77 goals in 340 games, he joined the Wanderers. Though he took over the No.11 shirt from Doug Holden who moved to the right-wing, Pilkington failed to reproduce the form that had made him one of the best wide men in the top flight. With Bolton struggling against relegation, Pilkington, who had scored 11 goals in 86 games joined Bury. He later played for Barrow and non-League Chorley before returning to his first club Leyland Motors as their manager. He was later appointed manager of Chorley.

1995   Bolton lost the League Cup semi-final first leg against Swindon Town at the County Ground 2-1, this after Alan Stubbs had given them the lead.

FEBRUARY 13th

1915   Ernie Jones and Ted Vizard each scored twice in Bolton's 4-1 FA Cup second round replay win over Millwall.

1943   Bolton crashed to a 7-1 defeat at Blackburn Rovers in this wartime league clash - this just a week after a George Hunt hat-trick had helped them to a 3-1 victory!

1963   Due to the 'big freeze', the Wanderers hadn't played any football since 8 December 1962 and so arranged to play a friendly against Manchester United in Cork, to get some match practice - for the record, United won 4-2.

FEBRUARY 14th

1959   Bolton's post-war record crowd of 58,692 saw the Wanderers draw 2-2 with Preston North End in a fifth round FA Cup tie, with the Wanderers finally getting through to the quarter-finals in a second replay at Ewood Park.

FEBRUARY 15th

1930   George Gibson netted a hat-trick as Bolton beat Leeds United 4-2. The Wanderers other goal was scored by debutant Jack Milsom, who had been a prolific marksman in the club's Central League side.

FEBRUARY 16th

1946   A Nat Lofthouse hat-trick helped the Wanderers to a 5-0 win at Bradford Park Avenue.

1963   Following the 'big freeze', Bolton's first League match after their 1-0 defeat of Tottenham Hotspur on 8 December 1962 was against Arsenal at Highbury, a match the Gunners won 3-2.

FEBRUARY 17th

1906   Albert Shepherd netted his second four-goal haul of the season as Bolton beat Sunderland 6-2.

1987   The Embankment floodlights were dismantled and new pylons erected to accommodate the new Normid Superstore Development. Matching pylons were built at the Great Lever End the following close season.

FEBRUARY 18th

1933   Bolton's highest attendance of 69,912 saw the Wanderers go down 4-2 at home to Manchester City in an FA Cup fifth round tie. Bolton's goals were scored by Jack Milsom and Ray Westwood.

1953 Nat Lofthouse netted a hat-trick for the Wanderers in a 5-3 home win over Middlesbrough.

FEBRUARY 19th

1919 Birth of Ernie Forest *(right)*. The Sunderland-born half-back played his early football with Unsworth Colliery before joining the Wanderers during the summer of 1937. IIe made his League debut against Chelsea in September 1938, but appeared in only a handful of matches prior to the outbreak of the Second World War. One of 15 Bolton players to join the Territorial Army, he was among the British Expeditionary Force in Dunkirk.

After the hostilities he became a regular in the club's half-back line where his performances led to him being selected for an England trial game. After missing just one game of the 1946-47 season, he began to suffer with a spate of injuries and having scored one goal – on the opening day of the 1946-47 season in a 4-3 defeat at Chelsea - in 73 League and Cup games, he joined Grimsby Town. After a year with the Mariners, he joined Millwall before returning to the north-west to end his career with Darwen.

1944 Jim Currier scored four of Bolton's goals in a 5-1 home defeat of Southport in a wartime Northern Section game.

1964 The Wanderers, who had already been beaten 1-0 at home by Manchester United, travelled to Old Trafford hoping for revenge, but the Reds, who were pushing Liverpool hard for the League Championship, completed the double by winning 5-0.

2000 Eidur Gudjohnsen scored the only goal of the FA Cup sixth round tie against Charlton Athletic at the Reebok, to send the Wanderers into their first FA Cup semi-final for 42 years.

FEBRUARY 20th

1904 Sam Marsh and Walter White each scored two of Bolton's goals in a 4-1 FA Cup second round defeat of Southampton.

1937 A crowd of 60,979 saw Bolton's hopes of progress in the FA Cup crumble as they were beaten 5-0 at home by Manchester City.

FEBRUARY 21st

1925 Joe Smith and David Jack scored two goals apiece in a 5-1 home win for the Wanderers over Burnley. Bolton's other scorer was James Cassidy.

1974 Birth of Ivan Campo *(left)*. The much-travelled Spanish international, who had played for CD Logrones, Alaves, Vallencia, Valladolid and Real Mallorca prior to joining the Wanderers on loan from Real Madrid. He took some time to settle into his new surroundings. Though big things were expected of him, he seemed to struggle to come to terms with the pace and directness of Premiership football.
However, all that changed when Sam Allardyce switched him to a holding role between the defence and midfield and from then on, the Spaniard with the distinctive hair style, was a revelation. Having scored against Liverpool on his home debut, the new role suited his tremendous range of passing, whilst his tough-tackling added some much needed aggression to the Bolton team. In the close season, after much negotiating, Campo joined the Wanderers on a permanent basis.

1989 Bolton were struggling against Wrexham in the Freight Rover Trophy when Mark Winstanley scored with a spectacular long-range goal. The Wanderers' defender scored again in a 3-1 extra-time win for the Whites.

FEBRUARY 22nd

1907 Birth of Jack Milsom. The Bedminster-born centre-forward had spells with both Bristol Rovers and Kettering before joining Rochdale in the summer of 1928. In his first season at Spotland he scored 25 goals and in December 1929, this prompted the Wanderers to pay £1,750 for his services. Despite scoring on his Bolton debut, in a 4-2 win over Leeds United, and netting six goals in a Central League game against Wolverhampton Wanderers, he could not force his way into the Bolton side on a regular basis. Just when it seemed he would be given an extended run in the side he broke his leg and had to wait until the 1931-32 season before becoming an established first team player. He was the club's leading scorer for the next six seasons with a best of 35 goals in 46 games during the Wanderers' promotion-winning season of 1934-35. The scorer of nine hat-tricks for the Wanderers, he also scored four goals against Liverpool in an 8-1 win on the final day of the 1931-32 season and against West Ham United in 1933-34 and Burnley in 1934-35. Milsom had scored 153 goals in 255 League and Cup games when he left Bolton in February 1938 to end his career with Manchester City.

1908   A Sam Marsh hat-trick in the FA Cup third round tie with Everton wasn't enough as the 3-3 draw resulted in the Merseyside club winning the replay after extra-time.

FEBRUARY 23rd

1929   The Wanderers were leading 3-0 at Fratton Park against a struggling Portsmouth side with George Gibson having netted two of the goals.
But Pompey came back strongly and the game ended all-square at 4-4 with Bolton hanging on desperately for a point!

FEBRUARY 24th

1880   Birth of David Stokes. He was playing for Brierley Hill Alliance when he joined First Division Aston Villa on Birmingham and District League forms. Though he was on Villa's books, he continued to turn out for Brierley Hill and in December 1901, Bolton secured his services. Villa reported the Wanderers to the League for poaching and the Burnden Park club was fined 10

guineas, while the Midlands club had to give Stokes a free! After making his Wanderers' debut in a 2-1 win at Wolves, Stokes scored the first of 46 goals for Bolton in a 2-2 draw with Aston Villa! Over the next 15 seasons, he missed very few games for the Wanderers and was ever-present in seasons 1905-06 and 1906-07. He won a Second Division Championship medal in 1908-09 and represented the Football League XI on a number of occasions. He continued to play for the Wanderers after the First World War but in September 1920, after taking his total of first team appearances to 420, he left to rejoin Brierley Hill Alliance. The following year, Wolves brought him out of non-League obscurity and he appeared in seven games of their 1920-21 league campaign.

FEBRUARY 25th

1893   Birth of Billy Jennings. A former Welsh schoolboy international, he joined the Wanderers in the summer of 1912 and made his League debut in a 1-1 draw against Derby County in November of that year.
Just as he seemed to have established himself in the Wanderers' side, he was injured in the Boxing Day clash against Sheffield United and forced to miss the rest of the season. When Jennings won the first of his 11 full international caps for Wales, he was still in the Wanderers' Central League side but when League football resumed after the First World War, he won a regular place in the first team at half-back.
When Bolton won the FA Cup in 1923, Jennings played in all seven Cup ties on the club's run to Wembley and was a member of the side when the Wanderers beat Manchester City 1-0 in 1926, to take the Cup for a second time. He had played in 287 League and Cup games for Bolton when in 1931 he decided to hang up his boots.
After two years out of the game he was appointed coach at Notts County, a post he later held at

Cardiff City before being appointed manager of the Ninian Park club.

1966 Bolton completed the double over Preston North End thanks to another hat-trick hero. Welsh international Wyn Davies had netted a treble in the game at Burnden Park, whilst in the encounter at Deepdale, Francis Lee scored all Bolton's goals in a 3-1 win.

1996 The Wanderers went down 6-0 at Burnden Park to Manchester United to equal the club's worst-ever home defeat.

FEBRUARY 26th

1992 Bolton, who had scored two goals in the last ten minutes of their FA Cup fifth round tie against Southampton at Burnden Park to force a draw, travelled to The Dell for the replay. Leading 2-1 with just a minute to play, the Wanderers conceded an injury-time equaliser to the Saints, who then went on to win 3-2 after extra-time.

FEBRUARY 27th

1897 Jim McGeachan was suspended by the Wanderers for refusing to travel to Sheffield for the League game against Wednesday.

1907 A crowd of 54,470, Bolton's first-ever home gate to exceed 50,000 saw the Wanderers lose 3-0 to visitors Everton.

1934 Birth of Stan Anderson. He captained Sunderland, Newcastle and Middlesbrough and was capped twice by England. A tough-tackling half-back, he played in 402 league games for the Black Cats and also appeared in two FA Cup semi-finals. He joined Newcastle United in November 1963 and played an important part in their Second Division Championship-winning season of 1964-65. After joining Middlesbrough

as player-coach, he was appointed their manager in April 1966. He brought about a revival at Ayresome Park, leading the Teeside club back to the Second Division in 1966-67 but after twice going close to promotion to the top flight, he left to manage AEK Athens. He joined Bolton as coach under manager Ian Greaves. When Greaves was dismissed in January 1980, Anderson took over as caretaker-manager before the appointment was made official the following month. At the end of that season though, the Wanderers were relegated. Despite being given the money to strengthen the squad, results didn't improve and in March 1981, George Mulhall returned to Burnden Park as Anderson's assistant. It was his return that coincided with the club's run to safety and the following summer Anderson was sacked.

FEBRUARY 28th

1925 Joe Smith netted yet another hat-trick as the Wanderers beat Manchester City 5-0 at Burnden Park.

FEBRUARY 29th

1951 Birth of Phil Neal. Beginning his League career with Northampton Town, Phil Neal clocked up 206 first team appearances for the Cobblers before joining First Division Liverpool for £65,000 in October 1974. He made his debut for the Reds against Everton the following month as a replacement for the injured Alec Lindsay at left-back. From his second appearance for the club in December 1974 until injury caused him to miss Liverpool's game with Sunderland in October 1983, Phil Neal *(right)* played in 366 consecutive League games. Neal was an intelligent positional player who denied the winger any space. Capped 50 times by England, he won almost every honour while playing for Liverpool. He won seven League Championship

medals and was on the winning side in four League Cup Finals. He won a UEFA Cup winners' medal and four European Cup winners' medals - only an FA Cup winners' medal eluded him. Halfway through the 1985-86 season, he left Anfield to join Bolton as player-manager. Neal continued to play for the Wanderers until 1988-89, lending his experience to the club's younger players.

His first few years in management were quite eventful. In 1986 he led the side to Wembley where they lost 3-0 to Bristol City in the Freight Rover Trophy Final. In 1986-87 the club were relegated to the Fourth Division for the first time in their history but bounced back at the end of the following campaign. There was another visit to Wembley in 1989 when the Wanderers beat Torquay United 4-1 to lift the Sherpa Van Trophy. Neal left the club at the end of the 1991-92 season, having helped bring stability to the Wanderers along with a measure of success but the pressure of poor results and declining attendances prompted the bombshell.

After a period of involvement with the England management team, Neal took charge of both Coventry City and Cardiff City.

2004 Middlesbrough, who had not won a major trophy in their 128-years history, beat the Wanderers 2-1 in the Carling Cup Final played at the Millennium Stadium.

The Teesiders were in front inside two minutes from a tap-in by Joseph-Desire Job after a Zenden cross. A further five minutes and Bolton were two down when Emerson Thome was harshly adjudged to have brought down Job. Zenden took charge only to slip as he struck the ball and accidentally knock it sideways with his right foot before guiding it past Jussi Jaaskelainen. As Big Sam argued, it should have been a free-kick to Bolton.

The Wanderers responded well and for the rest of the first-half they troubled Boro's defence. The

Wanderers' 21st minute goal was most unexpected, however, coming from an innocuous Kevin Davies shot that had no right to finish in the net. An easy take for Mark Schwarzer but the ball somehow bounced off his glove and squeezed inside the post. On the half-hour, Per Frandsen surged into the Middlesbrough box and struck a post before Youri Djorkaeff fired just wide. Moments later the Frenchman was denied by Schwarzer as the Wanderers finished the first-half on top.

Sadly, first-half promise turned to frustration for the Wanderers after the break, though Kevin Nolan headed a Nicky Hunt cross straight at Schwarzer. Middlesbrough replaced Job with former Wanderers' favourite Michael Ricketts who took to the field to a chorus of boos from Bolton fans.

Wanderers' manager Sam Allardyce introduced Pedersen and Moreno as attacking threats but to no avail. It was Bolton's third substitute Stelios Giannakopoulos who replaced Nicky Hunt who came closest to grabbing an equaliser but his shot blocked by the hand of Ugo Ehiogu was missed by referee Mike Riley.

The tension increased afterwards with Michael Ricketts being booked for kicking the ball away but for Sam Allardyce, dejected but magnanimous in defeat, the hours, days, weeks, even years of preparation had been destroyed in seven painful minutes.

MARCH 1st

1890 Burnley, who finished next to the bottom of the First Division and had to take part in the 'Test Matches', the forerunner of today's play-offs, beat the Wanderers 7-0 at Turf Moor!

1915 The Wanderers suffered another 7-0 defeat on this date, this time against Sheffield Wednesday at Hillsborough.

1941 Birth of Warwick Rimmer *(below)*. A nephew of the former Sheffield Wednesday player Ellis Rimmer, he made his Wanderers debut in the club's first- ever Football League Cup game at Hull City in October 1960.

Strong in the tackle, the Merseyside-born wing-half soon established himself in the Bolton side and was ever-present in three seasons.

Though he twice suffered relegation with the Wanderers, he captained the side that won the Third Division Championship in 1972-73 when his experience helped the young Paul Jones at the heart of the Bolton defence.

One of the club's most loyal servants, he played in 528 League and Cup games, scoring 17 goals for Bolton, but in March 1975 he left to join

Crewe Alexandra. After making 128 league appearances for the Railwaymen, he coached and managed the Gresty Road club before coaching in Sierra Leone. He returned to Burnden Park as the Wanderers' Commercial Manager before serving Tranmere Rovers in a similar capacity and later as their youth development officer.

1958 One of the most historic games in the history of Bolton Wanderers was the FA Cup sixth round tie against League leaders Wolverhampton Wanderers at Burnden Park. Though Bolton were outplayed for much of the game, goals from Dennis Stevens and Ray Parry gave them a 2-1 victory, though it has to be said, rarely had a team had such luck!

1971 A crowd of just 943 saw Bolton beat Rangers Freja of Denmark 2-1.
The Danish side fielded a goalkeeper by the name of Bone who wore spectacles! His task was made all the more difficult as the game was played in a snowstorm.

MARCH 2nd

1889 Davie Weir, Wanderers forward, scored on his international debut for England in a 6-1 win over Ireland at Goodison Park. He also netted on his only other appearance as England went down 3-2 to Scotland.

1912 Prior to the home game against West Bromwich Albion, which the Wanderers eventually won 2-0 after an uphill struggle, Sam Greenhalgh refused to play out of position on the left-wing and was suspended by the club for six weeks.

MARCH 3rd

1992 The Wanderers travelled to the Victoria Ground and beat Hartlepool United 4-0, their best away win for over four years. Bolton's goals were scored by Andy Walker (2), Tony Kelly and Michael Brown. The game though was watched by a crowd of just 2,244.

MARCH 4th

1893 Davie Weir scored three of Bolton's goals in a 5-2 defeat of Accrington Stanley.

1929 Birth of Harold Hassall. He played his early football for Mossley Common and Astley and Tyldesley Collieries before being signed by Huddersfield Town in the summer of 1946. Shortly after making his League debut for the Terriers, he found himself replacing the injured Town keeper in the match against Preston North End and saving a penalty taken by the great Tom Finney! Whilst with Huddersfield, Hassall won the first of his five full caps for England, scoring in a 3-2 defeat by Scotland. In January 1952, Hassall was transferred to the Wanderers, who paid £27,000 for his services. He won an FA Cup runners-up medal in 1953 as Bolton lost 4-3 to Blackpool and over the next couple of seasons was an important member of the Bolton side. He netted a hat-trick in a 6-1 defeat of Portsmouth in November 1953 and had taken his tally of goals to 34 in 109 games when on New Year's Day 1955 he sustained a serious knee injury in the game against Chelsea that ended his playing career.
After falling back on his teaching qualifications, he was appointed manager-coach of the England youth team before later being asked by FIFA to report on the 1966 World Cup games. Hassall who became a lecturer in Physical Education at Padgate Teacher Training College was a member of a study team that helped emerging countries with all aspects of the game of football.

1959 Freddie Hill netted a hat-trick including a penalty as the Wanderers beat Chelsea 6-0.

1960 Birth of Dave Felgate. He graduated through the youth system at Burnden Park but was unable to break into the first team and was loaned out to gain experience with both Rochdale and Crewe Alexandra. In September 1980 he joined Lincoln City for a fee of £25,000 and while at Sincil Bank won his only full cap for Wales against Romania when he replaced the injured Neville Southall. After appearing in 198 league games for the Imps, he had a short loan spell with Cardiff City before signing for Grimsby Town in the summer of 1985. However, in February 1986 he returned to Burnden Park on loan and kept a clean sheet on his debut in a 4-0 win over Newport County.

After helping the club reach the final of the Freight Rover Trophy he rejoined Grimsby before signing for the Wanderers on a permanent basis. Despite the Wanderers suffering relegation to the Fourth Division in his first season in the team, he helped them win promotion and the Sherpa Van Trophy in 1989. Missing very few games while with the Wanderers, he had made 300 appearances when he left to play for Chester. Felgate later played for Wigan Athletic before joining Leigh RMI for whom he was outstanding in the FA Cup games against Fulham in 1998-99.

MARCH 5th

1994 John McGinlay scored all Bolton's goals in a 3-2 home win over Charlton Athletic.

MARCH 6th

1915 Joe Smith scored twice from the penalty-spot as Bolton beat Hull City 4-2 in an FA Cup fourth round tie.

1943 Nat Lofthouse netted his first hat-trick for the club in a 4-1 defeat of Burnley in a wartime league fixture.

1963 The club's third round FA Cup tie against Sheffield United at Bramall Lane was played at the 13th attempt after the atrocious weather had taken its toll. For the record, Francis Lee scored Bolton's goal in a 3-1 defeat.

1965 Bolton's first appearance on BBC TV's 'Match of the Day' saw them beat Charlton Athletic 3-1 at The Valley with goals from Lee (penalty), Bromley and Butler.

MARCH 7th

1872 Birth of Robert Tannahill. Initially an outside right, he joined the Wanderers from Kilmarnock in February 1893 and made a goalscoring debut in a 9-2 friendly win over Bolton Wednesday. He soon became a regular in the Bolton side but was switched to inside-forward and played there against Notts County in the 1894 FA Cup Final. He reverted to the wing the following year and appeared in that position in the 1896 FA Cup semi-final matches against Sheffield Wednesday, scoring in both meetings. In 1897, Tannahill, who had scored 11 goals in 80 first team games, lost his place to Scottish international Billy Thompson and joined Tottenham Hotspur. He was a regular in the North London club's Southern League side but after helping them finish third in 1897-98 he left to play for Millwall Athletic. He later returned to league action with Chesterfield before ending his career with Grays United.

1951 Billy Hughes became Bolton's first Northern Ireland international when he played against Wales in Belfast.

MARCH 8th

1890 John McNee scored Bolton's goal in their 2-1 FA Cup semi-final defeat against Sheffield Wednesday at Perry Barr, Birmingham.

1995 The Wanderers overturned a first leg defeat of 2-1 by Swindon Town to beat the Robins 3-1 on the night and 4-3 on aggregate. All this after the Wiltshire club had extended their aggregate lead after scoring first in the Burnden Park clash. Bolton's scorers were McAteer, Paatelainen and McGinlay.

1997 Bolton beat Swindon Town 7-0, just one goal short of equalling the club's best-ever League win.

MARCH 9th

1889 Kenny Davenport netted a hat-trick for the Wanderers in a 7-3 home win over Notts County. Bolton's other scorers were Barbour (2), Turner and Brogan.

1946 Burnden Park became the scene of one of the worst disasters the English game has known, yet though 33 people were killed, many people present at the game were unaware of the tragedy. An estimated 85,000 crowd had poured into Burnden Park - the official 'gate' figure is only 65,419 - for the second leg of an FA Cup sixth round tie against Stoke City. The crowd was so tightly packed that many spectators tried to get out of the ground. As the pressure mounted, two crash barriers collapsed. Spectators were hurtled forward and many were trampled underfoot. Dead and injured were laid out on the running track, doctors being summoned from the crowd to attend to them. The game was just 12 minutes old when the referee was informed of the full extent of the disaster. He took the players off the field but after consultation with the police, play was resumed after a 12 minute break. It was felt that this was the wisest decision. Play continued until its finish with no interval being taken. In addition to the 33 fatalities, 500 were injured, 24 of whom were taken to hospital. The Mayor of Bolton opened a Relief Fund and a

total of almost £40,000 were raised. The match itself ended goalless, so Bolton having won the first leg 2-0, went through to the semi-finals.

1963 Three days after their FA Cup exit at the hands of Sheffield United, the Wanderers gained revenge when a Freddie Hill hat-trick helped Bolton to a 3-2 win over the Blades.

1968 Birth of Youri Djorkaeff *(pictured overleaf)*. The French international, who has won 82 caps for his country, played for a number of clubs including Grenoble, Strasbourg, AS Monaco and Paris St Germain before joining the Wanderers, initially on a short-term deal, from German League side Kaiserslautern in February 2002. It was a truly inspirational move by manager Allardyce as the Frenchman playing in his favoured role just behind an out-an-out striker, showed just why he was virtually every honour at club and international level. There is no doubt that his performances were instrumental in the Wanderers retaining their Premiership status and he was particularly outstanding when scoring both goals in Bolton's win at Charlton Athletic at the end of March.
His form throughout the 2002-03 season was of an extremely high standard and along with Jay Jay Okocha he was the focal point of the Bolton side. His touch and passing range were phenomenal and after scoring a stunning overhead goal in the draw against probably his favourite team Charlton Athletic, he ended the season as joint-top scorer with seven goals. Continually showing the reasons why the Wanderers management team are keen to tie him to the club, Youri has now scored 11 goals in 49 League and Cup games.

MARCH 10th

1888 Just prior to the League days, the Wanderers drew 5-5 at home to Derby County, who it

transpired were their first opponents in the Football League.

1894 Bolton won their FA Cup semi-final against Sheffield Wednesday at Fallowfield, Manchester 2-1 with both their goals being scored by the unusually named Handel Bentley. It was an outstanding result for the Wanderers, who had failed to beat the Owls in either of their League meetings that season.

1945 Nat Lofthouse, who scored 30 goals in 31 games during the course of this wartime league season, netted a hat-trick in a 6-1 home win over Southport.

MARCH 11th

1893 The Lancashire Cup second round tie against Bury was abandoned after a spectator ran across the pitch and kicked Wanderers' half-back James Turner. Despite the fact that Bolton were winning 3-1, the FA ordered a replay at Pikes Lane - Bolton winning 1-0 thanks to a last minute strike!

1906 Birth of Willie Cook. After playing his early football for his local team, Dundee North End, Cook joined Forfar Athletic before returning to play for Dundee. The left-winger joined Bolton in December 1928 and on his debut, had a hand in all of the Wanderers' goals in a 5-0 win over Leicester City. At the end of his first season with the club, he won an FA Cup winners' medal after Bolton had beaten Portsmouth 2-0 in the Wembley final.
Capped three times at full international level for Scotland during his time with the Wanderers, Cook helped the club win promotion to the First Division in 1934-35 following their relegation two seasons earlier. But after just one season back in the top flight, Cook left Burnden Park to play for Blackpool.
Cook, who had scored 40 goals in 262 games for

Bolton, helped the Seasiders win promotion to the First Division in his first season at Bloomfield Road before returning to his native Scotland to see out his career with Dundee.

MARCH 12th

1932 Willie Cook and George Gibson scored two goals apiece for the Wanderers in a 5-1 home defeat of Birmingham. Bolton's other scorer was Jack Milsom.

1949 Wanderers' leading scorer Willie Moir netted his third hat-trick of the campaign as Middlesbrough were beaten 4-1.

1994 Bolton reached the FA Cup sixth round for the first time for 35 seasons but went down 1-0 at home to Oldham Athletic as a fluke goal settled the local derby in the Latics' favour.

MARCH 13th

1897 Burnden Park was introduced to a different sport. Prior to the Wanderers' League game with Burnley which Bolton won 2-1 with goals by Miller and Wright, a lacrosse match took place that saw Bolton beat North Manchester 1-0.

1902 Birth of Alex Finney. He was playing for New Brighton against Chorley in the Lancashire Junior Cup Final at Burnden Park in 1922 when he was noticed by the Wanderers. The Rakers unaccountably forgot to place the full-backs name on the retained list and Bolton lost no time in signing him. After making his League debut in a 2-0 defeat at Birmingham in September 1922, he soon established himself in the side and formed a good understanding with right-back Bob Howarth. Finney was the mainstay of the Bolton defence that kept the Hammers at bay in the 1923 FA Cup Final when, at the age of 22, he was the youngest member of the side. In 1923-24 he was the club's only ever-present as they finished fourth in Division One after challenging for League Championship honours for most of the season. A cartilage operation cost Finney his place in the 1926 FA Cup-winning team but he was back for Bolton's 2-0 win over Portsmouth in 1929.

A year earlier, Finney had played for the Football League XI when they beat the Irish League at St James Park by 9-1. He played the last of his 530 League and Cup games for the Wanderers on New Year's Day 1937, the last player on the club's books to have played in the Cup Finals of the 1920s.

1920 Frank Roberts scored both Bolton's goals from the penalty-spot in a 2-1 home win over Aston Villa.

1925 Birth of John Ball. He began his career with Wigan Athletic during the Second World War before joining Manchester United in February 1948. He had made 22 First Division appearances for the Reds when Bolton signed him in September 1950.

Taking over the problem right-back position, Ball was a first team regular at Burnden Park for the next five seasons, being ever-present during 1953-54 and 1954-55. Though he lost his place to a young Roy Hartle who played in every round of the club's run to the 1953 FA Cup Final, Ball was back for the match against Blackpool which the Seasiders won 4-3.

Whilst with the Wanderers, Ball represented England at 'B' international level and was chosen twice by the Football League. Ball eventually lost his place to Hartle after a couple of games of the 1955-56 campaign but he continued to play in the Central League and help out at first team level whenever needed.

He had played in 212 games for the Wanderers when he left Burnden Park to manage his hometown club, Wigan Athletic.

MARCH 14th

1885 Kenny Davenport became Bolton's first England international when he played against Wales at Ninian Park, Cardiff.

1891 James Munro and James Cassidy scored two goals apiece in Bolton's 7-1 rout of West Bromwich Albion. The Wanderers' other scorers were Robert Turner, James Brogan and John McNee. Not surprisingly, Albion finished bottom of the First Division.

1925 Joe Smith and David Jack each scored twice in Wanderers' 4-0 defeat of Aston Villa at Burnden Park.

1931 The Wanderers scored five goals in the space of 21 minutes as they beat Sheffield United 6-2, with Harold Blackmore netting a hat-trick. This was also Ted Vizard's penultimate appearance in a Bolton shirt, the Welsh winger having made his debut 20 years previously.

1974 Birth of Mark Fish. The South African international defender was signed from Lazio for a fee of £2.5 million in September 1997. He was at the time, Bolton's joint-record signing and was a great coup for the club as Manchester United were also chasing his signature. He was an instant success with the Wanderers, his form leading to him representing South Africa in the 1998 World Cup Finals in France. In his second season at the Reebok, unpleasant club versus country wrangles did not help his cause and he frequently had to make lengthy trips to play in the African Nations Cup. Despite this, he always returned as quickly as possible to fight for the Bolton cause.

Fish *(right)*, who became Bolton's most capped player after making 34 of his 60 international appearances for South Africa whilst at the Reebok, went on to play in 127 games before

opting for a move back to the Premiership with Charlton Athletic. A regular at the heart of the Addicks' defence where he has formed a solid partnership with Richard Rufus, he scored Charlton's goal in the draw with the Wanderers last season.

MARCH 15th

1890 Bolton's Kenny Davenport helped himself to two goals as England beat Ireland 9-1 in Belfast.

1903 Birth of Jack Rimmer. He began his career with his home-town club, Southport where he had scored seven goals in 19 first team games before the Wanderers signed him in the summer of 1930. The flying winger, who went on to win England Amateur international honours whilst working in his father's building business, made his Bolton debut in a 1-1 draw against Chelsea in February 1931.

His appearances in his early days with the club were limited due to the fine form of Ray Westwood and Willie Cook but when the former moved to inside-forward in 1933, Rimmer became a regular in the Bolton side. After playing in 13 games in Bolton's promotion winning season of 1934-35, he found himself understudying Cook and though he stayed with the club for a further couple of seasons, he only made sporadic appearances.

He had scored 16 goals in 83 games when in February 1937 he moved to Burnley, but he failed to make an appearance in the Clarets' League side.

1961 The only French side to play at Burnden Park was Le Havre. They visited Bolton for the second leg of the Friendship Cup. The sides had drawn 1-1 in France but Bolton took the Cup by winning 4-0.

MARCH 16th

1914 Joe Smith scored on his England debut as Wales were beaten 2-0 at Ninian Park.

1935 George Walton scored Bolton's goal in a 1-1 FA Cup semi-final tie against West Bromwich Albion played at Leeds United's Elland Road ground.

1949 Birth of Alan Gowling. He began his career with Manchester United, winning England schoolboy and amateur international honours and appearing in the 1968 Mexico Olympics. Whilst he was still learning the game he became an economics graduate at university and in 1968-69, he forced his way into a United side containing Best, Law and Charlton. Whilst with United, he won England Under 23 honours but in June 1972 he left Old Trafford to join Huddersfield Town for a fee of £60,000. Under the managership of Ian Greaves, Gowling became a regular goalscorer at Leeds Road and in the summer of 1975, First Division Newcastle United paid £70,000 for his services. Forming a prolific partnership with Malcolm Macdonald, he helped the Magpies reach the League Cup Final in 1976 before two years later joining the Wanderers for a then club record fee of £120,000. After helping the Whites win promotion to the First Division, he scored the club's first goal back in the top flight, albeit in a 2-1 home defeat at the hands of Bristol City. During his stay with the Trotters, Gowling became a dual purpose player, either leading the attack or marshalling the centre of defence. Elected chairman of the PFA, Gowling went on to score 31 goals in 165 games before joining Preston North End where he spent his last season in first-class football.

MARCH 17th

1956 Nat Lofthouse and Dennis Stevens scored two goals each in a 4-0 home win over West Bromwich Albion. The two Bolton forwards - Lofthouse 32 and Stevens 13 - scored 45 of the club's 71 League goals.

1973 For the home game against Rochdale, both linesmen were situated on the Burnden side of the ground. The referee, Ron Tinkler ordered both linesmen to patrol the one line for the last half-an-hour of the match.
The referee explained that he was unable to see his linesman on the Manchester Road side of the ground due to the sun.

MARCH 18th

1922 The Wanderers inflicted the first home defeat on the League Champions elect, Liverpool at fortress Anfield. Goals from David Jack and Joe Smith (penalty) gave Bolton a 2-0 win. However, the match was very heated and the referee had to call both teams into the centre-circle to give them a cooling-down talk!

MARCH 19th

1904 A goal by Bob Taylor gave the Wanderers a 1-0 FA Cup semi-final win over Derby County at Wolves' Molineux Ground. It was a remarkable result as the Wanderers were a mid-table Second Division club and the Rams were riding high in the top flight.

1995 Though Bolton ended the season in third place in Division One and were promoted via the play-offs, their away form produced only five wins. This 1-0 win at Millwall who were difficult to beat at The Den came courtesy of a John McGinlay special.

MARCH 20th

1935 Having drawn 1-1 in their first meeting, the Wanderers met West Bromwich Albion at Stoke's

Victoria Ground for this FA Cup semi-final replay. Despite dominating the game for long periods of play, it was Albion who went through to the final, winning 2-0.

1942 Birth of Wyn Davies. Welsh-speaking Wyn began his career with his home-town team Caernarfon before being spotted by Wrexham. He scored on his league debut for the Robins. In his last match for the club he was one of three players who scored a hat-trick in a 10-1 win over Hartlepool United. He joined Bolton in a transfer deal worth £20,000 in cash, plus Ernie Phythian, who was valued at £10,000, moving to the Racecourse Ground. During his time at Bolton, Davies became affectionately known as 'Wyn the Leap' due to his amazing heading talents in the No.9 shirt. He was a regular in the Wanderers' side for four and a half years. In 1964 he won the first of 34 caps for Wales when he played against England at Wrexham. He scored his first hat-trick for the Wanderers in a 3-0 home win over Southampton and ended that 1964-65 season as the Wanderers' top scorer with 25 goals. His performances for the Wanderers led to his name being linked with a number of top clubs and in October 1966 after scoring 74 goals in 170 games, he joined Newcastle United for a club record fee of £80,000. He was the Magpies' first superstar of the modern game and though his ball skills never matched his aerial ability, he held the ball up well and controlled the forward line. As Newcastle surged into European competition, Davies became one of the most feared strikers on the continent, scoring 10 goals in 24 games and helping the club win the Inter Cities Fairs Cup in 1969. Once the club had been eliminated from Europe in 1970, Davies was sold to Manchester City. He later crossed the city to play for Manchester United and then had spells with Blackpool, Crystal Palace and Stockport County before ending his league career with Crewe Alexandra.

1946 Birth of Brian Bromley. He was aged just 16 when, in March 1963, he made his league debut for the Wanderers in a 3-2 home win over Sheffield United, in one of the club's youngest-ever forward lines. In that match Freddie Hill netted all the club's goals and though Bromley kept his place for the next two games, he returned to the reserves after Billy Russell joined the club from Sheffield United. In 1964 Bromley was selected for the England youth side and towards the end of the 1963-64 campaign, won a regular place in the Bolton side. Following the club's relegation to Division Two, Bromley was a virtual ever-present in the Wanderers' side for the next three seasons, taking his tally of goals to 26 in 184 first team appearances before being sold to Portsmouth for £25,000. His three seasons at Fratton Park brought him little success but after joining Brighton and Hove Albion, he was a member of their Third Division promotion-winning side. However, the Seagulls were relegated immediately and Bromley joined Reading, ending his league career with a brief loan spell with Darlington.

MARCH 21st

1896 Robert Tannahill scored Bolton's goal in the FA Cup semi-final against Sheffield Wednesday at Goodison Park. The match ended all-square at 1-1 and had to be replayed.

1936 The Wanderers went down 7-0 against Manchester City at Maine Road, thus equalling their worst-ever League defeat. Bolton keeper Fred Swift was opposed by his more renowned brother Frank in the City goal.

1953 Bolton played Everton in the FA Cup semi-final at Maine Road and by half-time were 4-0 up, courtesy of goals by Lofthouse (2), Moir and Holden. The Blues missed a penalty just before the interval but in the second-half, pulled three goals back. The Wanderers hung on to win through to the final against Blackpool.

1958   Birth of Tony Caldwell. An electrician by trade, he played his local football with Irlam Town and was scoring prolifically for Horwich RMI when Bolton signed him for a bargain £2,000 in 1983. After impressing on a pre-season tour to Ireland, the Salford-born striker was given his League debut in the opening game of the 1983-84 season against Wimbledon, which the Wanderers won 2-0. He scored in a Bolton victory at Bradford City the following week but really hit the headlines in the club's next home game when he scored five of Bolton's goals in an 8-1 victory over Walsall at Burnden Park to equal James Cassidy's club record that had stood for 93 years. Not surprisingly, Caldwell ended the season as the club's top scorer with 23 goals in 38 games, a feat he was to achieve in each of his four seasons with the club.

He had scored 78 goals in 176 games including a hat-trick in a 7-2 win over Plymouth Argyle in September 1984 when he left Bolton to join Bristol City for £27,500 - a fee decided by a tribunal transfer. But at Ashton Gate as with subsequent clubs Chester City, Grimsby Town and Stockport County, he failed to find his goalscoring touch.

MARCH 22nd

1941   Nat Lofthouse aged 15 years 207 days played his first game for the Wanderers at Bury. Bolton won 5-1 with the young Lofthouse scoring the club's last two goals.

1958   Ralph Gubbins replaced the injured Nat Lofthouse for the FA Cup semi-final against Blackburn Rovers at Maine Road. The stand-in became the Bolton hero, scoring both goals in a 2-1 win for the Wanderers.

MARCH 23rd

1890   Birth of Ernie Whiteside. When the Lytham-born player arrived at Burnden Park, he had a reputation as a first-class sprinter. When playing for his home-town team, had turned out at centre-forward but his first game for the Wanderers against West Bromwich Albion in September 1908 was at outside-left. Though he was at this time playing the majority of his football for the club's reserve side, he was converted into a wing-half and when he won a regular place in the Bolton side in 1909-10, it was in this position. Though the club was relegated that season, Whiteside was an important member of the side that won promotion back to the top flight a year later and who finished fourth in Division One in 1911-12.

He was an integral member of the side that continued to challenge for League Championship honours the following season but after losing his place to Walter Rowley, Whiteside moved to York City where he ended his playing career, he had played in 88 League and Cup games for Bolton.

1899   In the first FA Cup semi-final ever played at Burnden Park, Sheffield United beat Liverpool 1-0, after the club's had drawn 1-1 in the first meeting at Fallowfield.

1907   Everton beat West Bromwich Albion 2-1 in Burnden Park's second FA Cup semi-final.

1929   Goals from Billy Butler, George Gibson and Harold Blackmore gave Bolton a 3-1 victory over Huddersfield Town in the FA Cup semi-final played at Anfield.

1946   The Wanderers went down 2-0 to Charlton Athletic in the FA Cup semi-final played at Villa Park.

MARCH 24th

1879 Birth of Bob Struthers. Having played his early football with a number of Merseyside teams including Temple, Kirkdale and Rockferry, he joined First Division Everton but enjoyed little success with the Goodison club. He moved into the Southern League with Gravesend United before joining Portsmouth. It was from Pompey that Bolton signed him in the summer of 1901 and he made his league debut in a 2-0 defeat at Small Heath on the opening day of the 1901-02 season.

After that, he was relegated to the club's reserve side, with Charlie Ostick regaining his first team place. However, midway through the following season, Struthers won a regular first team spot and appeared in the club's 1904 FA Cup Final side and the team that won promotion to the First Division a year later. He went on to appear in 141 games for the Wanderers before leaving in August 1907 to play for Bradford Park Avenue. In his only season with the Yorkshire club, they won election to the Second Division of the Football League

1923 A goal from David Jack was enough to beat Sheffield United in the FA Cup semi-final played at Old Trafford. It took the Wanderers through to Wembley's first FA Cup Final.

MARCH 25th

1899 The Wanderers lost 3-1 to neighbours Bury in the final of the Lancashire Cup played at Burnden Park.

1938 Birth of Peter Deakin. A member of the Bolton side that reached the FA Youth Cup semi-final in 1956, he made his First Division debut for the Wanderers at inside-forward two years later, deputising for the injured Ray Parry in a 4-0 defeat at Aston Villa. The scorer of some vital goals for the Wanderers, he spent most of his time at Burnden Park as an understudy, first to Parry and then to Freddie Hill. This had a bearing on the Normanton-born schemer's decision to take up teaching and become a part-timer with the Wanderers. Deakin went on to score 15 goals in 73 League and Cup games until in March 1964 he left to play for Peterborough United. He spent two seasons at London Road before having a season back in his native Yorkshire with Bradford. He then had a second spell with 'Posh' before ending his first-class playing career with Brentford.

1959 Bolton Wanderers were the visitors to Manchester United for the first game under the Old Trafford floodlights. United, who were League leaders were expected to win comfortably but a Ray Parry thunderbolt and an own goal by Bill Foulkes gave the Wanderers a 2-0 win.

MARCH 26th

1881 Bolton beat Manchester Wanderers 10-0. It was the first time that the club had reached double figures!

1887 The Wanderers went down 3-0 at home to Preston North End in the final of the Lancashire Cup.

1892 James Cassidy had the distinction of scoring Bolton's first-ever penalty, when he converted the Wanderers' opening goal in a 2-0 defeat of Notts County.

1906 Walter White and David Stokes scored two goals apiece as the Wanderers beat Birmingham 5-2. Bolton's other scorer in a very one-sided game was Jack Atkinson.

1932 Jack Milsom netted a hat-trick as the Wanderers beat Sheffield United 3-1 at Burnden Park.

MARCH 27th

1900 Birth of Billy Butler. Possibly the greatest of all Bolton's wingers, he began his career with his home-town club Atherton for whom he signed after being demobbed from the army. The Wanderers spotted him playing for Atherton in the Lancashire Combination and brought him to Burnden Park in April 1920 where they converted him from a centre-forward to outside-right. He made his Bolton debut in a 2-0 home defeat by Chelsea in January 1922 after which he became a virtual ever-present in the Wanderers' side for the next 12 seasons. He won an England cap against Scotland in 1924, when he partnered David Jack and was also the holder of three FA Cup Final winners' medals from the 1920s, scoring the opening goal in the 1929 final when Bolton beat Portsmouth 2-0. After the Wanderers were relegated in 1933, Billy Butler asked to go on the transfer list and having scored 74 goals in 449 League and Cup games, left Burnden Park to join his former team-mate Joe Smith who was manager of Reading. When Smith left to join Blackpool, Butler replaced him as manager of Reading but resigned four years later for personal reasons. He later managed Torquay United before emigrating to South Africa where he coached and managed a number of clubs.

1926 The Wanderers won through to the FA Cup Final with a 3-0 semi-final win over Swansea Town at White Hart Lane. Bolton's scorers were Joe Smith (2) and Bill Baggert.

1976 Bolton beat Chelsea 2-1 but it was the London club's players who were responsible for the Wanderers' two goals, with Hay and Graham Wilkins putting through their own goal!

1979 Frank Worthington and Alan Gowling both scored twice in a 4-2 home win over Arsenal with Worthy's two goals coming from the penalty spot.

MARCH 28th

1896 Having drawn 1-1 with Sheffield Wednesday, the Wanderers replayed their FA Cup semi-final against the Owls at the Town Ground, Nottingham. Wednesday won 3-1 with Robert Tannahill again scoring Bolton's goal.

1914 Joe Smith netted his third hat-trick of the season as the Wanderers beat Bradford City 3-0 at Burnden Park. It was sweet revenge for the Trotters who had been beaten 5-1 at Valley Parade earlier in the season.

1925 The Wanderers took part in an experiment in a friendly match against Manchester City. There was no offside in operation 40 yards from the goal and Bolton ran out winners 3-0.

MARCH 29th

1894 Birth of Jimmy Fay. The Southport-born defender played his early football for local sides, Blue Star and Southport Working Lads. In 1903 he joined Chorley and after turning professional played for both Oswaldtwistle Rovers and Oldham Athletic. With the Latics, Fay did not miss a single game in four seasons from 1907-08 to 1910-11. In 1909-10 while playing at inside-forward he was the club's leading scorer with 26 goals. That helped the Latics win promotion to the top flight but after just one more season at Boundary Park, he left to join the Wanderers in September 1911. At Burnden Park, Fay was the club's regular centre-half but missed part of his second season with the Wanderers when he required a hernia operation. During the war years, Fay was to be found playing for Southport Central but returned to Burnden Park when the hostilities ceased in 1918. The following year, aged 35, he represented the Football League XI against the Scottish League at Ibrox. He spent another couple of seasons with the Wanderers, taking his tally of matches in which he scored five goals to 136 before returning to Southport Central. From 1922 to 1952, Jimmy Fay was secretary (and chairman 1922-1929) of the PFA, having been a founder member of the old Players' Union in 1907. Earning himself the title of 'Gentleman' James Fay, he later became a JP whilst continuing to operate his sports outfitting business.

MARCH 30th

1895 Bolton and Bury played out a goalless draw in the Manchester Cup Final played at Newton Heath.

1906 Bolton won the Manchester Cup, beating rivals Bury 3-0 in the final played at Clayton.

1947 Birth of Ronnie Phillips *(below)*. The Worsley-born winger made his Bolton debut as a replacement for Gordon Taylor on the left-wing in a 3-1 win over Cardiff City at Burnden Park in January 1967. Phillips and Taylor then became rivals for that position until the arrival of Terry Wharton from Wolves restricted Phillips' first team appearances.

Ronnie Phillips' best season without doubt was the club's 1972-73 Third Division Championship-winning campaign, when he missed just one game and scored some vital goals. Midway through the following season, Peter Thompson joined the Wanderers from Liverpool and Phillips was the one to make way for the England international. In January 1975 he had a loan spell with Chesterfield but six months later joined Bury for a fee of £12,000. Phillips had played first team football for Bolton for nine seasons, scoring 19 goals in 175 games. After just over two years at Gigg Lane, he joined Chester before ending his career with Barrow.

MARCH 31st

1894 The Wanderers appeared in their first-ever FA Cup Final but a crowd of just 23,000 saw the Bolton players freeze on the day. Notts County won 4-1 with James Cassidy netting for the Wanderers in the final minute of the match. Notts County were the first Second Division side to win the trophy.

APRIL 1st

1908 Albert Shepherd netted his third hat-trick of the season as the Wanderers thumped Newcastle United 4-0.

1916 Joe Smith netted his first hat-trick of the wartime games as the Wanderers beat Bury 4-3. The two clubs met four times over the course of the 1915-16 season but this was Bolton's only success!

47

1969 In Roy Hartle's testimonial match - an International XI played an All Stars XI - making a nostalgic return to Burnden Park was former favourite Francis Lee, who hit five goals for the All Stars, who ran out 10-9 winners!

APRIL 2nd

1895 Birth of John Reid Smith. Signed from Scottish giants Glasgow Rangers as a replacement for Frank Roberts, who had left to play for Manchester City, Smith had previously played for Albion Rovers, Kilmarnock and Cowdenbeath. He never really settled at Ibrox Park and when Bolton offered £3,000 for his services, he was more than happy to try his luck south of the border. He scored a last minute winner on his Bolton debut against Manchester City in November 1922 and at the end of the season, scored the club's second goal in the 1923 FA Cup Final win over West Ham United. He continued to be a regular scorer for the Wanderers and in 1924-25 he netted 21 goals in 35 games including a hat-trick in a 4-2 home win over Sheffield United. He scored another treble in the 5-0 defeat of West Ham United at Burnden Park in November 1924 and against Birmingham the following season when the Wanderers won 5-3. Smith's final hat-trick for the club came in the opening game of the 1926-27 season as Bolton beat Leeds United 5-2 at Elland Road. He had scored 87 goals in 174 appearances, a total reduced by a number of niggling injuries that forced him to miss quite a number of games, when he left to join Bury in March 1928. At Gigg Lane, he scored 108 goals in 157 games, including a quickfire hat-trick on his debut for the Shakers.

1995 The Wanderers reached the Football League Cup Final at Wembley for the first time in their history. Though Alan Thompson scored a spectacular goal for Bolton, two strikes from Steve McManaman won the game for Liverpool. This game saw the debut as a substitute of the ever-popular Gudni Bergsson.

2000 Bolton reached the FA Cup semi-finals for the first time since 1958.
Their opponents at Wembley were Premiership side Aston Villa and though the Wanderers and Dean Holdsworth in particular had the chances to score, the game remained goalless after extra-time. However, it was Villa who won the penalty shoot-out 4-1 with only Holdsworth converting his spot-kick!

APRIL 3rd

1893 Birth of Frank Roberts. The Sandbach-born forward played his early football with local clubs Sandbach Villa and Sandbach Ramblers before joining Crewe Alexandra. His goalscoring exploits for the Railwaymen led to the Wanderers signing him in May 1914. He made his Bolton debut the following October as he and Joe Smith spearheaded the Wanderers' attack as they reached the FA Cup semi-final where they lost 2-1 to Sheffield United. During the First World War, Roberts served in the North Lancashire Regiment, whilst in 1919-20, the first season of peacetime football, he was the club's leading scorer with 26 goals including a hat-trick in a 6-3 win at Aston Villa. In 1920-21, he was ever-present as the Wanderers finished third in Division One, as he and Joe Smith scored 62 goals between them. Roberts' share was 24 whilst Smith's total of 38 made him the Division's highest scorer. In October 1922, after taking over the management of licensed premises, Frank Roberts was suspended by the board. He had scored 80 goals in 168 games when he left Burnden Park to play for Manchester City. He was their leading scorer in three of his five seasons with the club and played against the Wanderers in the 1926 FA Cup Final. After helping City win promotion to the First Division in 1928 he joined Manchester Central before later ending his career with Horwich RMI.

1897 Bolton lost 3-1 to near neighbours Bury in the final of the Manchester Cup played at Hyde Road.

1898 Birth of David Jack. Though he is most famous for scoring the first goal in a Wembley Cup Final as the Wanderers beat West Ham United 2-0 in 1923, he contributed far more to the game than that. The son of the former Wanderer's player, Bob Jack, he began his Football League career with Plymouth Argyle where his father was manager. Arsenal and Chelsea, with whom he had played during the First World War, both wanted to sign him, but he opted for his home-town club and signed for the Wanderers in December 1920 for a then record fee of £3,500. He made his Bolton debut the following month in a goalless draw at Oldham Athletic and became a first team regular thereafter. For the next seven seasons, Jack shared the goalscoring responsibilities with Joe Smith and was the club's top league scorer in five of them, with a best return of 26 in 1924-25. David Jack netted in six of Bolton's seven FA Cup ties on the way to winning the trophy for the first time in 1923.
A year later, he won the first of four England caps while he was at Burnden Park. He scored the winning goal in the 1926 FA Cup Final but in October 1928 after having scored 161 goals in 324 games, he joined Arsenal for a then record £10,340 transfer. He went on to win both League Championship and further FA Cup winners' medals with the Gunners. He later managed Southend United, Middlesbrough and League of Ireland club Shelbourne. He then worked as a sportswriter before retiring in April 1955. Jack also worked for the Inland Revenue as he had done in the early part of his career. One of the most famous of all Bolton Wanderers' players, David Jack died in September 1958.

1953 Nat Lofthouse netted three of Bolton's goals in a 5-0 defeat of Sunderland. The Wanderers went on to complete the double over the Wearsiders, who finished the season five places higher than Bolton!

1961 Northern Ireland international centre-forward Billy McAdams scored all Bolton's goals in a 3-0 home win over Aston Villa.

APRIL 4th

1876 Birth of Bob Jack. He began his career with his home-town team, Alloa Athletic before joining Bolton in 1895. He made his debut in a 2-1 win over Small Heath, replacing the injured James Cassidy in the Wanderers' attack. A member of the Bolton side that reached the 1896 FA Cup semi-final, he was the club's leading scorer in 1896-97 with 11 goals from his position at outside-left. He helped the Wanderers win back their place in Division One in 1899-1900 but midway through the following season, he lost his place to William Tracey and after scoring 29 goals in 125 games, he left to play for Preston North End. After a year at Deepdale, he moved to Glossop but twelve months later he joined Southern League Plymouth Argyle. After a brief spell managing the Devon club, he took up a similar post with Southend United before rejoining the Pilgrims for a much longer - 1910 to 1938 - spell as manager.

1900 The Wanderers again lost to Bury in the final of the Manchester Cup, losing 4-0 at Hyde Road.

1911 Birth of Bill Ridding. As a player he had been a centre-forward playing for Tranmere Rovers and both Manchester clubs before a double cartilage injury forced his retirement at the age of just 22. His association with the Wanderers began in 1946 when he was appointed trainer and after a temporary spell as manager following Rowley's resignation, he was officially appointed secretary-manager of the Wanderers in February 1951. He also acted as the club's trainer.

In 1953 he led the Wanderers to Wembley in the FA Cup Final only for them to lose 4-3 to Blackpool after they had led 3-1 with just 20 minutes to play. Five years later, he took the club to Wembley again, with a team he had put together for £110 and this time had the pleasure of being on the winning side against Manchester United. The abolition of the maximum wage in 1961 proved disastrous for clubs like Bolton and Ridding *(below)* had to fight to hold on to the Wanderers' better players.

In August 1968 he left Burnden Park to concentrate on his physiotherapy practice, later joining Lancashire County Cricket Club in that capacity before dying in September 1981, at the age of 70.

1947 Birth of Roy Greaves *(right)*. The Saturday after he made his League debut at Leyton Orient, the 18-year-old Greaves scored both Bolton's goals in a 3-2 home defeat by Southampton. He then settled into the Wanderers' side at inside-forward, becoming a regular in 1967-68, when he topped the club's goalscoring charts. He was again top scorer the following season.

Despite these achievements, he failed to win over the majority of the home fans and was often subjected to mindless criticism. The turning point in his career came when manager Jimmy Armfield moved him into midfield after relegation to the Third Division in 1981. When the Wanderers won the Third Division Championship in 1972-73, Greaves was ever-present and a cornerstone of the side that spent the next five seasons in the leading pack in Division Two before winning a place in the top flight.

By then, Roy Greaves had become captain and it was he who lifted the Second Division Championship trophy aloft at the end of the 1977-78 season. In his debut season in the First Division, he missed only one game but the following term a combination of injuries and advancing years cost him his place.

He had scored 85 goals in 575 games when in March 1980 he left Bolton to play for the Seattle Sounders in the NASL. After his stint in the United States, he returned to become player-manager at Rochdale, thus giving him the distinction of having played in every division of the Football League.

1958 Wing-half Derek Hennin moved to centre-forward for the home game with Aston Villa and

responded by netting a hat-trick in a 4-0 win for the Wanderers.

APRIL 5th

1934 For the visit of Preston North End - a game which ended goalless - the Burnden Park crowd were treated to a new form of match-day entertainment - a wireless!

1948 Birth of Roy McFarland. After beginning his playing career with Tranmere Rovers, he joined Derby County where he formed an excellent partnership with Dave Mackay, helping the Rams win the Second Division Championship in 1968-69. After winning the first of 28 caps for England he became an inspirational skipper as Derby won their first League Championship in 1972. He went on to appear in 530 games for the Rams, scoring 48 goals. In his first managerial role he took Bradford City to Division Three in 1982 but was then enticed to rejoin Derby as assistant manager. He took over as caretaker when Peter Taylor was sacked and remained at the Baseball Ground as Arthur Cox's assistant until 1993 when he became manager. But in June 1995, after 26 years service to the Rams, he left to take charge at Bolton with former team-mate Colin Todd remaining as his assistant.
The Wanderers' first season in the Premiership was always going to be hard and with just two wins before the turn of the year, Bolton were on course for a swift return to the First Division. The poor run of results culminated in a parting of the ways. He later managed Cambridge United and Torquay United before taking charge of Chesterfield.

APRIL 6th

1895 John Sutcliffe kept a clean sheet on his international debut as England beat Scotland 2-0 at Goodison Park.

1907 Walter White became Bolton's first Scottish international when he played against England at St James Park.

1917 It was Good Friday and the Wanderers played two games on the same day! In the morning they lost 2-0 at Stockport County in the Lancashire Section Primary Competition and in the afternoon won 2-1 at Oldham Athletic in the Subsidiary Competition. Nine Wanderers' players took part in both games.

1965 Birth of Andy Walker. One of the game's most lethal finishers, he began his career with Motherwell before joining Celtic. During the 1987-88 season, Walker scored 31 goals as the Bhoys won the League and Cup double - and he won the first of three full caps for Scotland. After failing to fit in with the plans of the new Celtic boss Liam Brady, Walker *(right)* had a loan spell at Newcastle United before joining the Wanderers in January 1992 on a similar basis. He made his debut as a substitute in a 2-2 draw at Exeter City, scoring with his first touch, minutes after coming off the bench. The following month he signed for the Wanderers on a permanent basis for £160,000, after which he could do no wrong. He scored 15 goals in 24 league games and after netting after just 47 seconds in the opening game of the 1992-93 season against Huddersfield Town, he went on to score 26 league goals as the Wanderers won promotion to the First Division. His total of 33 goals equalled a post-war club record set by Nat Lofthouse twice during the 1950s. Sadly, his season came to an end when he damaged his cruciate ligament in the match against Swansea City. He recovered to take his tally of goals to 55 in 87 games before rejoining Celtic for a tribunal set fee of £550,000.

2002 German international Fredi Bobic scored a well taken hat-trick in the crunch match against Ipswich Town as the Suffolk club found

themselves 4-0 down at the interval! It was the club's first top flight treble since Freddie Hill netted three goals in 1962.

APRIL 7th

1907   Albert Shepherd scored on his England debut but they went down 2-1 to the Auld Enemy at Hampden Park - it was his only appearance for his country.

1920   Having beaten Aston Villa 2-1 at Burnden Park, courtesy of two Frank Roberts' penalties, the Wanderers travelled to Villa Park and came away with a 6-3 victory. Frank Roberts netted a hat-trick including another goal from the penalty spot!

1945   Nat Lofthouse scored all Bolton's goals in a 4-1 win over Blackpool at Bloomfield Road in a wartime league game.

APRIL 8th

1895   The Wanderers won the Manchester Cup for the first time, beating Bury 3-2 in the Hyde Road final.

1920   Birth of Harry McShane. He was just 17 years old when he made his Football League debut for Blackburn Rovers but he didn't appear in another League game for the Ewood Park club because of the outbreak of the Second World. On the resumption of League football in 1946, McShane joined Huddersfield Town, but after just one season with the Terriers he signed for the Wanderers. Replacing Bill Wrigglesworth on the left-wing, his early days at Burnden Park were disappointing and he lost his place in the side after just a handful of appearances. He eventually found his form and over the next two seasons, was a regular in the Wanderers side after switching to outside-right following the signing

of Bobby Langton. McShane went on to score seven goals in 99 games before leaving to play for Manchester United. He was a member of United's League Championship winning side of 1951-52 and remained at Old Trafford until February 1954 when he joined Oldham Athletic. The father of actor Ian McShane, he later had a spell as player-coach of Chorley before becoming a scout for Manchester United.

1964   Birth of John McGinlay *(below)*. He played his early football with Nairn County before spending a season in New Zealand playing for Hanimex. On his return he joined then Gola League side Yeovil Town and spent three and a half seasons with the Somerset club before returning north of the border to play for Elgin City.

His goalscoring achievements led to Shrewsbury manager Ian McNeill paying £25,000 for his services in February 1989.

The following season he scored in both games against the Wanderers but in the summer of 1990 after scoring 31 goals in 68 games for the Shrews he joined Bury for a fee of £175,000. While with the Shakers, McGinlay hit a hat-trick against the Wanderers at a rain-soaked Burnden Park in a 3-1 win for the Gigg Lane club, but in January 1991, Bruce Rioch, who was then manager of Millwall paid £80,000 to take him to the Den.

The London club reached the play-offs that season but in September 1992, Rioch, who had by now become boss at Burnden Park, paid £125,000 for his services. McGinlay ended his first season with 22 goals as the Wanderers won promotion and reached the fifth round of the FA Cup. His goals in both matches against Liverpool and the penalty-kick that beat Preston North End in the final game of the season endeared him to the hearts of the Bolton fans.

In 1993-94 he netted 33 goals to equal the post-war club record held by Nat Lofthouse and Andy Walker for total goals in a season. His record included hat-tricks against Charlton Athletic and Middlesbrough. In 1994 he won the first of 13 Scottish caps when he scored in a 2-1 defeat of Austria. McGinlay, who netted another hat-trick in the 6-1 League Cup win over Spurs, went on to score 118 goals in 245 games, including the last goal at Burnden Park before joining Bradford City for £625,000 in November 1997.

APRIL 9th

1921   Joe Smith scored all Bolton's goals in a 3-1 home defeat of Newcastle United.

1938   Birth of Brian Birch. He was just 16 years of age when he replaced the injured Doug Holden for his League debut in a 3-3 draw against Aston Villa in September 1954. Most of his early football was played in the club's Central League side, though he was still a member of the club's youth team when they reached the semi-finals of the FA Youth Cup. It was 1957 before he won a regular place in the Bolton side, going on to play in every round of the FA Cup as the Wanderers reached the Wembley final. At 20 years of age, he was the 'baby' of the side that beat Manchester United 2-0. He then found himself sharing the winger's duties with Neville Bannister and then following the signing of Brian Pilkington, he found himself back in the reserves as Holden reverted to the No.7 shirt. Birch remained at Burnden Park until 1964, taking his tally of goals to 28 in 191 League and Cup games before being allowed to join Rochdale. He spent two seasons at Spotland before entering non-League football with Ellesmere Port.

1955   Eric Bell, who had just received notification of his selection by the FA for the close season tour to the Caribbean, broke his leg in Bolton's 2-2 draw at Preston North End.

APRIL 10th

1940   George Hunt netted the club's first hat-trick in wartime football as the Wanderers beat Burnley 5-1 in front of a Burnden Park crowd of just 700.

1993   Goals from Tony Kelly and Andy Walker helped the Wanderers to a 2-0 win over Wigan Athletic at Springfield Park. This was Andy Walker's 33rd goal of the season - it turned out to be his last because he was injured in the club's next game at home to Swansea City.

APRIL 11th

1885   Bolton beat Blackburn Rovers 5-1 in the Lancashire Cup semi-final played at Darwen but were then disqualified for fielding ineligible players.

1942 George Hunt, who was a prolific scorer for the Wanderers during the wartime years, found the net in the opening minute in the match against Blackpool at Bloomfield Road, but the Seasiders hit back to win 7-1.

1979 In an extraordinary fightback, Bolton beat Manchester United at Old Trafford by 2-1 with both the Wanderers' goals scored by Frank Worthington, the second goal in injury time. The previous December, the mercurial Worthington had netted two of Bolton's goals in a 3-0 home win.

1989 A Julian Darby goal gave Bolton a 1-0 win over Blackpool in the Sherpa Van Trophy Northern Area Final first-leg at Burnden Park.

APRIL 12th

1919 Frank Roberts, who scored 18 goals in 19 appearances in this last season of wartime football, netted a hat-trick in Bolton's 3-1 win over Oldham Athletic.

1964 Birth of Chris Fairclough. The Nottingham-born defender began his career with his home-town club Nottingham Forest, for whom he made 134 appearances despite being out of the game for 18 months with injury. Also whilst at the City Ground, he won five of his seven England Under 21 caps. In July 1987 he joined Tottenham Hotspur for a fee of £387,000 but after David Pleat left the club, Fairclough *(right)* too moved on, joining Leeds United for £500,000.
He became a member of the most successful Leeds side since the Don Revie era as they won the Second Division Championship prior to pipping Manchester United for the League Championship in 1992.
He suffered with injury in his last season at Elland Road but had made 195 appearances for the Yorkshire club when he joined Bolton for

£500,000 in the summer of 1995. Despite the club's poor performance, Fairclough proved to be a consistent player at the heart of the Bolton defence. He was the club's only ever-present in 1996-97, winning the player's Player of the Year award. Injuries hampered his progress the following season and after scoring eight goals in 106 games he was allowed to join Notts County on a free transfer. Things didn't work out for him at Meadow Lane and after a loan spell with York City, he joined the Minstermen on a permanent basis, later ending his career with the Bootham Crescent club.

APRIL 13th

1895 Cup Finalists West Bromwich Albion were beaten 5-0 by the Wanderers with Peter Turnbull, who had recently joined the club from Burnley, netting a hat-trick. Albion were handicapped when their keeper James Reader was sent-off for pushing Willie Joyce.
This was the last Football League game to be played at the Pikes Lane ground.

APRIL 14th

1868 Birth of John Sutcliffe. He won international honours at both rugby and soccer. He played rugby union for both Bradford and Heckmondwyke and while with the latter won an England cap against New Zealand in 1889. Towards the end of that year, the Yorkshire club were suspended for professionalism and so Sutcliffe decided to try his hand at soccer and joined the Wanderers. He arrived at the club as a forward but after his rugby instincts became apparent, he was switched to goalkeeper and made his debut in December 1889, in a 7-0 home win over West Bromwich Albion at Pikes Lane. The following season he became the club's regular keeper, a position he held for the next 11 seasons. Sutcliffe, who played for the Football League on three occasions, won the first of five full caps for England in March 1893 when he played against Wales. However, he also had the unwanted distinction of being the first Bolton play to receive his marching orders at Burnden Park when he was sent-off for dissent in a 3-1 defeat of Sheffield Wednesday. Sutcliffe went on to appear in 364 games for the Wanderers before leaving to join Millwall in the summer of 1902. He later had spells with Manchester United and Plymouth Argyle, then in the Southern League, before becoming coach at Southend United. After the First World War he was appointed trainer at Bradford City.

1891 Birth of Walter Rowley. After playing his early football for Oldham Athletic, Rowley joined Bolton Wanderers in 1912, playing his first game a year later against West Bromwich Albion. He was the Wanderers' 12th man in their 1923 FA Cup Final victory over West Ham United, missing the match after just finishing a suspension following his sending-off in the fifth round victory over Huddersfield Town. He had scored seven goals in 191 games when injury forced his retirement in 1925. Appointed coach to the club's reserve team, he later became the first team coach before being appointed manager in the summer of 1944. At the end of his first season in charge, the Wanderers beat Manchester United 3-2 on aggregate to take the League North Cup; in 1946 they reached the semi-finals of the FA Cup. The Wanderers continued to make steady progress under Rowley but in October 1950 he was forced to resign because of ill-health. He was awarded life membership of the club for services rendered before later returning to management, first with Middlesbrough and then Shrewsbury Town.

1894 Bolton lost 2-1 to Everton in the final of the Lancashire Cup played at Ardwick.

1912 Birth of Ray Westwood. After playing his early football for both Stourbridge and Brierley Hill Alliance, Ray Westwood was given a trial by Aston Villa. Fortunately for the Wanderers, this came to nothing and on the recommendation of former centre-half Jack Round, the Wanderers secured his services on amateur forms in the summer of 1928. He turned professional three years later and made his first team debut in a 1-1 draw against Manchester City. Forming a formidable partnership with Willie Cook, Westwood's performances led to him representing the Football League XI and winning six full caps for England, the first against Wales in September 1934. In 1934-35 when the

Wanderers finished runners-up to Brentford in the Second Division and so won promotion to the top flight, Westwood scored 30 goals in 38 league games, including four in the 8-0 rout of Barnsley. During the 1937-38 season when the Wanderers finished seventh in Division One, Westwood was the club's top scorer with 23 goals in 33 games including hat-tricks against Chelsea (Home 5-5) and Grimsby Town (Home 3-1). He continued to play for the Wanderers after the Second World War, taking his tally of goals to 144 in 333 League and Cup games before moving to join Chester.

After ending his career with Darwen, he returned to his home-town of Brierley Hill to run a newsagents.

APRIL 15th

1891 Bolton Wanderers won the Lancashire Cup, beating Darwen 3-1 in the final at Anfield.

1927 Wanderers' recent signing from Hamilton Academicals, George Gibson, netted a well-taken hat-trick as Bolton beat Everton 5-0.

APRIL 16th

1932 Jack Milsom scored his second hat-trick in the space of four games as the Wanderers beat Blackpool 3-0 at Bloomfield Road.

1963 Birth of Peter Valentine. He began his career with his home-town club, Huddersfield Town but after two seasons at Leeds Road, he was given a free transfer. He joined the Wanderers in the summer of 1983 and he became a regular at the heart of the Bolton defence during John McGovern's reign as manager. Because of the club's lack of success, there were numerous team changes at Burnden Park and in May 1985, Valentine became one of the casualties when he was given a free transfer after 81 appearances in a Bolton

shirt. His only goal for the club came in the 8-1 thrashing of Walsall when Tony Caldwell scored five of the goals. Valentine's replacement at Burnden Park was another signing from Huddersfield, Dave Sutton, whilst Valentine moved to neighbours Bury. He gave the Gigg Lane club great service, going on to appear in 319 games for the Shakers before later playing for Carlisle United and Rochdale, where he ended his first-class career.

1973 Stuart Lee netted a hat-trick for the Wanderers as they beat Halifax Town 3-0 on their way to winning the Third Division Championship.

1989 Nat Lofthouse was the Guest of Honour at the annual dinner of the PFA at London's Hilton Hotel. The Lion of Vienna was receiving a special merit award in recognition of his service to Bolton Wanderers and to his 50 years in the game.

APRIL 17th

1882 Bolton beat Bootle 12-0, the seventh time the club had reached double figures since it played its first match in December 1879.

1886 The Wanderers won the final of the Lancashire Cup beating Blackburn Rovers 1-0 in the final at Deepdale.

1888 At a meeting in Manchester, Bolton Wanderers became one of the 12 clubs to form the Football League, the brainchild of William McGregor, a member of the Aston Villa club.

1909 Billy Hughes and Billy Hunter scored two goals apiece in the Wanderers 4-1 home victory over Stockport County. Bolton went on to win their last two games to win the Second Division Championship, whilst County just avoided having to apply for re-election.

APRIL 18th

1892 James Cassidy netted a hat-trick in the final game of the season, as Bolton beat Everton 5-2.

1989 A Steve Thompson penalty gave Bolton a 1-1 draw against Blackpool at Bloomfield Road and a place in the Sherpa Van Trophy Final at Wembley, with a 2-1 aggregate win.

1997 Just one hour before Prime Minister John Major paid an official visit to the club's new stadium, Reebok signed a contract to name Bolton's new home Reebok Stadium. A press release announced the agreement as a multi-year, multi-million pound deal, the most lucrative naming rights contract ever signed in the United Kingdom.

APRIL 19th

1922 Birth of Willie Moir. Spotted playing football for the RAF team at Kirkham by Wanderers' scout Bob Jackson, Willie Moir joined Bolton in 1943. During the war years he 'guested' for both Aberdeen and Dundee, whilst in 1945 he played for Bolton in the North v South Cup Final. When League football resumed in 1946, Moir, who was predominantly right-footed, played most of his football at outside-left after having made his league debut in a 4-3 defeat at Chelsea on the opening day of the 1946-47 season. However, two seasons later he was switched to inside-right and scored all four goals including one from the penalty-spot in a 4-2 win at Aston Villa. He was ever-present during that campaign and ended the season as the First Division's leading scorer with 25 goals, a total which included another four goal haul in a 6-1 defeat of Sheffield United and a hat-trick in a 4-1 win over Middlesbrough. Forming an ideal partnership with Nat Lofthouse, Moir continued to find the net, his form winning him international recognition when he played for Scotland against England in April 1950. He had

scored 134 goals in 358 games when he left to become player-manager of Stockport County.

1975 Birth of Jussi Jaaskelainen *(right)*. The Finnish international goalkeeper joined the Wanderers from VPS Vaasa in November 1997. Following Keith Branagan's ligament problems, Jaaskelainen was thrown in at the deep end, proving himself to be a promising young keeper with a series of assured displays. Though he started the 1999-2000 season as second choice behind Branagan, his form was such that he displaced the London-born keeper after he had suffered a bad leg injury. An excellent shot-stopper, he worked hard at his all-round game - his positioning, kicking, distribution and confidence in one-on-one situations, making him one of the game's top keepers. Sadly in January 2001, he suffered a cruciate ligament injury in the game against Tranmere Rovers and was forced to miss the remainder of the season. Thankfully he returned to full fitness and over the last couple of seasons his consistency between the posts for the Wanderers has been phenomenal.
Jaaskelainen was ever-present in 2002-03 season and has appeared in 184 games for the Wanderers, at the time of writing. He continues to enhance his ever-growing reputation with some outstanding performances.

APRIL 20th

1907 Newly crowned League Champions Newcastle United visited Burnden Park for their final game of the season. The Wanderers ran out winners by 4-2 with goals from Marsh (2), White and Gaskell.

1991 The Wanderers were pushing hard for a play-off place and were expected to beat mid-table Leyton Orient, who had nothing to play for.
However, it took a David Reeves goal in injury-time to give Bolton the three points.

APRIL 21st

1913 The Wanderers lost 4-1 to Manchester United in the Manchester Cup Final played at Hyde Road.

1917 Jimmy Fay, 'guesting' for the Wanderers in this wartime fixture against Bury, scored four of Bolton's goals in a 6-0 win.

1979 Though Bolton lost 3-2 at home to Ipswich Town, Frank Worthington, who was this season's leading scorer in the First Division, won the 'Goal of the Season' award with a stunning strike against the Portman Road club

APRIL 22nd

1893 The Lancashire Cup Final against Preston North End at Ewood Park was unfinished. The Wanderers were losing 2-0 when following a crowd invasion, the referee had no choice but to call a halt to the proceedings.

1925 David Jack scored four times as local rivals Blackburn Rovers were comprehensively beaten 6-0.

APRIL 23rd

1892 The Wanderers lost 4-1 to Ardwick in the final of the Manchester Cup played at Newton Heath.

1904 Second Division Bolton's appearance in their second FA Cup Final against Manchester City, who were also chasing the First Division title, ended in a 1-0 defeat thanks to a disputed goal, after 20 minutes, from Welsh international winger Billy Meredith. The Wanderers claimed that he had been in an offside position when he received the ball before running clear to score.

1909 Birth of George Taylor. Captain of the England schoolboys, George Taylor signed for the Wanderers in a disused tramcar in a tramshed where his father worked. Though he made his league debut in a 3-3 draw at Blackpool in February 1931, it was 1933-34 before he began to establish himself as a first team regular because a broken ankle had kept him out for the entire 1932-33 campaign. In 1934-35, Taylor missed just one game as the Wanderers won promotion and the following season after some impressive displays in the top flight, he was chosen as a reserve for the England team. He had appeared in 244 League and Cup games for Bolton when the Second World War interrupted his career, though he did turn out in 75 wartime games for the Wanderers before hanging up his boots. Taylor was later appointed chief coach, a position he held when the Wanderers won the FA Cup in 1958. Even when he had retired, he still worked for the club on a part-time basis, thus serving Bolton Wanderers in a variety of capacities for over 50 years!

1957 The first of the modern day testimonials took place when Bolton beat an All Star XI 3-0. The game was played on behalf of Harold Hassall whose career had come to a premature end on New Year's Day 1955 when his right knee was shattered in a game against Chelsea.

1988 John Thomas netted his second hat-trick of the season as the Wanderers beat Newport County 6-0.

1994 Having recently won international recognition for Scotland, John McGinlay netted his second hat-trick of the campaign in a 4-1 home win over Middlesbrough.

APRIL 24th

1916 Frank Roberts scored his first hat-trick for the club in this wartime fixture as the Wanderers beat Stockport County 4-2.

1926 The FA Cup Final between Bolton Wanderers and Manchester City was expected to be the last one played at Wembley! A crowd of 91,447 saw David Jack score the only goal of the game to give the Wanderers victory.

1964 Bolton ended their stay in the top flight after a period of 29 years, going down 4-0 at home to Wolverhampton Wanderers.

APRIL 25th

1908 Notts County visited Burnden Park for the last game of the season in what was a relegation cliffhanger. A draw would have ensured Bolton another season of top flight football but Jimmy Cantrell's 50th minute strike gave County the points. Bolton's only hope now was that Chelsea avoided defeat at home to Notts County, but once again the Meadow Lane club won, this time 2-1, to send the Wanderers into Division Two.

1953 The last day of the season saw Bolton travel to the north-east to take on Newcastle United at St James Park - Nat Lofthouse scored his third hat-trick of the season as the Wanderers ran out winners 3-2.

1997 Charlton Athletic were Bolton's opponents in the last-ever game at Burnden Park. A crowd of 22,030 saw the Addicks hold a half-time lead but second-half goals from John McGinlay (2), Alan Thompson and Gerry Taggart gave the Wanderers a 4-1 win.

APRIL 26th

1978 A Frank Worthington goal was enough to give Bolton a 1-0 win against Blackburn Rovers at Ewood Park. This gave the Wanderers the two points they needed to confirm promotion to Division One.

APRIL 27th

1901 Burnden Park was the venue for the FA Cup Final replay between Tottenham Hotspur and Sheffield United. An extra stand was erected on the cycle track to accommodate the expected increase in spectators. Burnden Park could then house 47,000 but only 20,470 saw non-league Spurs take the cup. The day became known as 'Pie Saturday' as numerous pies remained unsold!

1929 The Wanderers won the FA Cup for the third time with a 2-0 win over Portsmouth with Billy Butler and Harold Blackmore, who had scored in every round of the competition, finding the net.

APRIL 28th

1900 Laurie Bell, who was the Wanderers' leading scorer with 23 goals, netted four in the final game of the season as Burton Swifts were beaten 5-0 - Bolton winning promotion to the top flight.

1923 Bolton met West Ham United in what was Wembley's first full final and it nearly became a disaster. Though 126,947 people paid for admission, thousands more burst down the doors to invade the stadium. It is believed that almost 200,000 were present at kick-off time when the pitch was completely covered by spectators! As the Bolton players stood on the edge of the pitch watching the police horse clear the playing area, someone tapped Jack (JR) Smith on the back. It was his brother, whom he hadn't seen for six years! It was largely due to the patience of the famous policeman on his white horse that the pitch was cleared but even so, spectators still encroached onto the pitch during play. However, it was felt safer to play the game than to announce to the horde that the match would be postponed. Within two minutes of the eventual kick-off time which was delayed by 40 minutes,

Images from 1923 (clockwise from top left): Aerial view of Wembley prior to kick-off, Bolton captain Joe Smith shakes hands with the West Ham captain, the team with the FA Cup back at Burnden Park, and the cover of the match programme.

David Jack had scored for the Wanderers. Both teams remained on the pitch at half-time and eight minutes after the break, Bolton scored again. Taking a pass from Ted Vizard, John Reid Smith rammed the ball home with his left foot with such force that it hit the crowd wedged behind the goal and rebounded onto the pitch. Many people didn't know a goal had been scored until West Ham kicked off again. Thus, in such bizarre circumstances did Bolton secure the FA Cup for the first time in their history.

1934 George T. Taylor and Ray Westwood netted two goals apiece as high-flying Bolton beat lowly Millwall 5-0. The Wanderers' other scorer was Jack Milsom. Bolton missed promotion by one point whilst the Lions were relegated to the Third Division (South).

APRIL 29th

1909 Bolton won the Manchester Cup defeating Stockport County 3-0 at Hyde Road.

1944 Birth of Francis Lee. He was just 16 years old when he made his debut for the Wanderers as an amateur in November 1960 after playing in only eight Central League games. Partnering the 35-year-old Nat Lofthouse, Lee scored a goal and got booked in a 3-1 win over Manchester City. He signed professional forms in the summer of 1961 and after winning a regular first team place at the start of the 1962-63 season he topped Bolton's goal charts for five successive seasons. He netted the first of his two hat-tricks for the club in a 5-4 defeat at West Bromwich Albion in September 1962 with two of his goals coming from the penalty-spot.
Lee *(right)* was one of the game's most deadly penalty takers, scoring 26 of his 106 goals in that fashion. His second hat-trick came in a 3-1 win at Preston North End in February 1967. Later that year, the goalscoring winger, who had put in a

number of transfer requests, left Burnden Park to join Manchester City, after appearing in 210 games for Bolton. The fee was £65,000.
At Maine Road he was one of the successes in a team that enjoyed one of the greatest era in the club's history. He hit three hat-tricks for City including a spectacular threesome in the Manchester derby of 1970-71. In 1971-72 Lee topped the First Division goalscorers with 33 goals including 15 from the penalty spot. For this achievement he was awarded the bronze boot in the Golden Boot competition. Lee was also a vital part of Sir Alf Ramsey's England squad and had gone to Mexico to defend the World Cup in 1970.

Lee scored 10 goals in his 27 international appearances. After scoring 143 goals in 320 games for City he joined Derby County, where he helped the Rams win the League Championship. After securing millionaire status via his thriving paper business he became Manchester City chairman, relinquishing his position in 1998.

1978 Crowd segregation came into force at Burnden Park for the first time in a match against Fulham. The game ended goalless, earning the Wanderers a point that secured the Second Division Championship.

APRIL 30th

1909 This Friday evening fixture, the last game of the season, saw the Wanderers travel to the Baseball Ground to take on Derby County. Billy Hughes scored the only goal of the game to give Bolton a 1-0 win and the Second Division Championship. The title had been won with an amazing run of consistency - Bolton winning 10, drawing one and losing one of their last 12 games.

1920 Joe Smith scored two of Bolton's goals in a 3-2 defeat of Liverpool.
This meant that he had equalled the Football League record of 38 goals in a season held by Bert Freeman who established that record while playing for Everton in 1908-09.

1927 In the final game of the season, Billy Wright scored a hat-trick in a 4-0 defeat of Huddersfield Town. This win lifted the Wanderers into a final position of fourth in Division One.

MAY 1st

1929 Bolton beat local rivals Bury 4-3 in the penultimate game of the season with Jack McClelland scoring twice. The Wanderers' other scorers were George Gibson and Ted Vizard. The Shakers who put up a brave fight, were relegated.

1953 Nat Lofthouse was voted 'Footballer of the Year' by the Football Writers' Association, collecting the award at the traditional eve of Wembley dinner.

1982 The Wanderers played their first game on Queen's Park Rangers 'plastic' pitch at Loftus Road. It turned out to be nothing short of a disaster as the Whites lost 7-1 - their goal being a penalty converted by Tony Henry!

MAY 2nd

1921 The Manchester Cup semi-final saw Bolton easily beat Mossley 8-0 to reach the final where their opponents were Manchester United.

1931 On the final day of the 1930-31 season, the Wanderers travelled to Highbury to play Arsenal who had already clinched the League Championship. Bolton were completely outplayed and lost 5-0.

1953 A day which will live forever in the hearts of Bolton Wanderers supporters - the FA Cup Final won 4-3 by Blackpool. In one of the most exciting of finals, the Wanderers broke away to open the scoring after only 75 seconds. Holden on the right, found Lofthouse in front of goal, and he scored with a snap shot from 28 yards which Farm in the Blackpool goal failed to gather. This, despite seeming to have the ball covered. Even though a hamstring strain reduced left-half Eric Bell to a passenger on the wing, Bolton continued to pour forward and Lofthouse almost doubled the Wanderers' lead, but his shot came back off a post. The Seasiders drew level when Hassall deflected a Mortsensen shot that appeared to be going wide. The Wanderers though, were ahead before the interval, as Willie Moir scored with a glancing header from Bobby Langton's cross. After the break, Bolton extended their lead when the injured Bell threw himself forward to head home Holden's cross. With a 3-1 lead, the destination of the Cup seemed settled, but with little over half-an-hour left, Stanley Matthews took over. In the 68th minute, the Seasiders reduced the arrears when Mortensen forced the ball home from close range after Stan Hanson had failed to hold Matthews' shot. The equaliser came with just one minute to play when Mortensen completed his hat-trick, striking home a free-kick from outside the Bolton penalty area. Two minutes into injury-time, Matthews dribbled his way along the bye-line before pulling the ball back for Perry to score the winner. The Wanderers had collapsed in one of the most exciting FA Cup Finals in history and Stanley Matthews had his Cup winners' medal!

1962   Bolton's first game on their tour of Greece, saw them go down 4-1 to AEK Athens.

1973   The Wanderers were involved in a testimonial at Burnden Park for the first time in 16 years, when after just winning the Third Division Championship, they took on Second Division champions Burnley on behalf of club captain Warwick Rimmer. A crowd of 13,314 saw Bolton come from behind to win 3-1.

MAY 3rd

1902   The Wanderers went down 4-2 at home to Preston North End in a game arranged to raise money for the Ibrox disaster fund.

1958   Bolton won the FA Cup Final, beating Manchester United 2-0. Having led the Wanderers to Wembley for the second time in five years, Bill Ridding, whose side cost no more than the £10 signing-on fee, faced a United side rebuilding after the Munich tragedy. Bolton took the lead as early as the third minute when Nat Lofthouse stabbed the ball home from six yards out after a speculative ball from Bryan Edwards was deflected into his path. Though the

Wanderers were the better side, two shots from Bobby Charlton, one that hit the inside of a post and one that brought a magnificent save out of Eddie Hopkinson, reminded Bolton that the game wasn't yet won. Then in the 57th minute came Bolton's second goal, one of the most controversial in Cup Final history. Dennis Stevens fired in a shot that United keeper Harry Gregg could only push vertically into the air and as he turned and jumped to gather the ball, Lofthouse bundled both Gregg and the ball over the line. Unbelievably by today's standards, the referee signalled a goal and though it was at a time when goalkeepers were considered fair game, many neutral observers believed it was a foul!

1967   Birth of Julian Darby. Appearing for the club in every outfield position, Bolton-born Julian made the first of his 345 appearances for the club at right-back against Blackpool in March 1986. In nine seasons with the Wanderers, Darby scored 52 goals, none more important than his 27th minute equaliser against Torquay United in the Sherpa Van Trophy Final at Wembley in 1989. After establishing himself as a first team regular in 1986-87 he missed very few games and in 1989-90 when the Wanderers reached the play-offs, he was ever-present. During the 1991-92 season, Darby was made the scapegoat by a section of the Bolton crowd for the overall failure of the Burnden side. After that his first team appearances became limited and in October 1993 he joined former manager Phil Neal at Coventry City after the Sky Blues had paid £150,000 for his services. He left Highfield Road in November 1995 to join West Bromwich Albion for £250,000 but he didn't settle at the Hawthorns and in the summer of 1997 after 44 appearances for the Baggies, he returned to the north-west to join Preston North End in a player-exchange deal. He had a short spell at Carlisle before returning to Preston North End as Youth Team Coach.

MAY 4th

1913 Bolton's only defeat on their seven-match tour of Austria and Germany came in their second match when they lost 2-1 to Victoria Berliner.

1929 On the final day of the 1928-29 season, the Wanderers travelled to Filbert Street to take on Leicester City, who had to win and hope Sheffield Wednesday lost, to win the League Championship. The Foxes had no trouble in beating a poor Bolton side 6-0.

1932 The Wanderers beat Blackpool 5-1 in a Lancashire Cup semi-final replay to reach the final where they met Manchester City.

1935 Ray Westwood scored Bolton's goal in a 1-1 draw at Blackpool on the final day of the season to ensure the Wanderers' promotion to the First Division. Westwood's 30th goal of the season was the club's 96th of the campaign - a new club record.

1997 Bolton drew their last game of their promotion-winning season 2-2 at Tranmere Rovers with former Middlesbrough midfielder Jamie Pollock scoring the club's 100th goal of the campaign. John McGinlay had earlier netted his 30th goal of the season.

MAY 5th

1923 Following their success in the first Wembley Final, Bolton visited Chorley, where the home side displayed the Lancashire Combination Championship alongside the FA Cup. For the record, the Wanderers ran out 8-0 winners.

1927 Bolton, who had finished fourth in Division One, entertained an International XI at Burnden Park. The game, an 11-goal thriller saw the visitors win 7-4.

1928 Sheffield United were the visitors to Burnden Park for the final game of the season. There was controversy when Blades' captain Billy Gillespie was sent-off for head butting Jimmy Seddon who was carried off injured. The Wanderers player returned a few minutes later only to receive his marching orders as a joint offender in the incident!

1948 The Wanderers lost the Manchester Cup Final after extra-time, 2-1 to Manchester United.

1951 Bolton travelled to Stamford Bridge to take on Chelsea. The Pensioners needed to win this last game of the season to have any hope of staying in the top flight. They beat the Wanderers 4-0 and Sheffield Wednesday and Everton were relegated.

MAY 6th

1922 The final game of the 1921-22 season saw Bolton entertain Middlesbrough. The Wanderers were one point behind the Teeside club but won an entertaining game 4-2 to leapfrog their opponents and finish the season in sixth place.

1933 The Wanderers needed to beat Leeds United and hope that fellow relegation rivals lost on the last day of the season. Bolton beat Leeds 5-0 with Jack Milsom netting a hat-trick and Ray Westwood the other two goals but unfortunately so did all the Wanderers' rivals, meaning that Bolton joined Blackpool in dropping to Division two.

1967 Bolton ended their home fixtures this season with a resounding 5-0 defeat of Millwall with Northern Ireland international centre-half John Napier scoring two of their goals from well-worked set pieces.

1986 A Tony Caldwell goal gave the Wanderers a 1-0

win against Wigan Athletic at Springfield Park in the Northern Area semi-final first leg of the Freight Rover Trophy.

MAY 7th

1924 Bolton again embarked on a continental tour at the end of a hectic season, playing teams in Czechoslovakia and Germany. Winning all six of their matches, their biggest victory was an 8-0 rout of Fortuna.

1932 Jack Milsom took his season's tally of goals to 18 in 19 games by scoring four times in the final game of the season as the Wanderers beat Liverpool 8-1 - the second such scoreline against the Anfield club that season.

1938 A similar situation to that of seven years previously, Bolton travelled to Highbury to play Arsenal in the last game of the season. The only difference this time was that the Gunners needed to win to lift the League Championship. Bolton had beaten Arsenal 1-0 at Burnden Park but again lost 5-0 to the Champions elect.

1988 Robbie Savage scored the goal that gave the Wanderers a 1-0 win at Wrexham on the final day of the season, thus enabling them to win promotion from the Fourth Division at the first attempt.

MAY 8th

1936 Birth of George Mulhall. The pacy winger began his career with Aberdeen, for whom he scored 42 goals in 150 games and won a Scottish League Cup winners' medal in 1959 before leaving to join Sunderland in 1962. At Roker Park, he continued to find the net, scoring 66 goals in 284 first team outings and helped the club win promotion to the top flight in 1963-64. In October 1971, the Scottish international joined

Halifax Town as player-coach before being appointed manager eight months later. He arrived at Burnden Park in October 1974 as assistant to Ian Greaves before four years later, leaving to manage Bradford City. In March 1981 he returned to Bolton for a second spell with the club and in June of that year, was appointed manager. Despite a number of problems - six players released and six players placed on the transfer list and the chief coach and scout leaving - Mulhall saved the club from relegation. However, there was conflict between Mulhall and the board over the sale of Paul Jones and in June 1982 he parted company with the club. He later worked as chief scout, youth development officer and assistant manager at Huddersfield Town before taking charge of Halifax Town.

1948 The Wanderers won the Lancashire Cup when Southport were beaten 5-1 at Haig Avenue with Scottish international forward Willie Moir scoring a hat-trick.

1969 Bolton ended their close season tour of Denmark in which they won all their three games with a 4-3 defeat of Freja Randers.

1985 The Wanderers had a great chance of reaching Wembley in that season's Freight Rover Trophy. Drawn at home to Mansfield Town, they crashed out of the competition, losing 2-1 to the Stags, with Tony Caldwell netting for Bolton.

1993 A John McGinlay penalty helped the Wanderers beat a spirited Preston North End side 1-0 on the final day of the season. The three points was enough to help the club win promotion to the First Division.

1994 Bolton lost 3-2 at home to Barnsley on the final day of the campaign.
It was the club's first defeat in 19 games played on a Sunday!

MAY 9th

1986 Goals from George Oghani and Tony Caldwell gave Bolton a 2-1 win on the night (3-1 on aggregate) over neighbours Wigan Athletic in the Freight Rover Trophy semi-final, second leg, in front of a Burnden Park crowd of 12,120.

MAY 10th

1888 Birth of Jack Feebury. Joining the Wanderers from Hucknall, he spent a season in the club's reserve side before making his debut in a 3-0 win over Woolwich Arsenal in September 1909 as a replacement for Jack Slater. The Bolton defender was noted for his powerful shooting and in August 1913 he won a Players' Union kicking contest. His 80 yard right-foot kick won him the title and when challenged by a spectator to do the same with the other foot, he duly obliged. During the First World War he 'guested' for Notts County but when League football resumed in 1919-20, full-back Feebury scored in four consecutive games! He had scored 16 goals in 192 League and Cup games when in May 1920 he left to play for Exeter City. He later had a spell with Brighton before ending his career with Mid-Rhondda.

1922 Having drawn 4-4 against Stockport County at Edgeley park in the semi-final of the Manchester Cup, the Wanderers won the replay at Burnden Park 6-0.

1922 Birth of Dan Murphy. Discovered playing in Warrington junior football, Dan Murphy made his Bolton debut during wartime football. Playing at left-half, he kept his place in the side until the return of George Taylor but then had a spell 'guesting' for Bury before returning to Burnden Park. He won his first honours in 1945 as the Wanderers won the Football League North Cup and played in the North v South Final. After completing his National Service, he found his appearances at first team level limited and in January 1952, after scoring just one goal - against Middlesbrough in October 1949 - in 76 games, he left to play for Crewe Alexandra. He made 106 appearances for the Railwaymen and then played in 109 games for Rochdale, before ending his playing career with Macclesfield.

1939 The Wanderers drew 1-1 with Preston North End in the final of the Lancashire Cup but there was no replay due to the outbreak of the Second World War.

1941 A Wanderers Second World War Football League (North) side containing players such as Lofthouse, Hubbick, Howe, Atkinson and Ralph Banks, lost 8-0 at Chester!

MAY 11th

1902 Birth of Jack McClelland. Though he began his career with Raith Rovers and later played for Southend United, it was at Middlesbrough that he made his name. In 1925-26 he was ever-present in the Ayresome Park club's side, scoring 32 goals in 38 games and though he was overshadowed the following season by George Camsell, who scored 59 goals, in March 1928 the Wanderers paid £63,000 for his services. Replacing John Reid Smith, who joined Bury, he scored on his debut in a 2-2 draw at Burnley and netted eight goals in the last 10 games of the season. Although his goals dried up the following season, he was an important member of the Bolton side that won the FA Cup in 1929, beating Portsmouth 2-0. However after scoring 19 goals in 65 games, he was allowed to join Preston North End, going on to score 22 goals in 53 games for the Deepdale club. There followed spells with Blackpool and Bradford before he joined his last club Manchester United, the Reds just having won promotion to the First Division.

1921 The Wanderers won the Manchester Cup, beating Manchester United 2-0 in the final which was played at Burnden Park.

1929 Bolton again reached the final of the Manchester Cup but lost 2-0 to Manchester United, a team they had already met four times in various competitions that season.

1958 Eddie Hopkinson had a disastrous game for England, conceding a number of soft goals in a 5-0 defeat against Yugoslavia in Belgrade - it cost him his place in the England side for the 1958 World Cup Finals in Sweden.

MAY 12th

1905 Birth of George Nicholson. He was a latecomer to first-class football, having played for the Washington Colliery Club, that produced a number of fine players. Nicholson was 25 years old when he made his Football League debut in a 2-2 draw against Liverpool at Anfield in September 1931. He remained a regular throughout that 1931-32 season, playing most of his games at right-half. With the return of Harry Goslin, Nicholson was forced to miss the entire 1934-35 campaign. But when Nicholson did win back his place in the Bolton side, it was not a return he would wish to remember as the Wanderers lost 7-0 at Manchester City. In fact, it proved to be the last of his 71 League and Cup appearances for the club, his only goal coming in a 4-3 defeat at Leeds United in December 1932. He then had a season playing for Cardiff City before returning to the north-west to join Oldham Athletic. He was still waiting to make an appearance for the Latics when the Second World War broke out.

1934 The Wanderers won the Lancashire Cup for the eighth time, beating Oldham Athletic 4-2 in the final at Maine Road.

1956 The club embarked on a tour of Norway, winning three and drawing one of the four matches. Their best result was a 6-1 defeat of Lyn Oslo.

1978 Having just won promotion to the First Division, the Wanderers played an Everton-Liverpool select side on behalf of Peter Thompson.
Liverpool brought along the European Cup and fielded nine of the side that had beaten Bruges. A crowd of 20,516 saw some entertaining football as the sides played out a 5-5 draw. Bolton keeper Jim McDonagh played up front in the second-half and scored the final goal of the game!

MAY 13th

1904 Birth of Harold Blackmore. He joined the Wanderers in unusual circumstances: the Burnden Park club had visited Exeter City to play the Grecians in Robert Pollard's benefit game and lost 3-2, with Blackmore scoring two of Exeter's goals. Immediately after the game, the Wanderers paid £2,150 to bring Blackmore to Burnden Park, the Silverton-born forward having scored 44 goals in 74 games for the Devon club. He made his Bolton debut in April 1927, scoring in a 3-2 defeat of Sheffield Wednesday. The following season, he scored eight goals in 12 games including four in a 7-1 home win over Burnley, but it wasn't until 1928-29 that he won a regular place in the Bolton side.
That season, he was the club's leading scorer with 37 goals in 43 League and Cup games, including hat-tricks against Portsmouth (Home 4-2), Aston Villa (Away 5-3) and Birmingham (Home 6-2) as well as netting the second goal in the FA Cup Final win over Portsmouth. He also headed the Wanderers' goalscoring charts in 1929-30 with 30 goals, four of which came in the 5-0 defeat of Everton and in 1930-31 when a similar total included him finding the net in seven successive games.
Blackmore had scored 122 goals in 165 games

before later playing for Middlesbrough, Bradford and Bury.

1940 In the first season of wartime football, the Wanderers recorded their biggest win in the North-West Division with an 8-1 win at Southport, with Walter Sidebottom netting four of Bolton's goals.

1953 Birth of Paul Jones *(right)*. Without doubt the best footballing centre-half to have played for the Wanderers since the Second World War. He joined the club straight from school in Ellesmere Port and after working his way through the ranks, was one of a number of teenagers who made their debut in the 2-1 win over Sheffield United in January 1971.

Replacing John Hulme at the start of the following season, Jones missed very few matches over the next 12 seasons and was ever-present in seasons 1972-73, 1974-75 and 1976-77. He won a Third Division Championship medal in 1973 and five years later, a Second Division Championship medal, though he sustained an injury that restricted his appearances during that campaign. He received a call-up into the England squad during Don Revie's reign as manager but never played. During the club's stay in the First Division, Jones had a spell playing at right-back but he lacked the pace to fill the role on a regular basis. Following the club's relegation to the Third Division, Jones, who had scored 43 goals in 506 games, left the Wanderers to play for Huddersfield Town. After that he had spells with Oldham Athletic and Blackpool before playing non-League football for a number of clubs.

1990 The Wanderers met Notts County in the play-off semi-final first leg.
A crowd of 15,105 saw them draw 1-1 with Tony Philliskirk scoring Bolton's goal from the penalty spot.

2001 Bolton faced West Bromwich Albion in the play-off semi-final first leg at the Hawthorns. The Wanderers were 2-0 down with just ten minutes to play, but a goal from Gudni Bergsson and a Per Frandsen penalty levelled things up.

MAY 14th

1927 Bolton won the Lancashire Cup, beating neighbours Bury 1-0 at Burnden Park with John Reid Smith scoring the all-important goal.

1932 The Wanderers beat Manchester City 3-2 at Maine Road to lift the Lancashire Cup with all their goalscorers - McKay, Gibson and Cook - being Scots!

1938 Bolton won the Manchester Cup, beating Manchester United 2-1 in the final at Old Trafford.

1995 England goalkeeping legend Peter Shilton became Wanderers' oldest-ever player when at the age of 45 years 239 days, he played in the First Division play-off semi-final first leg against Wolves at Molineux. For the record, Bolton lost 2-1 but with Keith Branagan restored to the side, won the return leg 2-0.

2000 The first leg of the play-off semi-final against Ipswich town, saw the Wanderers held to a 2-2 draw at the Reebok. Bolton's scorers were Dean Holdsworth and Eidur Gudjohnsen.

MAY 15th

1882 Birth of Walter White. A Scottish international, he missed very few games in his six seasons with the Wanderers after joining them from Hurlford Thistle in the summer of 1902. After playing in the 1904 FA Cup Final defeat by Manchester City, he scored 24 goals in 33 League games in 1904-05 as the Wanderers won promotion to the First Division.
Included in his total were hat-tricks against Burton United (Home 7-0) and Doncaster Rovers (Away 4-0). His goalscoring feats continued in the top flight as he netted 25 goals in 38 games including a spell of seven goals in five games. White had scored 93 goals in 217 games when following the club's relegation in 1907-08, he left to play for Everton.
He helped the Merseyside club to the runners-up spot in the League in 1908-09, his first season and to the FA Cup semi-finals the following

season. He left soon afterwards to join Fulham where he ended his career having played in 193 games for the Cottagers.

1958 One of the club's best results on their pre-season tour of Europe was the 3-2 defeat of French side, Olympique Lyonnais.

MAY 16th

1990 Having drawn 1-1 at Burnden Park in the play-off semi-final first leg, the Wanderers travelled to Meadow Lane, facing an uphill struggle. Despite a brave performance, they went down 2-0.

1999 A goal from Michael Johansen gave the Wanderers a 1-0 win over Ipswich Town in the play-off semi-final first leg in front of a Reebok crowd of 18,295.

2000 Having been held to a 2-2 draw in the first leg of the First Division play-off semi-final at the Reebok, Bolton travelled to Portman Road for the return game against Ipswich Town. The Wanderers led 3-2 but with just one minute remaining, Town drew level and went on to win the game 5-3 after extra-time. During the course of the game, the referee awarded Ipswich three penalties - one of which was saved by Jussi Jaaskelainen and booked ten and sent-off two of the Bolton side!

MAY 17th

1922 The Wanderers won the Lancashire Cup, beating Bury 3-1 in the final played at Gigg Lane.

1955 Birth of Neil Whatmore. He was still an apprentice when he made his League debut for the Wanderers in April 1973, scoring twice in a 3-2 win at Swansea City, with the club well on its way to the Third Division Championship. He immediately became a regular in the Bolton side

following their promotion to Division Two and in 1976-77 his 31 goals in League and Cup made him the third top scorer in the entire Football League. Six of his goals were scored in the League Cup including the strike at Everton in a 1-1 draw in the first leg of the semi-final. Whatmore *(below)* was ever-present and top scored with 19 goals as Bolton won the Second Division in style in 1977-78. He moved into midfield for the club's return to the top flight but then top scored in each of the next two seasons before leaving to join Birmingham City for £340,000 in August 1981. The goals were slow in coming at St Andrew's and after a loan spell with Oxford United, he returned to Bolton in a similar capacity. He had taken his tally of goals to 121 in 338 games before joining Oxford on a permanent basis. After spells with Burnley and Mansfield Town, he rejoined Bolton again before becoming reserve team coach at Field Mill.

1987 Aldershot were Bolton's opponents in the two-legged play-offs. The Wanderers, who went down 1-0 in the first leg at the Recreation Ground, could not force victory at Burnden Park, drawing 2-2 after extra-time with Tony Caldwell netting both goals and so were relegated to the Fourth Division for the first time in their history.

MAY 18th

1913 At the end of the 1912-13 season in which the Wanderers finished eighth in Division One, the club embarked on a tour of Germany and Austria. The final game of that tour saw Bolton beat the German Association 12-0 with Billy Hughes scoring five of the goals.

1940 On the final day of the first North West Division of War Regional League football, Bolton beat Accrington Stanley 4-1 with George Hunt and Walter Sidebottom netting two goals apiece.

1956 The Wanderers ended their four-match tour of Norway with a 5-0 win over Stavanger to finish with the following playing record:

P. W. D. L. F. A.
4   3   1   0   18 4

MAY 19th

1924 On their tour of Europe, the Wanderers met Scottish First Division side, Aberdeen at Leipzig. The Wanderers, who played 10 games on the continent during the month of May were unbeaten, winning all their games including the Dons 3-1 in the process.

1945 In the first leg of the Wartime League North Cup, Nat Lofthouse scored the goal of the game when he bundled both the ball and the Manchester United keeper Jack Crompton into the net!

1991 Bolton met Bury in the play-off semi-final first leg at Gigg Lane. The game ended all-square at 1-1 with Tony Philliskirk netting from the spot for the Wanderers.

1999 Having won the play-off semi-final first leg against Ipswich Town 1-0, the Wanderers travelled to Portman Road for the return match. The Tractor Boys ran out 3-2 winners after 90 minutes to send the match into extra-time. The game ended 4-3 in Town's favour but the Wanderers went through on the away goals rule.

MAY 20th

1895 Birth of Jimmy Seddon. He played his first game for the Wanderers against Middlesbrough in February 1914 but didn't have the best of debuts as he gave away a penalty in a 1-1 draw. During the First World War he served in France and contracted trench foot, an affliction that was to trouble him throughout the rest of his footballing career. Seddon didn't turn professional until the summer of 1919 but then was a first team regular for the next 12 seasons, appearing in 375 League and Cup games. He went on to gain three FA Cup winners' medals, captaining the Wanderers in 1929 when they beat Portsmouth 2-0. He won six full international caps for England, his first against France in Paris shortly after the Wanderers had beaten West Ham United in the 1923 FA Cup Final. After playing his last game for the Wanderers in January 1932 against Middlesbrough, the team he had made his debut against 18 years earlier, he went as coach to Dordrecht in Holland before holding a similar post with Altrincham. He was later appointed trainer to Southport and then Liverpool reserves.

1901 Birth of Jack Round. He played his early football for Cradley Heath whilst working down the pit. The Wanderers signed him in January 1924 as an understudy to Jimmy Seddon. He eventually made his Bolton debut almost a year later as the Wanderers went down 2-0 at Sheffield United. A number of injuries to Seddon allowed Round to gain valuable First Division experience but in all honesty, it was a pity for Round that a player of Seddon's class was at the club for so long. By the start of the 1930-31 season, a campaign that saw Seddon still the club's first choice centre-half and after scoring two goals in 59 games, Round left to join Port Vale. He was a regular in the Valiants' side for the next five seasons before moving to play for Third Division (North) side Carlisle United. He was still with the Cumbrian outfit when in December 1936, he died from a perforated appendix.

1922 The Wanderers retained the Manchester Cup, beating Eccles United 3-1 in the final played at Old Trafford.

1956 Nat Lofthouse became the first substitute used by England in an international match. In the game against Finland in Helsinki, he replaced

73

Manchester United's Tommy Taylor and scored twice in a 5-1 win!

1963 Bolton won the Manchester Cup for the very last time, beating Fourth Division promotion winners Oldham Athletic 4-1 in the Boundary Park final.

MAY 21st

1929 The Wanderers, who won all five of the Norwegian close season tour games, beat Skien 2-1 and finished their trip to Scandinavia with the following record:

P. W. D. L. F. A.
5 5 0 0 17 2

1939 Fifteen of the Wanderers' playing staff joined the Territorial Army while players such as Stan Hanson, Ernie Forrest, Albert Geldard, Harry Goslin, Don Howe, Jack Roberts and Ray Westwood joined the Bolton Artillery and were posted overseas soon after the outbreak of war in September.

1958 The Wanderers took on Flamengo de Rio of Brazil in a Paris tournament and drew 1-1 after extra-time with Doug Holden scoring the Bolton goal. A penalty competition ended in a 3-3 draw but the Wanderers won on the toss of a coin. Unfortunately they lost 2-1 in the final to Racing Club, Paris.

MAY 22nd

1960 Having finished the season in sixth place in Division One, the Wanderers embarked on a five-match tour of Germany. It was a difficult trip but one of their best displays was against VFB Stuttgart, whom they beat 3-2.

1991 After drawing 1-1 at Gigg Lane in the play-off semi-final first leg against Bury, the Wanderers beat the Shakers 1-0 in the return at Burnden

Park with Tony Philliskirk netting the only goal of the game.
It was his 28th goal of the season and took the Wanderers to the play-off final at Wembley where they lost 1-0 to Tranmere Rovers.

MAY 23rd

1875 Birth of Laurie Bell. He first made his name as a prolific scoring centre-forward with Dumbarton before continuing to score on a regular basis with his next club, Third Lanark. Whilst with Third Lanark, Bell represented the Scottish League XI before coming south of the border to play for Sheffield Wednesday.
His stay with the Owls was brief and he moved to Everton, scoring twice on his debut for the Merseyside team as they beat Bolton 2-1. He went on to top Everton's scoring charts that season before joining the Wanderers in the summer of 1899.
He made his debut in the club's first-ever game in Division Two and scored the club's first-ever goal in that section as the Wanderers beat Loughborough Town 3-2. He ended his first season with Bolton as the club's top scorer with 23 goals, netting a hat-trick in the return game with Loughborough as the Wanderers ran out 7-0 winners and four goals in the final game of the campaign as Burton Swifts were beaten 5-0. Though he wasn't as prolific over the next couple of seasons, he was an important member of the Bolton side until he broke a leg during the Manchester Cup semi-final tie against Newton Heath. He had scored 45 goals in 103 games when he left Burnden Park to play for Brentford. He later had a spell with West Bromwich Albion before returning north of the border to end his career with Hibernian.

1939 The Wanderers ended their five-match unbeaten tour of Norway with a 4-0 win over Stavanger.

MAY 24th

1889 During a close season tour of Scotland, the Wanderers beat Glasgow Thistle 6-1. Their other two games though ended in heavy defeats, 5-1 by Celtic and 8-3 by Dumfries Wanderers.

1941 Bolton lost a high-scoring game against Manchester City at Maine Road, 6-4.

1965 Birth of Mark Patterson. He made his name as a left-winger with his first club Blackburn Rovers, netting a hat-trick in a 6-1 defeat of Sheffield United in April 1986. The following year, he was a member of the Blackburn side that beat Charlton Athletic in the Full Members Cup Final at Wembley. He had scored 20 goals in 101 League games for Rovers when in June 1988 he joined neighbours Preston North End for £20,000. Patterson was a regular in the North End side during 1988-89 as they reached the Third Division play-offs only to lose to Port Vale in the semi-final. In February 1990, Bury paid £80,000 for his services and he helped the Shakers to the Third Division play-offs, where they lost to Tranmere Rovers. In January 1991, Bolton manager Phil Neal paid £65,000 to bring him to Burnden Park and though his early days were hampered by injury, he helped the Wanderers win promotion in 1992-93. He was an important member of the Bolton side for the next few seasons but his last game for the club during the 1995-96 season ended in disappointment as he missed a penalty in a shoot-out against Norwich City in the Coca Cola Cup. He had scored 14 goals in 215 games when in December 1995 he joined Sheffield United for £150,000. He helped the Blades pull away from the relegation zone to become play-off contenders but then following a loan spell with Southend United, he returned to the north-west for a second spell with Bury. There followed a loan spell with Blackpool before he signed for Southend on a permanent basis. On leaving Roots Hall, he joined non-League Leigh RMI as player-manager.

1986 The Wanderers played Bristol City in the final of the Freight Rover Trophy at Wembley. It was the club's first final since their 1958 FA Cup success and though Tony Caldwell struck the bar early in the game, the Robins, who were Bolton's bogey side, won 3-0.

MAY 25th

1924 Whilst on their close season European tour, the Wanderers met Leeds United in Amsterdam and beat the Yorkshire club 3-1.

1952 Nat Lofthouse earned the title, the 'Lion of Vienna'. Before a capacity crowd of 65,000 in the Prater Stadium, the stage was set for a match that both England and Austria desperately wanted to win. Austria began with a series of attacks. Lofthouse scored, Huber equalised and the stadium erupted. Sewell restored England's lead. Hysterical scenes greeted Austria's second equaliser scored by Dienst. Austria attacked with renewed frenzy but to no avail. One raid ended when England goalkeeper Gil Merrick plucked the ball off Dienst's head and threw it upfield to Tom Finney. Finney's shrewd through-ball put Lofthouse clear. With the desperate defence in pounding pursuit, Lofthouse slid the ball under the advancing Musil before being felled by a crunching tackle. It was a great triumph but as Nat regretfully said: 'I never saw the ball enter the Austrian net for the best goal of my life'.

MAY 26th

1932 Birth of Ian Greaves. He began his footballing career with Manchester United, winning a League Championship medal in 1955-56 and in 1958 played in the FA Cup Final against the

Wanderers. After making 75 appearances for the Reds, he joined Lincoln City before later ending his playing career with Oldham Athletic. His first managerial post was at Huddersfield Town and in 1970 he took the Terriers to the Second Division title but after two seasons in the top flight, the Yorkshire club suffered relegation in consecutive seasons to the Third Division. After a boardroom struggle, Greaves *(below)* parted company with the then Leeds Road club.

After a couple of months of unemployment, Greaves was appointed assistant-manager to Jimmy Armfield at Burnden Park and when he

left to manage Leeds United in October 1974, Greaves became Wanderers' manager. At Bolton, Manager of the Month awards came his way in January 1975, November 1976, August 1977 and in October 1977 and after taking the Wanderers to a League Cup semi-final in 1976-77, he was named Second Division Manager of the Season as the club won that division's Championship in 1977-78.

He broke the club transfer record four times before his dismissal in January 1980, with Bolton firmly rooted at the foot of the First Division. There were many who likened his departure to a 'death in the family'.

1945 The second leg of the wartime League North Cup against Manchester United took place at Maine Road because Old Trafford was out of use due to bomb damage. Two goals from Malcolm Barrass, his second in injury-time, gave the Wanderers a 2-2 draw and an aggregate victory of 3-2.

1953 Birth of Don McAllister. After being rejected by Coventry City, Don McAllister had better luck with his local club, Bolton Wanderers. The Radcliffe-born defender soon established himself in the club's Central League side and captained the club to victory in the Lancashire Youth Cup Final. He made his first team debut for Bolton against Norwich City in the final game of the 1969-70 season before winning a regular first team place midway through the following season. After the club were relegated, McAllister was instrumental in the club winning the Third Division Championship in 1972-73.

Earning a reputation as one of the best defenders in Division Two, he had appeared in 177 League and Cup games for the Wanderers, when in February 1975 he joined Tottenham Hotspur for a fee of £80,000. He helped the North London club win promotion to the top flight in 1977-78 and re-establish themselves as a First Division force. But following a bad injury, McAllister, who had played in 202 games for Spurs, left White Hart Lane to join Charlton Athletic. He played his last game of League football for the Addicks in a 4-1 defeat of the Wanderers - the match that sent the club back to the Third Division at the end of the 1982-83 season.

MAY 27th

1959 Bolton's best result of their 10-match South African tour was a 6-1 win over the Border FA, this came after the Wanderers had lost two matches in succession - 2-1 to Eastern Transvaal and 1-0 to Natal - their only defeats on the trip.

1969 Burnden Park was used for a cricket match, when a Lancashire XI took on a Wanderers XI in aid of Eddie Hopkinson's testimonial.
Drivers on Manchester Road had to be extremely watchful as players, especially West Indies captain Clive Lloyd smashed a number of sixes way out of the ground.

MAY 28th

1928 Bolton's best result on their six-match tour of Scandinavia was a 4-0 defeat of Elfsborg.

1989 The Wanderers won the Sherpa Van Trophy Final at Wembley, beating Torquay United 4-1 after the Devon club had taken the lead.
Bolton's scorers were Julian Darby, Dean Crombie, Trevor Morgan and an own goal by Torquay's Morrison.

2001 Bolton returned to the Premiership with a convincing 3-0 victory over Preston North End in the First Division play-off final at the Millennium Stadium in Cardiff. Gareth Farrelly scored Bolton's opening goal and late strikes from Ricardo Gardner and Michael Ricketts put the matter beyond doubt.

MAY 29th

1957 Nat Lofthouse took over as landlord of 'The Castle Hotel' even though the Wanderers' board had said that if he wanted to go into the licensing trade, he could forget about playing for Bolton Wanderers! Luckily good sense prevailed and at the end of the next season, the Wanderers won the FA Cup, with Nat Lofthouse scoring both goals in a 2-0 win over Manchester United.

1995 Bolton met Reading in the First Division play-off final at Wembley.
Reading stormed into a two-goal lead after just 12 minutes and had the opportunity of making it 3-0 just before half-time when they were awarded a penalty - goalkeeper Keith Branagan produced an outstanding save from Lovell's spot-kick. In the second-half, Bolton got on top and goals from Coyle and De Freitas levelled the scores. As the game went into extra-time, there was only going to be one winner as De Freitas and Paatelainen scored in a 4-3 win for the Wanderers.

MAY 30th

1959 Birth of Phil Brown. He began his League career with Hartlepool United and after making his debut against Peterborough United in March 1980, went on to appear in 217 games before joining Halifax Town in the summer of 1985. Appointed the Shaymen's captain, he was the club's leading scorer in 1986-87 with 14 goals, one of which came against Bolton when he earned the Yorkshire club a second replay in the first round of the FA Cup. The Wanderers paid £17,500 for Brown's services in June 1988 and after making his Bolton debut in a 2-0 defeat at Southend United on the opening day of the 1988-89 season, he appeared in 171 consecutive League games before injury ruled him out of the game against Bournemouth in April 1991. The Bolton manager at the time of Phil Brown's arrival at Burnden Park was Phil Neal and he had no hesitation in handing him the captain's armband. At the end of his first season with the club, Brown *(below)* led them to success in the Sherpa Van Trophy and later through two disappointments in the Third Division promotion play-offs. Brown scored 17 goals in 332 games for the Wanderers before joining Blackpool as player-coach. He is now back with Bolton as assistant-manager to Sam Allardyce.

MAY 31st

1953 Having won all five games of their German tour, the Wanderers met a Dutch XI before returning to these shores and ran out winners 6-1.

1999 Bolton went down 2-0 to Watford in the First Division play-off final at Wembley.

JUNE 1st

1908 The Wanderers ended their Netherlands tour with a 10-1 victory over Dordrecht. They won all their five matches, scoring a remarkable 31 goals and conceding just three!

1991 Bolton returned to Wembley for the Third Division play-off final against Tranmere Rovers but went down to the only goal of the game scored by Chris Malkin.

JUNE 2nd

1923 Following their FA Cup Final victory over West Ham United, the Wanderers embarked on a close season tour of Switzerland. They won seven and drew one of their eight matches, with their biggest win being 6-0 against Mullhouse.

1945 The Wanderers visited Stamford Bridge to play Chelsea for the North v South Cup Winners Final. The proceeds from the match went towards the King George Fund for Sailors. Bolton, who were a goal down, came from behind to win 2-1 with goals from Hunt and Hamlett (penalty) but instead of receiving medals, they went home with saving certificates instead!

JUNE 3rd

1923 Bolton played the last game of their Switzerland tour, beating an Alsace XI 3-0.

1928 The Wanderers ended their Scandinavian tour with a 3-1 victory over Oslo. They had lost just one of their six matches played over a period of 13 days.

JUNE 4th

1882 Birth of John Edmondson. The Wanderers' goalkeeper began his career with his home-town club, Accrington Stanley before moving to Manchester City in the summer of 1902. Though his first team opportunities were limited owing to the fine form of Jack Hillman, Edmondson was one of a number of City players suspended in an illegal payments scandal at the club. The ban was eventually lifted and in December 1906, the Wanderers paid £600 to bring him to Burnden Park. He kept a clean sheet on his Bolton debut as Liverpool were beaten 3-0 on New Year's Day 1907. Edmondson went on to be the club's first-choice custodian for the next nine seasons and was ever-present in Bolton's Second Division Championship-winning season of 1908-09. He had appeared in 259 first team games when he retired in 1915.

JUNE 5th

1889 Birth of Bob Glendenning. The tough-tackling wing-half began his career with Barnsley, making his league debut for the Tykes in November 1908. He soon established himself as a first team regular with the Yorkshire club and played in both of their FA Cup Final appearances - when they lost to Newcastle in 1910 and when they beat West Bromwich Albion two years later. In March 1913, he left Oakwell to join the Wanderers as the club sought to strengthen the side in a concerted push for the League Championship. Glendenning made his Bolton debut in a 2-0 win over Spurs but five defeats in the club's last seven matches of the season, ended his hopes of picking up another medal. A first team regular up to the outbreak of the First World War, he was appointed captain in October 1914 and led the club to the FA Cup semi-finals that season, only for the Wanderers to lose 2-1 to Sheffield United. Glendenning had appeared in 83 first team games when he retired to take over the Ainsworth Arms for former Wanderer Sam Marsh.

JUNE 6th

1898 Birth of Bruce Longworth. Though he was born in Newcastle-under-Lyme, Bruce Longworth was brought up in Bolton and 'guested' for the Wanderers in three wartime matches whilst serving in the army.
He made his League debut in a 2-1 defeat at Burnley in September 1919, replacing the injured Walter Rowley at wing-half. It was during the course of the 1920-21 season when the Wanderers finished third in Division One that Longworth established himself in the Bolton side. He helped the Wanderers beat Manchester United in the Manchester Cup Final and gave a good account of himself in the following season's Lancashire Cup Final which the Wanderers lost to Manchester City. He eventually picked up a Lancashire Cup winners' medal as the Wanderers beat Bury in 1922. The following season he lost his place to Harry Nuttall and so missed out on an FA Cup Final appearance. He had taken his total of first team appearances to 82 when he left to join Sheffield United. He spent two years at Bramall Lane but never really established himself in the Blades' side. He then joined Bury but injury prevented him from making a first team appearance and forced his premature retirement.

1959 On their tour of South Africa, the Wanderers beat the national side 1-0.

1969 Charlie Hurley became Bolton's first Republic of Ireland international when he played against Hungary in Dublin.

JUNE 7th

1889 Birth of Ted Vizard. He played rugby for Penarth and football for Barry Town before he was recommended to the Wanderers by an old school friend and invited to Burnden Park for a month's trial. The Wanderers signed him in September 1910 and two months later he made his League debut in a 3-0 home win over Gainsborough Trinity. In January 1911, only two months after making his Bolton debut, Vizard won the first of his 22 Welsh caps, his last coming in October 1926 when he was 37 years old. During the First World War, Vizard served in the RAF and 'guested' for Chelsea alongside Joe Smith. The pair formed a great left-wing partnership and helped the Stamford Bridge club win the 1919 London v Lancashire Cup Final. In February 1919, the management of Bolton Wanderers was put in Vizard's hands until normal League football returned and Charles Foweraker was appointed. Ted Vizard was a member of Bolton's successful FA Cup winning teams of 1923 and 1926 and though not a prolific scorer, he did score 13 goals in 1925-26 including a hat-trick in a 3-0 defeat of Arsenal. He made the last of his 512 League and Cup appearances (during which he scored 70 goals) on 21 March 1931. He was then 41, which makes him the oldest outfield player to appear in a first team game for the Trotters. He then took charge of the 'A' team before leaving Burnden Park in April 1933 after almost 23 years' service. Vizard became manager of Swindon Town and later took charge of Queen's Park Rangers and Wolverhampton Wanderers.

1941 During the war many curious things occurred, among them the continuance of the season right into June. Thus in 1940-41, Bolton's last competitive match saw them go down 3-2 at Oldham Athletic.

JUNE 8th

1866 Birth of James Turner. Signed from local side Black Lane Rovers in the summer of 1888, Turner's early games in the club's reserve side were at outside-left where he often partnered his brother Richard.

He scored on his first team debut as the Wanderers beat Notts County 7-3 in March 1889 but his appearances over the next couple of years were spasmodic until 1891 when after reverting to wing-half, he won a regular spot in the Bolton side. In March 1893 Turner was at the centre of a furore which saw the Lancashire Cup tie at Bury abandoned. He was involved in an attack on a Bury player and this incensed the home crowd who rushed onto the pitch to attack him!

Later that month he won his first England cap when he played against Wales at Stoke - in fact, Turner went on to win three full caps with three different clubs. After missing the 1894 FA Cup Final through injury, Turner, who had scored 12 goals in 108 games, left Burnden Park to join Stoke. He later played for Derby County, helping the Rams to third place in Division One and the FA Cup semi-finals in his first season at the Baseball Ground. In 1898 he played in the Derby side that lost to Nottingham Forest in the FA Cup Final before later rejoining Stoke where he ended his first-class career.

1953 Nat Lofthouse scored two of England's goals in a 6-3 win over the United States in New York. His good friend, Preston North End's Tom Finney also netted twice.

JUNE 9th

1977 Fences were installed at Burnden Park, initially behind each goal.
They stood 8ft high and cost in the region of £17,000. This came after pitch invasions, notably

in the promotion clashes against Chelsea in February and Wolverhampton Wanderers in May.

JUNE 10th

1915 Birth of Alf Anderson. Signed from Hibernian, he was another player who attempted to fill the position of outside-left vacated after the retirement of Welsh international Ted Vizard. It cost the Wanderers £2,500 to bring the diminutive winger to Burnden Park in January 1937. A regular member of the Bolton side for the next couple of seasons until losing his place to Ted Rothwell, he had scored five goals in 57 games when in March 1939 he was allowed to return north of the border to join Third Lanark. During the Second World War, Anderson returned to the north-west to 'guest' for Rochdale.

1971 Birth of Bruno N'Gotty. The French international defender had played for Lyon, Paris St Germain, AC Milan and Venezia before joining the Wanderers on loan from Marseilles in September 2001.
Equally adept at playing right-back or in the centre of defence, his experience shone through and it came as no surprise when in January 2002, the deal was made permanent. Last season, he was forced to miss a number of games midway through the campaign due to a calf injury but returned to action in the New Year, scoring an important header in the home draw with Manchester United. Regardless of where he plays, Bruno continues to display a high level of performance to which the Wanderers fans have come to expect in his first team appearances.

1975 Birth of Henrik Pedersen *(right)*. The Danish international looked immediately suited to the English game following his arrival at the Reebok in the summer of 2001. Signed from Silkeborg, he flitted in and out of the Bolton side during his first season with the club prior to being allowed

to rejoin Silkesborg on loan towards the end of the Danish season and help his former club in their fight against relegation from Denmark's top flight. After competing for a first team place with Holdsworth and Ricketts in 2002-03, Pedersen won a place in the side to play Leeds at Elland Road. He scored twice in a 4-2 win and after that retained his place in the starting line-up for the remainder of the season. A hardworking centre-forward, he ended the season as the club's joint-top scorer and has now scored nine goals in 49 first team games.

JUNE 11th

1873 Birth of Archie Freebairn. After playing his early football for Wheatburn and Partick Thistle, the Glasgow-born half-back joined the Wanderers in the summer of 1894. He made his Bolton debut in the 2-2 home draw with Stoke on the opening day of the 1894-95 season and was a model of consistency for the next five seasons when he missed just two games. During the course of that spell, his 136 consecutive league appearances were a club record. During the 1898-99 season, Freebairn was appointed club captain in place of Di Jones but despite one or two encouraging results, he couldn't prevent the Wanderers being relegated for the first time in their history. In 1899-1900 he played his part in helping the club win promotion at the first attempt and was a member of the Bolton side that lost 1-0 to Manchester City in the 1904 FA Cup Final. Freebairn played the last of his 315 League and Cup appearances for the Wanderers in a 3-2 home defeat by Birmingham in March 1907 and though he stayed on at Burnden Park for a further three years, they were spent playing reserve team football.

JUNE 12th

1969 'Happy' was the name chosen by Nat Lofthouse and Wanderers' captain Dave Hatton from those submitted by supporters for the new club emblem. The club shop became the Happy Shop and there was a Happy Burnden Beat in full swing where record requests and messages could be sent.

JUNE 13th

1959 Having won the first game against the South African national side, the Wanderers completed the 'double' with a 2-1 win in Johannesburg.

JUNE 14th

1941 Birth of Charlie Cooper. Though he spent 10 seasons at Burnden Park, Farnworth-born full-back Charlie Cooper was never a first team regular, being used as cover for a number of players. Cooper made his Wanderers' debut in a 2-0 defeat at Sheffield Wednesday in October 1960, going on to play in five successive First Division games before a disastrous display at Arsenal, where the Wanderers lost 5-1, saw him return to the reserves. Cooper's break came at the beginning of the 1966-67 season, by which time the Wanderers were in Division Two.
After a couple of seasons as the club's first-choice right-back, he lost his place to John Ritson and in July 1969 after appearing in 90 games, he joined Barrow. He made 54 appearances for the Holker Street club before hanging up his boots. His son, also called Charlie, played for Horwich RMI before joining Chorley. He was a member of the Magpies' side that beat Wolves in the FA Cup at Burnden Park in 1986.

JUNE 15th

1979 Work started on the Great Lever End terrace as 4,342 seats were installed and the pitch, a poor drainer despite its camber was dug up.
Undersoil heating and sprinklers were installed, though at one stage it seemed inevitable that a plastic pitch would be laid on the Burnden turf.

JUNE 16th

1925 Birth of George Higgins. The Dundee-born left-back served in the Royal Marine Commandos before moving to Blackburn Rovers in 1946. He had played in the same Navy team as Rovers' Eddie Quigley, who was later to play and manage the Ewood Park club. Due to the consistent form of Bill Eckersley, Higgins couldn't hold down a regular first team spot and in July 1951 joined

Bolton for a fee of £10,000. In his first season at Burnden Park, he missed just two League games as the Wanderers finished fifth in Division One after challenging for the title for much of the campaign. In 1953 he lost his place to Ralph Banks and so missed out on Bolton's FA Cup Final appearance against Blackpool, although he did play in the semi-final victory over Everton. He had played in 74 games for the Wanderers when in May 1954 he was given a free transfer and joined Grimsby Town. He later had a spell as player-manager of Scarborough before returning to Blundell Park as the Mariners' assistant-trainer in the summer of 1960.

1972 Birth of Bo Hansen. Signed from Danish club Brondby for £1 million in February 1999, he had scored 12 goals in eight games for the side prior to his transfer and figured in all of their European Champions' League games. Though he had been signed to replace Nathan Blake and Arnar Gunnlaugsson who had been sold by the club, he didn't make too many first team appearances that season, his outings being limited to a handful of starts and substitutions. He made more appearances in 1999-2000 playing alongside Eidur Gudjohnsen but it was the following season when Wanderers fans saw the best of Hansen. Featuring mainly on the wings or just behind the front two, he was a revelation, scoring a number of important goals. Though he was less prolific after that, he did score a wonder goal against Middlesbrough whilst wearing a pair of Michael Ricketts' golden boots! Hansen had scored 17 goals in 119 games when he was allowed to return to his homeland to play for Midtjylland.

JUNE 17th

1954 England's first World Cup match against Belgium in Basle ended all-square at 4-4 with Nat Lofthouse scoring two of England's goals - Manchester City's Ivor Broadis also netted twice.

1958 Tommy Banks was a member of the England side that played the Soviet Union in Gothenburg in a World Cup play-off for a place in the quarter-finals. Though the Wanderers' full-back had an outstanding tournament, England, who had drawn all their three group games, lost 1-0.

1959 Bolton's tour of South Africa saw them win eight of their ten games with one of the best results being a 5-0 win over Southern Rhodesia.

JUNE 18th

1971 Birth of Jason McAteer. The Republic of Ireland international joined the Wanderers from non-League Marine and made his first team debut in November 1992 when he came on as a substitute for Scott Green in a 4-0 defeat of Burnley. His full first team debut came the following week in another 4-0 victory, this time against Rochdale in an FA Cup second round tie in which he scored a goal. After that, McAteer became a regular in the Bolton midfield and in 1993-94 he appeared in every league game and scored in both FA Cup matches against mighty Arsenal. His performances that season saw him win the first of 51 full caps for the Republic of Ireland when he played against Holland. In 1994-95 he was instrumental in the club reaching the League Cup Final where they lost to Liverpool and promotion to the Premiership via the play-offs. Sadly, the Birkenhead-born midfielder appeared in just four Premier League games to take his total of appearances for the Wanderers to 145 before leaving Burnden Park to join Liverpool for £4.5 million - a new club record fee for an outgoing transfer. He went on to appear in 139 games for the Reds before Blackburn Rovers paid £4 million for his services in January 1999.
Injuries hampered his progress at Ewood Park and in under three years he made just 83 League and Cup appearances. Transferred to

Sunderland for £1 million in October 2001, the popular McAteer continued to suffer from injury problems, notably an abdominal hernia which required surgery.

JUNE 19th

1959 Birth of Jeff Chandler *(right)*. The London-born winger began his career with Blackpool and scored on his league debut for the Seasiders in a 2-1 win over Blackburn Rovers in September 1977.

Two years later, Leeds United paid £100,000 to take him to Elland Road but despite winning two caps for the Republic of Ireland whilst with the Yorkshire club, he failed to settle and in October 1981 he crossed the Pennines to join the Wanderers for a cut-price £40,000. He made his debut in a 3-0 win over Leicester City and over the next four seasons missed very few games, being an ever-present in 1983-84. That season saw him score 17 goals and that coupled with 20 he netted in 1984-85, prompted Derby County to sign him for £38,000, the fee being fixed by a tribunal. He helped the Rams win promotion to Division Two in 1985-86 before following a loan spell with Mansfield Town, he rejoined the Wanderers. Yet in only his fourth game back, he damaged ligaments which forced him to miss most of that promotion-winning season. He had scored 48 goals including one in the Sherpa Van Trophy Final win over Torquay United, in 211 games, when he left to join Cardiff City.

1959 Birth of Ray Deakin. An England schoolboy international, he spent four years with Everton without making a first team appearance and in August 1981 left to join Port Vale. After just one season at Vale Park,
he left to play for the Wanderers who signed him on a free transfer. He made his Bolton debut against Crystal Palace, having won the No.3 shirt from Mike Bennett. Deakin became a

regular in the Bolton side and despite the club's relegation to the Third Division, he maintained his place in the side, being made captain for a spell. The emergence of Jimmy Phillips forced Deakin to move to a central defensive role and it was in that position that he made the last of his 121 appearances.

In May 1985 he joined Burnley as the Clarets prepared for life in Division Four for the first time ever. An ever-present in his first two seasons with the club, he led them to victory over Orient -

the match that was make or break for the club's very survival and led them out at Wembley for the Sherpa Van Trophy Final against Wolves. He went on to appear in 271 games for Burnley before being released.

JUNE 20th

1956 Birth of Peter Reid *(below)*. A member of the successful Huyton Boys' side that won the English Schools' Trophy in 1970, he had the chance to join a number of clubs as an apprentice but opted for the Wanderers. He made his first team debut in October 1974 as a substitute in a home match against Orient.

An ever-present for the next two seasons, Reid's cultured midfield play and his intense desire to be involved at all times were features of Bolton's Second Division Championship-winning side of 1977-78.

On New Year's Day 1979, Reid collided with Everton goalkeeper George Wood on a snow-covered Burnden Park and broke his leg. He eventually returned to the side on a weekly contract but broke his leg again in Bolton's match with Barnsley.

Reid had scored 25 goals in 261 games for the Wanderers when in December 1982 he joined Everton for £60,000. In 1984-85 he was voted the Players' 'Player of the Year' as Everton won the League Championship and European Cup Winners' Cup. In 1986 he replaced Bryan Robson in England's World Cup side and on his return to Goodison helped the Blues win their second League title in three years. On the departure of Howard Kendall in June of that year, he became Everton's player-coach. He had scored 13 goals in 228 games when he left to join Queen's Park Rangers. He later became player-coach at Maine Road before becoming Manchester City's manager. He later took charge at Sunderland, taking the Wearsiders into the Premier League as runaway First Division Champions. After a spell as manager of Leeds United, he is currently working in the media.

1956 Birth of Mike Walsh. After working his way up through the ranks, he made his Bolton debut as a substitute in a 3-2 win at Nottingham Forest in February 1975. Though he started his career as a left-back he was also able to play both at centre-half and in midfield, though the next two seasons following his debut were spent deputising for first team regulars. Following an injury to Paul Jones, Walsh started Bolton's Second Division Championship-winning season of 1977-78 alongside Sam Allardyce at the heart of the defence and missed just one game as the Whites finished two points ahead of runners-up Tottenham Hotspur. During Bolton's two seasons back in the top flight, Walsh was an ever-present, playing in 126 consecutive League games before injury ended the run. Despite the Wanderers' defence coming under a lot of pressure, Walsh *(below)* was in commanding form and it came as no surprise when he moved to Everton for £90,000 with Jim McDonagh returning to Burnden Park in the deal.

Capped five times by the Republic of Ireland, he had loan spells with Norwich City and Burnley before joining Manchester City; he later played for Blackpool. In December 1990 he entered football management with Bury.

JUNE 21st

1959 The Wanderers ended their South African tour by beating Northern Rhodesia 5-3 to finish with the following record.

P.	W.	D.	L.	F.	A.
10	8	0	2	27	10

JUNE 22nd

1882 Birth of Bob Clifford. He was 19 years old when he made his Bolton debut as a right-half in the match against Preston North End in January 1904, a match the Wanderers lost 3-1. He remained in the League side for the rest of the season, often switching to centre-half to accommodate Archie Freebairn. Though he didn't play in any of the club's successful FA Cup ties of 1904, he did play in the final itself when he replaced the injured John Boyd. The following season he missed just two games as the Wanderers won promotion to the First Division. Despite an early season injury, Clifford wasn't phased by the higher grade of football. He moved to centre-half on a permanent basis and held that position for a couple of seasons. He had scored six goals in 167 League and Cup matches when in November 1908 he along with Walter White, joined Everton. At Goodison he made 45 appearances, the majority after being moved to full-back before leaving to end his first-class career with Fulham.

JUNE 23rd

1869 Birth of James Cassidy. The Kilmarnock-born forward began his career with his home-town club before joining Glasgow Hibernian. Here his goalscoring feats attracted a number of clubs from south of the border but it was the Wanderers who signed him in 1889. His first league game for the Wanderers saw them beaten 6-3 by West Bromwich Albion but in only his fifth game for

2001 PLAY-OFF FINAL WINNERS

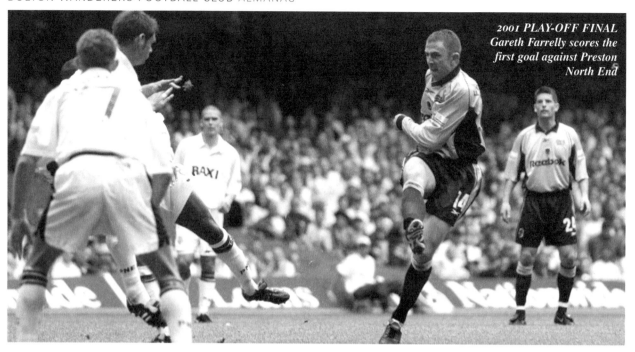

2001 PLAY-OFF FINAL
Gareth Farrelly scores the
first goal against Preston
North End

2001 PLAY-OFF FINAL
A young fan celebrates!

2001 PLAY-OFF FINAL
Michael Ricketts
scores the second goal

FINAL DAY OF THE SEASON 2002/03
Per Frandsen opens the scoring
against Middlesbrough

FINAL DAY OF THE SEASON 2002/03
Above: Jay-Jay Okocha scores the second from a free-kick.
Sam Allardyce salutes the crowd at the final whistle as
Premiership safety is secured.

*2004 CARLING CUP SEMI-FINAL
FIRST LEG
Above: Jay-Jay Okocha opens the scoring
with a stunning free-kick.
Kevin Nolan hits the second.*

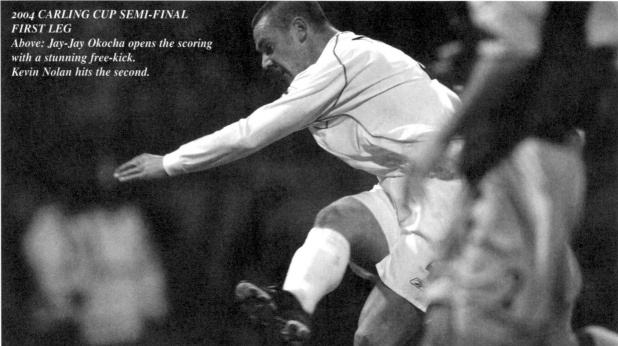

2004 CARLING CUP SEMI-FINAL
FIRST LEG
Bruno N'Gotty scores the fourth goal.

2004 CARLING CUP SEMI-FINAL
FIRST LEG
Jay-Jay Okocha completes the rout
with a stunning shot.

2004 CARLING CUP FINAL
Fans at the Millennium Stadium

2004 CARLING CUP FINAL
Youri Djorkaeff gets in a shot.

the club, he scored four times in a 7-1 win over Derby County. He ended his first season as the club's leading scorer with 20 goals in 19 League and Cup games - a feat he was to achieve on five occasions. Included in this total were five goals in the club's record 13-0 FA Cup rout of Sheffield United. When the Wanderers beat Notts County 2-0 in March 1892, Cassidy became the first Bolton player to score from the penalty spot. He also scored one of Bolton's goals in the 3-1 win over Everton in what was the first-ever Football League game played at Burnden Park. Cassidy had scored 101 goals in 219 games when he left Bolton to play for Newton Heath.

After a couple of seasons, he joined neighbours Manchester City before later ending his career with Middlesbrough.

JUNE 24th

1944 Birth of Dennis Butler. The nephew of the great Billy Butler and able to play on either wing, he made his Bolton debut as a 19-year-old in a 5-0 defeat at Aston Villa after replacing England international Brian Pilkington. As the Bolton youngsters battled for First Division survival, Butler was given a 17-match extended run in the side before disaster struck. The winger was forced to undergo a cartilage operation and after that, struggled to find any consistency. Following the signing of Terry Wharton from Wolves, Butler's first team appearances were restricted and after scoring 13 goals in 69 games, he signed for Rochdale in February 1968. He went on to score 39 goals in 156 League games before hanging up his boots to become coach at Bury. He later held a similar position with Port Vale before managing the Valiants for a brief period.

1982 Birth of Kevin Nolan *(right)*. A former Liverpool schools' player, he was the first of a number of fine Bolton Academy youngsters to make the grade.

He made his League debut for the Wanderers as a second-half substitute in the match against Charlton Athletic in March 2000, when he hit the woodwork with an audacious 30-yard effort. Although injuries forced him to miss the opening games of the 2000-01 season, he eventually established himself in the Wanderers' midfield, his performances earning him selection for England at Under 18 level. The following season proved to be an outstanding one for Kevin Nolan. After scoring on the opening day of the season as the Wanderers won 5-0 at Leicester City, he went on to become recognised as one of the best young midfielders in the country. A fearsome battler, with a tigerish tackle and a lethal shot, he found the net nine times during the course of that campaign. In 2001-02 he became a regular in the England Under 21 squad and though he found the campaign a little more frustrating will surely go on to win full international honours one day.

JUNE 25th

1889   Birth of Joe Smith. A magnificent centre-forward and inspirational leader, Joe Smith played his early football as an amateur with Newcastle St Luke's in the Staffordshire League before joining the Wanderers. Smith made his League debut for the Burnden Park club in a 2-0 defeat at West Bromwich Albion in April 1909 before establishing himself as a first team regular in 1910-11. His displays for the Wanderers in the years leading up to the First World War led to him winning the first of five full caps for England in February 1913 in a 2-1 defeat against Ireland. Smith played in 51 wartime games for the Wanderers, scoring 48 goals including six against Stoke in September 1916 as Bolton ran out winners 9-2. Along with Ted Vizard, he 'guested' for Chelsea while serving in the RAF and in 1918 they both helped the Stamford Bridge club win the London v Lancashire Cup Final. Joe Smith was Bolton's most consistent

goalscorer until Nat Lofthouse and his 38 goals in 1920-21 are still a club record. The total included hat-tricks against Middlesbrough (Home 6-2), Sunderland (Home 6-2) and Newcastle United (Home 3-1). In 1923 came Joe Smith's greatest honour when he became the first FA Cup Final captain to receive the trophy at Wembley. Three years later he lifted the Cup again but his career at Bolton was coming to an end. After heading the Wanderers' League scoring charts for the sixth time, Smith, who had scored 277 goals in 492 games, joined Stockport County in March 1927 for £1,000. For the Edgeley Park club, he scored 61 goals in 69 league games but in 1929 he joined Darwen and had a spell at Manchester Central before becoming manager of Reading. Four years later he took charge at Blackpool. Guiding the Seasiders to their best-ever League position and to the FA Cup Finals of 1948, 1951 and 1953, he was the longest-serving manager in the Football League when he parted company with the club in April 1958.

JUNE 26th

1897   Birth of Bob Haworth. Bolton manager Charles Foweraker's first signing, when he joined the Wanderers from Atherton Collieries in 1921, Bob Haworth made his debut in a 1-0 win against West Bromwich Albion at the Hawthorns. Haworth who had originally started out as a centre-forward, played at right-back in that game - a position he held virtually unchallenged for the next nine seasons.
During that time, he was a member of the Bolton side that won the FA Cup three times in the 1920s and after being ever-present in 1929-30, was appointed club captain in place of Jimmy Seddon. Haworth had played in the first 29 games of the following season when he broke his leg in a 4-1 defeat at Grimsby Town on 17 February 1931. It was his 357th and last appearance for the Wanderers, after which he had

a short spell with Accrington Stanley before retiring.

JUNE 27th

1900 Birth of Harry Greenhalgh. The Bolton-born defender made his name in local football, representing the Town's schools side and helping Chorley Old Road Congregational to win the Bolton Sunday School League. After moving to Atherton Collieries in the Lancashire Combination, Greenhalgh joined the Wanderers in April 1924. He made his League debut in a 1-0 win at Notts County in January 1925, taking over at right-back from the injured Bob Haworth. In 1926, Greenhalgh replaced Alex Finney in the Bolton side that beat Manchester City 1-0 to win the FA Cup Final. He also picked up Lancashire Cup medals in 1925 and 1927 before a spate of niggling injuries restricted his first team appearances. In February 1929 he broke his right leg at Derby County and though he stayed at the club after making a full recovery, playing Central League football, he did not add to his 80 first team outings.

JUNE 28th

1920 Birth of Ralph Banks. The older brother of England international full-back Tommy Banks, he played his early football for non-League South Liverpool prior to signing for the Wanderers during the early part of the Second World War. His first game in Bolton colours in January 1941 saw the Wanderers beat Oldham Athletic 2-1. There is no doubt that Farnworth-born Ralph Banks lost his best years to the war and his career was curtailed even further after the cessation of hostilities due to National Service. His most consistent season for the club was 1948-49 and though he later became understudy to Kinsell, Kennedy and finally George Higgins, he outlasted them all! The last of his 117 first team

appearances was in the 1953 FA Cup Final against Blackpool when he wore the No.3 shirt before handing it over to Tommy for the start of the following season. Though he failed to get on the scoresheet for the Wanderers, he netted one for his next club Aldershot before ending his playing days on the south coast with Weymouth.

JUNE 29th

1871 Birth of Alex Paton. After appearing at centre-forward for the Vale of Leven in the 1890 Scottish Cup Final, Alex Paton signed for West Manchester. It was from here that he joined the Wanderers later that year, making his Bolton debut in the opening game of the 1890-91 season as the Trotters beat Notts County 4-2. Having been converted to half-back, Paton was ever-present for the next three seasons and didn't miss a game until Boxing Day 1893 after 98 consecutive League and Cup games following his debut. Alex Paton was a fearless player; in 1894 he played in the FA Cup Final defeat by Notts County with his entire body virtually covered in bandages! He recovered to become a regular in the Bolton half-back line, again missing just one game in the next three seasons. At the end of the of the 1897-98 season he refused to re-sign after a disagreement over pay and although the differences were eventually resolved, he only played in a further five games as the club lost their First Division status for the first time in its history. Having had the distinction of appearing in both the English and Scottish FA Cup Finals, he ended his Bolton career with 15 goals in 241 League and Cup games.

JUNE 30th

1918 Birth of John Roberts. The Welsh international began his career with his local club Cwmburia before signing for the Wanderers in April 1936. After a series of impressive performances for the club's reserve side, he made his Bolton debut against Sunderland in February 1938.

Playing at inside-forward, Roberts hit a purple patch midway through the 1938-39 season when scoring six goals in as many games. Included in this total was a hat-trick in Bolton's 4-2 home win over Everton.

During the Second World War, Roberts served with the 53rd Field Regiment (RA), playing a number of games abroad and 'guesting' for Norwich City. When League football resumed in 1946-47, Roberts switched to centre-half where his performances led to him becoming the club's captain. After winning full international honours against Belgium, Roberts, who had scored 19 goals in 171 games, returned to South Wales to sign for his home-town club, Swansea Town. He later played non-League football for Llanelli whilst continuing to work in a Swansea steel works.

JULY 1st

1888   Birth of Billy Hughes. Signed from his local club, Stourbridge, he replaced Albert Shepherd, scoring on his debut in a 3-0 home win over Oldham Athletic in December 1908. That season, Hughes scored 16 goals to help the Wanderers win the Second Division Championship.

In 1909-10, Hughes found goals harder to come by as Bolton were relegated but the following season after forming a deadly strike partnership with Harold Hilton, he netted 21 goals in 28 games as the Wanderers returned to the top flight at the first time of asking. Over four consecutive home games in the months of December 1910 and January 1911, Hughes scored 11 goals including three hat-tricks.

Following the arrival of George Lillycrop from Barnsley, Billy Hughes found first team appearances hard to come by and in September 1913 after scoring 51 goals in 102 games, he was allowed to join Wolverhampton Wanderers. The

Trotters were later fined £25 by the Football League for misleading Hughes into assuming he would receive £200 in lieu of a benefit if he left Burnden Park.

1942   Birth of Terry Wharton. The Bolton-born winger followed his father John into the Football League, though he began his career with Wolverhampton Wanderers, for whom he scored on his debut in a 2-0 home win over Ipswich Town in November 1961. He was Wolves' first-choice right-winger for the next five and a half seasons, netting his first hat-trick for the club in March 1963 as West Bromwich Albion were beaten 7-0. After the Molineux club had suffered relegation in 1964-65, Wharton helped them return to the First Division two seasons later, netting another hat-trick in a 7-1 defeat of Cardiff City. He had scored 79 goals in 242 games when he joined his home-town club Bolton for a then record transfer fee of £70,000. He soon settled into the side and became the club's regular penalty-taker. He had two good seasons with the Wanderers, scoring a hat-trick in a 4-2 defeat of Luton Town on the opening day of the 1969-70 season. Failing to live up to his early promise, he had scored 30 goals in 110 games when in January 1971 he was allowed to join Crystal Palace for £12,000, later ending his career with a single game for Walsall.

JULY 2nd

1951   Australian-born Bolton goalkeeper Ken Grieves, equalled Lancashire's John Tyldesley's world record when playing cricket for the Red Rose county against Sussex at Old Trafford when he held six catches in an innings.

JULY 3rd

1867   Birth of David Jones. Known as Dai, he was born near Oswestry and at the age of 16 helped his

home-town team capture the Shropshire Cup.
A year later he moved to Chirk, where he became captain and helped them win the Welsh Cup in 1885. Whilst playing for Chirk, Jones worked as a miner but later left to play briefly for Newton Heath. He signed for the Wanderers in 1888, having earlier won the first of 15 full caps for Wales. Jones was the ideal full-back, cool under pressure and a strong tackler, able to kick with either foot. Appointed Bolton's captain, he hardly missed a game in his time with the club, though one miss that was down to him, was the club's first penalty miss in the match against Everton in January 1892. He skippered the Wanderers to the 1894 FA Cup Final and the following year, the first game played at Burnden Park was a testimonial in aid of Dai Jones.

In October 1898 after scoring eight goals in 255 games, he joined Manchester City. In his second season with the club, he helped them win the Second Division Championship but in August 1902, he gashed a knee in a practice game and contracted tetanus. Within 11 days, Jones was dead.

JULY 4th

1929   After winning the FA Cup for the third time this decade, the Wanderers were invited to open a new 65,000 all-seater stadium in Barcelona against the Catalonian Club. Unfortunately Bolton went down to a 4-0 defeat before the King of Spain.

JULY 5th

1882   Birth of Sam Greenhalgh. He had played local football for Eagley and Turton before joining the Wanderers in the summer of 1902. The following season he became a regular at centre-half in a Bolton team that failed to register a League win until January!
He was a member of the Bolton side that lost 1-0 to Manchester City in the 1904 FA Cup Final and a year later missed only two games as the Wanderers won promotion to the First Division. That season, Greenhalgh was also selected for the Football League XI against the Scottish League XI. In October 1905, he left Burnden Park to join Aston Villa, but within two years he was back at Bolton.
A member of the Wanderers' Second Division Championship-winning team of 1908-09, he captained them to promotion again two seasons later following a quick relegation.
In March 1912 he fell into dispute with the club after refusing to play on the wing in an emergency. After serving his six weeks' ban, he apologised to the board and went on to score 20 goals in 278 games before later playing non-League football for Chorley.

JULY 6th

1871   Birth of Jim McGeachan. The strong-tackling centre-half joined the Wanderers from Hibernian after promising to join Celtic and made his debut in a 2-1 home defeat by Small Heath in November 1894.
He soon established himself at the heart of the Bolton defence and had the distinction of scoring Bolton's first goal in a 3-0 win over Bury - it was the first goal to be scored in the First Division at Gigg Lane.
The following game saw him take part in the opening fixture at Burnden Park and he was a regular in the Bolton side until 1897. He was then suspended by the Bolton board for refusing to travel to Sheffield. Although he was later reinstated, he eventually lost his place to a fellow Scot, Bob Brown. Having scored five goals in 81 first team outings, McGeachan returned north of the border to rejoin Hibs but after just one game he returned to Burnden Park. But his first team days were over and he saw out his career in the club's reserve side.

JULY 7th

1889 Birth of John Slater. A versatile player, he made his Bolton debut when he came in at left-back for the injured John Stanley in the match against Everton in March 1907. In a little over a year, Slater had become a regular in the Bolton side and helped them win the Second Division title in 1908-09. The following season though he found his first team appearances curtailed by Herbert Baverstock and Billy Stott.

Over the next few seasons, he made just an handful of appearances and though he stayed at Burnden Park until August 1914, he had only made 99 appearances by the time he joined South Liverpool. With his football flagging, Slater became involved in a coal merchant's business before later working in cotton, pottery and the shipping business. In 1932, Slater became an MP for Eastbourne but having suffered heart trouble for a good number of years, he died suddenly at a banquet, aged 46.

JULY 8th

1986 One of the greatest changes to Burnden Park took place when the 16,000 capacity Railway Embankment was cut in half and a Normid Superstore was built on the spot where the 1946 Disaster had occurred.

JULY 9th

1889 Birth of Jimmy Jones. A sharp-tackling full-back, he began his career with Gateshead before joining Blackpool in June 1912. Although relatively small for a defender, he had tremendous pace and packed a powerful shot. He went on to play in 116 games for the Seasiders before Bolton paid £1,000 for his services in March 1920. He went straight into the Wanderers' League side, making his debut against Oldham Athletic. During the 1920-21 season he held the right-back position from the opening day of the season as the Wanderers made a concerted challenge for the League Championship. After losing his place to Alec Finney, Jones, who had played in 70 games for the Wanderers, joined New Brighton, curiously enough as a replacement for the gap left by Finney's departure!

JULY 10th

1966 Birth of goalkeeper Keith Branagan. He began his League career with Cambridge United and had made 134 first team appearances when Millwall paid £100,000 for his services in March 1988. Initially he was unable to break into the Lions' side but after a loan spell at Brentford, he established himself in the Millwall side. He had helped the London club to the play-offs when injury struck and though he regained full fitness following a further loan spell, this time with Gillingham, he found it difficult to regain his place.

Wanderers' manager Bruce Rioch brought Branagan to Burnden Park on a free transfer and he made his debut in a 2-0 home win over Huddersfield Town on the opening day of the 1992-93 season. He was ever-present that campaign as the Wanderers won promotion from the Second Division but he missed a good deal of the following season because of injury.

The following season, he was instrumental in the Wanderers reaching the League Cup Final and the play-offs, where he turned the game against Reading after saving a penalty. After that the Republic of Ireland international keeper remained the Wanderers' first-choice until injury cost him his place.

In April 2000, after playing in 263 games, Branagan *(right)* left to join Ipswich Town as cover for Richard Wright.

JULY 11th

1985 Local folk group, the Houghton Weavers, fronted by big Wanderers' fan, Tony Berry, launched the record 'The Lion of Vienna'.

JULY 12th

1919 Charles Foweraker was appointed manager of Bolton Wanderers. He entered football in a part-time capacity in 1895, acting as a gateman and a checker when Burnden Park opened, while also employed by the Lancashire and Yorkshire Railway Company. When Tom Mather was called up to join the Royal Navy in 1915, Foweraker stepped in and guided the club through the war years. In July 1919 he was appointed secretary-manager on a permanent basis at a salary of £400 per annum.

He was in charge of the Wanderers throughout their most successful period during the 1920s when the club won three FA Cup Finals at Wembley and were serious contenders for the League Championship.

In July 1938 he was awarded the Football League's Long Service Medal in recognition of more than 21 years' service to the Wanderers. The Lancashire FA also presented him with a similar award and he served as vice-president of that organisation for many years. Foweraker strongly believed in the development of players under military age and from this belief rose the greatest of all the Wanderers' heroes, Nat Lofthouse. In August 1944, Charles Foweraker, the most successful manager in the club's history, was forced to retire through ill-health, having completed 49 years' continuous service with the club. He died at his Bolton home in July 1950, aged 73.

JULY 13th

1885 Birth of Billy Hunter. Signed from Millwall Athletic, Hunter was an inside-forward when he arrived at Burnden Park in January 1909 and made his debut in that position in a 2-1 defeat at Gainsborough Trinity. After a handful of games, he was switched to outside-left replacing Marshall McEwan. He missed only one game in helping the Wanderers win that season's Second Division Championship. In 1909-10 he played a number of games at centre-forward, scoring 10 goals in 29 games but the arrival of Ted Vizard ended Hunter's run in the team and he spent the next two seasons as the Welsh international's understudy. His final game in Bolton colours came in October 1911 when he replaced David Stokes on the right-wing but sadly he sustained an injury that was to end his playing career. Having scored 16 goals in 55 games, he turned to coaching in January 1914 and he took up a post with the Dutch team Dordrecht. After the First World War, he worked for the Turkish FA.

JULY 14th

1966 Birth of Owen Coyle. He began his career with Dumbarton, scoring from the penalty-spot on his debut against Ayr United in February 1986. He spent three seasons with Dumbarton, topping their goalscoring charts in 1987-88 before leaving to play for Clydebank in September 1988. He again scored on his debut, as the Bankies just missed out on promotion to the Premier League. He had scored 34 goals in 68 games when Airdrie paid £175,000 for his services in February 1990. Coyle netted a hat-trick on his debut in a 6-0 home win over Ayr United and although he ended the season as the club's leading scorer, they just missed out on promotion.
In 1990-91 he scored 17 goals in the opening seven games of the season, a total which included four hat-tricks and although he missed a number of games through injury he was still the leading scorer as the club won promotion to the Premier League.
In July 1993 Coyle joined Bolton for a tribunal set fee of £250,000 and scored some vital goals in the club's run to the FA Cup sixth round. In 1994 he won full international honours when he played for the Republic of Ireland against Holland. He scored for the Wanderers in their

play-off final defeat of Reading and had scored 23 goals in 78 first team outings when he left to play for Dundee United in October 1995. After helping the Tannadice club win promotion to the Premier League he joined Motherwell, later rejoining Dunfermline Athletic. Coyle is now with Falkirk, having helped the Bairns win the Scottish First Division Championship last season.

JULY 15th

1866 Birth of Jocky Wright. Signed from Clyde, Jocky Wright was a left winger when he arrived at Burnden Park in the summer of 1895. Moved to inside-left, he was an ever-present in the club's first season at their new ground and in 1896 scored one of the goals in the 2-0 win over Bury, in the first FA Cup tie to be staged at Burnden Park. He continued to be a regular in the side until Sheffield Wednesday paid £200 for his services in October 1898. His debut for the Owls was in a famous game against Aston Villa which was abandoned after 79 minutes because of bad light. The remaining 11 minutes were played the following March! In 1899-1900, Wright was Wednesday's leading scorer with 26 goals as both they and the Wanderers won promotion to the First Division. In March 1902, after playing in 110 games for the Yorkshire club, Wright rejoined the Wanderers, taking his total of goals to 22 in 128 League and Cup games.

2001 The Wanderers suffered two heavy defeats on their tour of Denmark, the first being a 6-0 reversal at the hands of Lyngby.

JULY 16th

1952 Despite having a disappointing game against Italy in Florence as England drew 1-1, Nat Lofthouse became the transfer target of local club Fiorentina, who made an offer that the Wanderers' board turned down. Lofthouse, who enjoyed playing against the Italians, was on £14 a week, but the Italians were offering him £60 a week to start with!

JULY 17th

1940 Birth of Syd Farrimond. An England youth international, he made his League debut in a goalless draw against Preston North End at Deepdale in October 1958, replacing the injured Tommy Banks. It was 1961-62 before he won a regular place in the side, being ever-present that season. However, Farrimond didn't have the timing of the England international and his vigorous tackling often saw him sent-off on a number of occasions. A member of the Bolton side for the next 10 seasons, he occasionally lost his place to Charlie Cooper or Dave Hatton but always won it back at their expense. Farrimond went on to appear in 404 League and Cup games for the Wanderers, his only goal coming in a 1-1 home draw against Norwich City in March 1967. After losing his place to the up and coming Don McAllister, he left Burnden Park on a free transfer following a dispute over a loyalty bonus. He joined Tranmere Rovers and appeared in 134 league games for the Wirral-based club before embarking on coaching spells with Halifax Town, Sunderland and Leeds United.

2001 Two days after the heavy defeat at Lyngby, the Whites conceded another six goals, going down 6-1 to Odense.

JULY 18th

1872 Birth of John Somerville. Known as 'Surefoot' because of his reliable displays at right-back, John Somerville played in 293 League and Cup games for the Wanderers and appeared in the FA Cup Final of 1894 as well as helping the club win promotion to the First Division in 1898-99. When Frank Brettell left the club to join Tottenham Hotspur, Somerville was appointed Bolton's secretary-player. He had therefore been acting as secretary for 10 years when he added managerial duties to his role. His first season in charge proved extremely successful as the Wanderers collected their first championship trophy in winning the Second Division title after only a season's absence from the top flight.
The following season saw a complete contrast when Somerville found that the players who had helped the club win promotion in 1908-09 were not good enough to keep the Trotters in the First Division. In January 1910, with the club firmly rooted to the foot of the First Division, and beaten 4-1 in the FA Cup by Second Division Stockport County, the management of the club was handed over to Will Settle.
Somerville remained as secretary to the end of the season before going on to be a Football League linesman.

1998 Bolton began their tour of the Republic of Ireland with a 5-0 win over Galway.

JULY 19th

1975 The Wanderers started their tour of Europe with a 2-0 win over Westphalia Herne and followed it up with a 3-2 defeat of Hamburg before being heavily beaten 4-0 by Dutch side NAC Breda.

1993 An electronic scoreboard was erected at the corner of the Manchester Road Stand and Normid Development.

1996 The Whites began their programme of pre-season friendlies with a comfortable 5-0 win over Atherton LR.

1997 Bolton won an exciting pre-season friendly at Notts County's Meadow Lane ground 4-3.

JULY 20th

1938 Birth of Roger Hunt. The Liverpool goalscoring legend played in 403 League games for the Anfield side, scoring a then club record 245 goals including 41 in as many games during the 1961-62 season. He won League Championship medals in 1963-64 and 1965-66, a Second Division Championship medal in 1961-62 and an FA Cup winners' medal in 1965. He played in 34 full internationals for England and was a member of the 1966 World Cup winning side. Bolton did try to sign him during the early part of the 1969-70 season but Hunt refused to leave Anfield.

However, in December 1969, Hunt, who had supported the Wanderers as a boy, joined the Burnden Park club in a £32,000 deal. He made his Bolton debut in a Boxing Day fixture at Preston North End but could do little to revive the club's flagging fortunes.

Midway through the following season, he was dropped but returned to net a hat-trick in a 3-0 defeat of Birmingham City. However, the Wanderers were still relegated to the Third Division for the first time in their history before Hunt, who went on to score 25 goals in 84 games hung up his boots to concentrate on his family haulage business.

JULY 21st

1931 Birth of Jimmy Meadows. He began his playing career with Bolton YMCA before making his Football League debut with Southport.

In March 1951 he joined Manchester City and it was whilst he was with them that he won full international honours for England in a 7-2 win over Scotland. After injury forced him into premature retirement, Meadows took over the managerial reigns at Stockport County. Though he led the Hatters out of the Fourth Division, he left Edgeley Park in 1969 to take over as chief coach at Blackpool. He took over as Bolton manager in January 1971 and although the club won his first game in charge - with a team selected by Nat Lofthouse - Meadows was never to taste success at Burnden Park again. Many of the club's top players put in transfer requests while the club also sold Paul Fletcher and Terry Wharton. Meadows recruited former Olympic athlete Joe Lancaster in an attempt to boost the club's training programme but morale was at a low ebb. After three draws and seven defeats in his 10 games in charge, Meadows resigned. He did find success in his next managerial post when he won the Fourth Division Championship with Southport. He later had another spell in charge of Stockport County.

1965 Birth of Gudni Bergsson. He was a law student at Reykjavik University when he was invited to join Tottenham Hotspur on trial. He was playing as an amateur for his local club Valur, whom he helped win the Icelandic title in 1987 and the Icelandic Cup in 1988. With Spurs he appeared in 71 League games before joining the Wanderers for a fee of £115,000 in March 1995. Capable of playing at right-back or in the centre of defence, he made his Wanderers' debut as a substitute in the League Cup Final against Liverpool at Wembley. He returned there the following month to play his part in the play-off final win against Reading. After that he missed very few games and scored a number of vital goals, perhaps none more enjoyable than the one against Spurs at White Hart Lane which earned the Wanderers their first away point in the Premiership.

In 1996-97, he captained the Wanderers to the First Division Championship and then proceeded to defy his advancing years by winning numerous 'Player of the Year' awards. A superb reader of the game and with excellent distribution, he continued to delay his retirement and plans to return to Iceland to work as a lawyer until the end of the 2002-03 season. Iceland's second most capped player, having made 80 international appearances for his country, Gudni *(below)* went on to score 27 goals in 317 games for the Wanderers and was a key factor in helping the club to retain its Premiership status.

JULY 22nd

1886 Birth of Tom Barber. Despite being born within a stone's throw of Newcastle United's St James Park, Tom Barber began his Football League career with Bolton Wanderers. He made his debut at Fulham in October 1908 and over the next few seasons, became a reliable half-back and inside-forward for the club, culminating in him being an ever-present in 1911-12. Barber had scored 14 goals in 107 games when on Christmas Eve 1912, Aston Villa paid £1,950 for his services It was with the Midlands club that he recorded his greatest success, scoring the winning goal against Sunderland in the 1913 FA Cup Final. The profits from Barber's sale allowed the Wanderers to cover the cost of the Great Lever Stand. On leaving Villa, he had spells with Stalybridge Celtic and Merthyr Tydfil before signing for Walsall. He sadly died from tuberculosis aged just 39.

1972 Birth of Michael Johansen. He arrived at Burnden Park in August 1996 in a double deal with FC Copenhagen team-mate Per Frandsen. He became the Wanderers' fourth signing to have cost at least £1 million and soon became a great favourite with the Burnden crowd. Johansen had won a Danish League Championship medal in 1993 and scored one of the goals when they won the Danish Cup two years later. He made his League debut in a 1-1 draw at Port Vale on the opening day of the 1996-97 season, going on to score five goals in 33 games as the Wanderers won the Second Division Championship. Though he spent most of the following Premiership season on the bench, he did, when he came on as a substitute, prove to be a real handful for opposing defences with a terrific turn of pace. Despite the club's relegation, Johansen continued to play with great enthusiasm and scored some vital goals, perhaps none more important than the only goal of the game against Ipswich Town in the first leg of the play-off semi-final which helped the Wanderers get to Wembley. Having signed a pre-contract agreement in early 2000 to return to Denmark to play for FC Copenhagen, Johansen had scored 21 goals in 170 games when he left the Reebok Stadium at the end of the 1999-2000 season.

1993   After coming on as a substitute for David Reeves, Scott Green scored a hat-trick for the Wanderers in a 4-0 win over Atherton LR in a pre-season friendly.

1996   Construction work began on the Reebok Stadium.

JULY 23rd

1977   Bolton's pre-season tour of Germany didn't get off to the best of starts when they were beaten 5-1 by Bayreuth. In fact, despite only winning one of their four games, the Wanderers went on to win the following season's Second Division Championship.

1989   The club's first game in the Isle of Man Tournament saw them go down 1-0 to Scottish Division One side, Motherwell.

1993   The Wanderers' first match in that season's Lancashire Cup saw them beat Rochdale at Spotland 4-3.

JULY 24th

1941   Birth of Tony Dunne *(right)*. He joined Manchester United from League of Ireland club Shelbourne United for £3,500 in the summer of 1960. He made 530 first team appearances for the Red Devils, playing in the 1963 FA Cup Final winning side, the League Championship winning sides of 1964-65 and 1966-67 and in the 1968 European Cup Final when he gave one of the best displays of his career in United's 4-1 defeat of

Benfica. Capped 32 times by the Republic of Ireland, he left Old Trafford in August 1973 and joined the Wanderers on a free transfer. He made his Bolton debut in a 1-0 defeat at Bristol City on the opening day of the 1973-74 season. However, his form during that campaign was inconsistent and it was the following season before he showed his true capabilities. He was a regular member of the Bolton side in 1975-76 and 1976-77 when the Wanderers narrowly missed out on promotion to the top flight and was still there in 1977-78 when the Whites won the Second Division Championship. He won a further six caps for the Republic of Ireland while with Bolton but left the

club after playing in 192 games. In 1980 he returned to Burnden Park as first team coach, then as assistant-manager to Stan Anderson, leaving when he was replaced by George Mulhall in the spring of 1981.

1985 A larger than normal Chorley crowd was packed into Victory Park to see the Northern Premier League side take on the Wanderers in a pre-season friendly. Though the visitors came close on a number of occasions and the woodwork came to Chorley's rescue many times, the game was goalless.

1996 The Wanderers ventured north of the border for a friendly against Queen of the South and though they came under great pressure from the Scottish outfit, they came away with a 1-0 victory.

JULY 25th

1989 Bolton's only success in their three matches in the Isle of Man Tournament was a 1-0 win over League of Ireland side, Dundalk 1-0.

1992 The Wanderers visited Oakwell, the home of First Division Barnsley for a pre-season friendly and came away with a 2-0 victory.

JULY 26th

1928 Birth of Johnny Wheeler. The Liverpool-born wing-half was manager Bill Ridding's first signing when he joined the Wanderers from Tranmere Rovers in February 1951. He made his Bolton debut in a 2-1 home win over Liverpool and then held his place virtually unchallenged for the next five seasons. On 3 January 1953 he was asked to play as an emergency centre-forward and responded with a hat-trick in a 4-0 win over Blackpool. After winning Football League and England 'B' honours, Wheeler won full international honours when he was selected to play for England against Northern Ireland in Belfast. He went on to score 18 goals in 205 League and Cup games for Bolton before rather surprisingly being released to join his cousin Ronnie Moran at Liverpool. He made 164 League appearances for the Anfield club before taking up the post of assistant-trainer at Bury.

1994 Bolton entertained the mighty Liverpool in a pre-season friendly at Burnden Park and despite the big names of Bruce Grobbelaar, Ian Rush, Steve McManaman etc, the Wanderers won a one-sided match 4-1.

JULY 27th

1904 Birth of Billy McKay. Having played his early football with East Stirling, Billy McKay moved on to Hamilton Academicals where his impressive displays alerted a number of clubs south of the border. It was Bolton manager Charles Foweraker who persuaded McKay to come to Burnden Park and the tough-tackling Scot made his Bolton debut in a 1-1 draw with Manchester United at Old Trafford in December 1929. Initially, he failed to settle into a struggling Bolton team but eventually he won a regular place in the side, his creative play providing Harold Blackmore with numerous goalscoring opportunities. Finding himself in and out of the Wanderers' side, McKay, who had scored 17 goals in 109 games, asked to be placed on the transfer list and in March 1934 he joined Manchester United. He helped the Reds win the Second Division Championship in 1935-36 and after a quick relegation, helped them win promotion to the top flight again in 1937-38. He left United during the war years but then in 1946, played non-League football for Stalybridge Celtic.

1993 The Wanderers won their second match in the Lancashire Cup, beating Burnley 1-0 at Turf

Moor with Alan Thompson scoring the all-important goal.

JULY 28th

1944 Birth of John Byrom *(below)*. An instinctive goalscorer, he began his Football League career with his home-town of Blackburn Rovers where he scored 45 goals in 108 league games before Bill Ridding signed him for the Wanderers for a fee of £25,000.

Initially he had linked up well with Wyn Davies

and Francis Lee but within a couple of months, both players had left Burnden Park. It was 1969-70 before 'JB' achieved the hoped-for prolific returns, for after netting hat-tricks in the first two games of the season, he ended the campaign with 25 first team goals. The following season, Bolton were relegated and as the club's most saleable asset, he was made available for transfer.

Fortunately, he stayed to top the Wanderers' goalscoring charts in 1972-73 and win a Third Division Championship medal. On the club's return to the Second Division, he was again top scorer with 24 goals. In the FA Cup tie against Stoke City, he netted a hat-trick in Bolton's 3-2 win, popping up on his own goal-line in the last minute to clear and then salute the fans! Byrom had scored 130 goals in 351 games for the Wanderers before being given a free transfer in 1976 and returning to Ewood Park for a brief Indian summer.

1972 Birth of Fabian De Freitas. He arrived at Burnden Park from Volendam in August 1994 for what was then a club record fee of £400,000. In all, he had scored 40 goals in 150 games for the side from Stadium Monica but after five years with them, he wanted to try his luck in English football. A speedy forward, he made his Bolton debut in a 1-0 defeat against Middlesbrough but as that 1994-95 season progressed, he failed to hold down a regular first team spot. His appearance at half-time in the Wembley play-off final against Reading helped turn the tide after the Wanderers had been 2-0 down. He hit the equaliser and then his side's fourth goal that sent the Bolton supporters from the depths of despair to heaven. He had scored just nine goals in 49 first team outings when he was allowed to join Spanish Second Division side Osasuna for £225,000. He later returned to League action with West Bromwich Albion before returning to Holland to play for Cambuur.

1977 Bolton's only victory on their four-match tour of Germany came in their third game against Atlas Delmenhorst, a match the Wanderers won 2-1.

1989 Bolton needed to beat Swansea City to qualify from the group stages for the final of the Isle of Man Tournament, but went down 2-1 to the South Wales side.

JULY 29th

1987 Bolton's only pre-season friendly that didn't involve them playing in the Lancashire Cup, saw them travel to Port Vale, where they came away with a 3-2 victory.

1991 After taking a point from Sunderland in the opening match of the Isle of Man Tournament, Bolton couldn't break down a stubborn Shelbourne defence and a game the Whites were expected to win, ended goalless.

JULY 30th

1985 Bolton's last pre-season friendly saw them visit Southport's Haig Avenue ground where they ran out 5-2 winners.

1999 The Wanderers travelled north of the border to play Dunfermline Athletic in a friendly. The game which ended goalless after 90 minutes was decided by a penalty shoot-out; the Wanderers winning 5-4.

2000 After embarking on a two-match tour of the United States, the Wanderers beat Indiana Blast 2-0 before losing 1-0 to the United States Under 23 team - both matches were played in Indianapolis.

JULY 31st

1990 A good crowd turned up at Lancaster City's Giant

Axe ground to see their favourites play the Wanderers in a pre-season friendly.
Bolton ran out winners 5-1 with Phil Brown netting twice. Bolton's other scorers were Thompson, Cowdrill and Stubbs.

1995 Bolton embarked on a four-match tour of Scotland, winning their first match against Queen's Park 3-0.

AUGUST 1st

1994 The Wanderers' short pre-season tour of Scotland saw them win three and draw one of the four matches - although they won the penalty shoot-out after the goalless draw with Dunfermline Athletic. The club's best win was a 7-0 defeat of Ross County in which Paatelainen and Sneekes both scored twice.

AUGUST 2nd

1983 Bolton began their pre-season tour of Ireland with a 2-1 victory over Sligo Rovers. They then went on to win three and draw one of their four-match tour.

1991 After drawing their first two games in the Isle of Man Tournament - Sunderland (2-2) and Shelbourne (0-0), the Wanderers beat the Isle of Man XI 6-0 with both Julian Darby and David Reeves finding the net twice.

AUGUST 3rd

1907 Birth of Jack Tennant. He played his early football as a centre-forward for Washington Colliery where he was both born and worked before entering League football with Stoke. By the time he had arrived at the Victoria Ground, Tennant had been converted into a full-back but even so, he only made one appearance for the Potters before joining Third Division Torquay

United. His impressive displays for the Devon club, for whom he was ever-present in 1932-33 prompted Liverpool to secure his service in the summer of 1933. He had made 39 appearances for the Reds when Bolton paid £2,750 for his services in December 1935.

He soon made the right-back position his own, although on occasions he moved across to left-back as the club consolidated its position in the top flight. Tennant's only goal in 105 first team appearances came in a 3-1 defeat at Sunderland in October 1937 before early the following season, he left Burnden Park to rejoin his first club, Stoke City. He continued to play for the Potters until the end of the Second World War but hung up his boots prior to the recommencement of League football in 1946.

1913 Jack Feebury was noted for his powerful shooting and won a Players' Union kicking contest. His 80-yard right foot punt won him the title and when challenged by a spectator to do the same with the other foot, he duly obliged!

AUGUST 4th

1998 Jimmy Phillips, who made 411 first team appearances during his two spells with the Wanderers, was awarded a testimonial at the Reebok Stadium. Scottish giants Celtic were the visitors and a keenly contested game ended all-square at 1-1.

AUGUST 5th

1958 Birth of John Thomas. A carpenter by trade, he joined his first club Everton in the summer of 1977 but after being unable to break into the Toffees' first team, he had loan spells with Tranmere Rovers and Halifax Town before joining the Wanderers on a free transfer. He made his debut as a substitute in a 3-1 home win over Leyton Orient in December 1980. His early days

with the club saw him suffer more than his fair share of injuries but he was in the side that lost 2-1 to Grimsby Town midway through the 1981-82 season - Thomas scored Bolton's goal in that defeat, the club's 5000th League goal. In May 1982, Thomas joined Chester City and in his only season with the club, top-scored with 22 goals. He then joined Lincoln City and netted 21 goals in 71 games before signing for Preston North End for £15,000. He was a great favourite at Deepdale and his 27 goals in 1986-87 helped the Lilywhites win promotion. He joined Bolton for a second time in the summer of 1987 and top-scored the following season with 28 goals, including hat-tricks against Peterborough United and Newport County as Bolton won promotion to the Third Division. Thomas had scored 44 goals in 110 games when he joined West Bromwich Albion, later playing for Preston North End (again), Hartlepool United and Halifax Town.

AUGUST 6th

1887 Bolton lost 4-2 to Accrington in a friendly played at Raikes Hall Gardens, Blackpool - part of the illuminations attractions.

1960 Birth of David Burke. He made his debut for the Wanderers as a replacement for the injured Tony Dunne in a League Cup second round tie against Chelsea in August 1978. When Bolton entertained the Stamford Bridge club in the First Division later that season, Burke scored his only goal for the club in another 2-1 win. Following Tony Dunne's retirement, the England youth international established himself as the club's first-choice left-back, though he was also able to play on the left-side of midfield. However, after three seasons with the club in which he had appeared in 76 games, he left to play for Huddersfield Town. He went on to make 189 League appearances for the Terriers, helping them win promotion to the Second Division in

1982-83. In October 1987 he joined Crystal Palace for a fee of £78,000 and was captain in 1989 when they won promotion to the top flight via the play-offs.

David *(right)* returned to Burnden Park in the summer of 1990 and though at first he found it difficult to displace Barry Cowdrill, he went on to take his total of first team appearances in his two spells with the club to 214 before leaving to join Blackpool, where he ended his League career.

1984 The Wanderers, who won four of their five matches on their tour of Ireland, recorded their biggest victory with an 8-0 defeat of Moyola Park.

1985 The Wanderers beat Bury 1-0 in their second group match of the Lancashire Cup.

AUGUST 7th

1973 Birth of Florent Laville. Known as "The Rock", Florent Laville was loaned from Lyon during the January transfer window. He quickly lived up to his nickname, having an outstanding debut in the home draw with Manchester United. He remained at the heart of the Bolton defence until an unfortunate sending off against Arsenal resulted in him missing the final game of the season. It was certainly no coincidence that Bolton's record while he was in the side, resulted in four wins and four draws from ten games. During the close season, his transfer to the Wanderers was made permanent when they paid £500,000 for his services. Sadly, he had only played a handful of games at the start of the 2003-04 season when he was struck down by a cruciate ligament injury and forced to miss the rest of the season.

1976 Bolton's first-ever game in the Anglo-Scottish Cup against Blackpool ended goalless and was watched by a crowd of 9,402.

AUGUST 8th

1943 Birth of Alan Boswell. The agile goalkeeper began his career with his home-town team Walsall before joining Shrewsbury Town. In five seasons at Gay Meadow, Boswell made 223 League appearances, his displays leading to him being signed by First Division Wolverhampton Wanderers. He was just establishing himself as the Molineux club's first choice when he was badly injured in a clash with Everton's Joe Royle. When he regained full fitness, he found he couldn't displace Phil Parkes and in October 1969 he joined Bolton. Replacing the club's record appearance holder, Eddie Hopkinson at Aston Villa the following month, Boswell was something of an unorthodox goalkeeper, once coming out of goal to take a throw-in in the dying moments of a League Cup game at Leicester City. After the club's relegation to the Third Division, Boswell, who had made 56 appearances, lost his place to Charlie Wright and was transferred to Port Vale. He later played non-League football for Oswestry Town.

1998 Bolton's side for the opening game of the season away to Crystal Palace saw them field seven internationals - Juusi Jaaskelainen (Finland); Gudni Bergsson (Iceland); Mark Fish (South Africa); Claus Jensen and Per Frandsen (Denmark); Nathan Blake (Wales), whilst substitute Arnar Gunnlaugsson (Iceland) netted a 90th minute equaliser in a 2-2 draw.

AUGUST 9th

1957 Birth of Dean Crombie. He began his career with his home-town club Lincoln City but after just 33 appearances for the Imps, he made the short journey to Grimsby Town. An ever-present in the Mariners side that won promotion from the Fourth Division in 1978-79, he won a Third Division Championship medal the following

season as the Blundell Park club romped into Division Two. Following a brief loan spell with Reading, Crombie, who had appeared in 320 League games for Grimsby, joined the Wanderers in August 1987. He was a member of the Bolton side that won promotion from the Fourth Division at the first attempt in 1988-89 and then scored his first-ever goal for the club against Torquay United in the final of the Sherpa Van Trophy. The last of Dean Crombie's 126 first team appearances saw him sent-off for a professional foul in the League Cup tie at Coventry City. After rejoining Lincoln as player-coach, Crombie returned to Bolton to take charge of the club's youth team.

1969 For the opening game of the season against Millwall, the Wanderers appeared in an all-white kit. It certainly suited John Byrom who netted a hat-trick in a 4-1 home win. The game also saw Eddie Hopkinson make his 500th League appearance for the club.

1997 A Nathan Blake goal gave Bolton a 1-0 win at Southampton - the club's first victory on the opening day of a top flight season since a 4-0 defeat of Leeds United in 1958.

AUGUST 10th

1879 Birth of Sam Marsh. The prolific scoring forward played his early football for clubs, Daisy Hill and Atherton Church House before joining the Wanderers in 1902. Though the club were relegated at the end of his first season at Burnden Park, Marsh scored nine goals in a 10-game spell towards the end of the campaign and was the club's top scorer. In 1903-04 Marsh netted 21 League and Cup goals including hat-tricks against Gainsborough Trinity (Home 5-0) and Barnsley (Home 5-1). The following season he formed a prolific goalscoring partnership with Albert Shepherd and Walter White and scored 27 goals including a hat-trick against Burton United (Home 7-1) to top the scoring charts for a third successive season. Though he was to remain at Burnden Park until 1912, his first team appearances were restricted because of the arrival of John Owen. After captaining the reserves to success in the Manchester Cup in 1909, he returned to the first team at wing-half, but after scoring 81 goals in 201 League and Cup games and helping the club win promotion to the First Division, he left to play for Bury.

1961 Birth of David Hoggan *(right)*. He progressed through Bolton's junior ranks before making his first team debut in the Division One match against Bristol City at Ashton Gate in April 1980. It was a 2-1 defeat in this match that confirmed the Wanderers' relegation to Division Two. After winning a regular place in the Bolton midfield, Hoggan won selection for the Scotland Under 21 side and in January 1980 hit the headlines with two spectacular goals in the club's 3-3 draw at Nottingham Forest in a third round FA Cup tie. Though he was offered a new contract, he refused to sign in the hope of finding First Division football. However, the only club that showed an interest in him was Dundee United, but after just one day at Tannadice he returned to Burnden Park. He had scored 15 goals in 104 games when he left these shores in September 1983 to try his luck in the American Major Indoor Soccer League with Pittsburg Spirit.

AUGUST 11th

1880 Birth of John Picken. He had spent two seasons playing at inside-forward for Kilmarnock Shawbank before joining the Wanderers in 1899. He made his Bolton debut in a 2-1 home win over Newton Heath in what was the club's first-ever home game in Division Two. By the middle of that 1899-1900 season, Picken was a regular in the Bolton side, replacing Tom Barlow and

helping the side win promotion to the First Division. In 1900-01, he was the Wanderers' only ever-present, scoring some vital goals in the end of season games. In May 1903, after scoring 22 goals in 106 games, he joined Southern League Plymouth Argyle, later returning to Football League action with Manchester United. He was the Reds' leading scorer in 1905-06, helping them win promotion to the top flight. He also appeared in eight of United's games when they won the League Championship in 1907-08 and 14 in 1910-11 when they also won the title. This was his last season with United and after scoring 46 goals in 121 games, he joined Burnley, later ending his career with Bristol City.

AUGUST 12th

1921 Birth of Matt Gillies. He was on Motherwell's books as an amateur, prior to 'guesting' for Arsenal, Queen's Park Rangers and Chelsea during the Second World War. He played his first game for the Wanderers in a Football League (North) wartime fixture against a star studded Blackpool side and continued to appear for the club throughout the hostilities. Popularly known as 'Jimmy' he played all his games during 1946-47 at wing-half before switching to centre-half for the following campaign. His consistency at the heart of the Bolton defence earned him the captaincy but following the emergence of Malcolm Barrass, Gillies, who had appeared in 154 games, joined Leicester City for a fee of £12,000. His only goal in Bolton colours came in a 4-0 home win over Huddersfield Town in December 1946.

After appearing in 102 games for the Filbert Street club, he was appointed their coach prior to becoming manager in January 1959.

Under his guidance, Leicester reached the 1963 FA Cup Final where they lost 3-1 to Manchester United. Gillies later spent three years in charge of Nottingham Forest.

AUGUST 13th

1969 John Byrom netted his second hat-trick in the space of four days as the Wanderers beat Rochdale 6-3 in a first round League Cup tie.

1979 The Wanderers suffered their first home defeat at the hands of continental opposition when they lost 3-1 to Ajax of Amsterdam.

AUGUST 14th

1960 Bolton travelled to France to play Le Havre in the first match of the Friendship Cup. They came back with a share of the spoils in a 1-1 draw.

1973 Birth of Jay Jay Okocha *(below)*. The Nigerian international who had also played for Eintracht Frankfurt and Fenerbahce, joined the Wanderers on a free transfer from Paris St Germain in the summer of 2002.

He made his Bolton debut at Fulham on the opening day of the season and initially seemed to struggle to come to terms with life in the Premiership. A series of niggling injuries meant

that he only made sporadic appearances over the next few months but after returning to first team action in November, he began to influence games far more.

From his roving midfield role, Jay Jay was a revelation, scoring some absolutely stunning goals. His strike that gave Bolton the three points in the home match against West Ham United was one of the best strikes ever seen in last season's top flight matches. One of the most skillful players ever to wear the white of Bolton, he scored seven goals in 32 League and Cup games in 2002-03 before being named Wanderers' captain for the 2003/4 season. He has been instrumental in establishing Wanderers in the Premiership. His goal against Aston Villa in the first leg of the Carling Cup Semi-Final was a contender for "goal of the season".

AUGUST 15th

1970 The Wanderers opened the season in style, beating Luton Town 4-2.
Bolton-born winger Terry Wharton who had joined the club from Wolves for a record fee of £70,000, netted a hat-trick with two of his goals coming from the penalty-spot.

1992 Andy Walker scored the season's first goal with an opening day strike against Huddersfield Town of 47 seconds. The Wanderers went on to win 2-0 with Julian Darby netting Bolton's second goal.

AUGUST 16th

1972 Garry Jones netted twice in a 3-0 League Cup first round victory over Oldham Athletic. John Byrom was Bolton's other scorer - Wanderers won that season's Third Division title beating fourth placed Latics 2-1 at home and 2-0 away in the League.

1986 In an exciting Lancashire Cup tie at home to

Wigan Athletic, the Wanderers lost 4-3 in a seven-goal thriller.

AUGUST 17th

1895 Burnden Park was used for the very first time when the Wanderers held their ninth annual Athletic Festival. The incomplete entrances could not cope with all the local interest and the first chance of seeing the new ground. Admission was 6d (2.5p) and one shilling (5p) and a crowd of 20,000 paid £453 to see a local cycle mile handicap start the proceedings. The entertainment was varied and included a troupe of lady cyclists, a donkey riding a bicycle, a high stilt walker and a high diver!

1974 Centre-half Paul Jones scored two of Bolton's goals in a 3-0 home win over Portsmouth on the opening day of the season. During the early part of the campaign, Jones scored five goals in 11 games.

AUGUST 18th

1951 The Wanderers beat Aston Villa 5-2 in front of a Burnden Park crowd of 30,253. The versatile Harry Webster scored twice with Bolton's other scorers being Moir, Lofthouse and Langton (penalty).

1956 Bolton's opening game of the season against Blackpool, which the Wanderers won 4-1, was significant not only for Nat Lofthouse netting yet another hat-trick, but it was the debut of goalkeeper Eddie Hopkinson, who went on to establish a club record number of 519 appearances.

2001 On the opening day of the Premiership season, the Wanderers hit the headlines by beating Leicester City 5-0 at Filbert Street. It was the club's best-ever opening day win!

AUGUST 19th

1950 Despite a Nat Lofthouse hat-trick on the opening day of the season, the Wanderers lost 4-3 to Charlton Athletic.

1978 Bolton's first game back in the top flight after an absence of 14 seasons, saw them lose 2-1 at home to Bristol City with Alan Gowling netting the Whites' goal.

1995 Bolton played their first-ever Premiership game - going down 3-2 at Wimbledon - with Alan Thompson and Fabian de Freitas netting for the Wanderers.

AUGUST 20th

1870 Birth of Bob Brown. Known as 'Sparrow' he played his early football for local club Blantyre Thistle before coming south of the border to play for Sheffield Wednesday. He scored two goals in the Owls' opening League fixture as they beat Accrington 5-2. Though he started his career as an inside-forward, his versatility soon began to show and over the next couple of seasons he played in seven different positions for the Yorkshire club. After a short spell with Third Lanark, he joined Bolton in the summer of 1895 and played in the opening League game at Burnden Park. Following a season on loan with Burnley, Brown returned to Bolton to play primarily at centre-half.
However over the next five seasons, he was used as cover for a number of positions and by the time he played the last of his 136 first team games in which he scored 14 goals, he had appeared in every position except goalkeeper and full-back.

1949 James Bradley scored two of Bolton's goals in a 4-0 opening day defeat of Stoke City. He also

scored twice in the return game at the Victoria Ground which the Wanderers won 3-2 to complete the 'double' over the Potters.

AUGUST 21st

1965 The first appearance of a substitute at Burnden Park occurred in the opening League game of the season as Bolton beat Charlton Athletic 4-2. Charlton's Keith Peacock came on for injured goalkeeper Michael Rose.

1990 The Wanderers won the Lancashire Manx Cup, beating Preston North End in the final. David Reeves scored both Bolton goals in a 2-1 win at Burnden Park. In the group matches the Whites didn't concede a goal, drawing 0-0 at Wigan Athletic and then beating Blackpool 2-0 and Burnley 3-0 at Burnden Park.

AUGUST 22nd

1930 Birth of Harry Webster. He worked as an apprentice engineer before turning professional with the Wanderers. The Sheffield-born player made his League debut in March 1950 as a right-winger in the match against Manchester City at Maine Road. However, his best spell for the club came in season 1950-51 when he switched to inside-left. Sharing the goalscoring duties with Nat Lofthouse, he scored 15 goals in 31 games including 11 in a 14-match spell just before Christmas. Though he lost his place early the following season, he proved his worth by becoming an understudy for any of the forward positions. During the course of the 1953-54 season, a five-game spell playing at centre-forward for the injured Lofthouse, produced four goals. Most of his games around this time were for the reserves and in 1954-55 he helped the Wanderers win the Central League title. He had scored 38 goals in 101 games when in the summer of 1958 he left to play for Chester. He later ended his playing days with non-League Chorley.

1978　Frank Worthington scored both of the Wanderers' goals in a 2-2 draw at Southampton as the Whites twice came from behind to take a point.

AUGUST 23rd

1958　The Wanderers provided one of their best opening day performances for a good number of years with Nat Lofthouse netting twice in a 4-0 defeat of Leeds United.

1967　Francis Lee, Gordon Taylor and John Byrom scored two goals apiece as the Wanderers beat Hull City 6-1. Wearing the No.9 shirt that day was Bob Hatton, who though he scored goals for a number of League clubs, failed to hit the target in 14 appearances in that first half of the season.

1980　Brian Kidd, a £150,000 signing from Everton, netted a hat-trick for the Wanderers in a 4-0 home win over Newcastle United.

AUGUST 24th

1865　Birth of James Brogan. One of the Wanderers' first professional players, he was a Scotsman of Irish descent who played for the club before the formation of the Football League. After playing for Beith and Edinburgh Hibernian, Brogan signed for Heart of Midlothian and it was while they were on a tour of Lancashire that the forward impressed the Wanderers. He signed for the club in December 1884 and over the years proved himself a useful goalscorer whether he played at inside or outside left. In December 1888 he netted five of Bolton's goals as Sunderland were beaten 10-1 and it was this kind of form that led to his selection for Lancashire. He scored one of the goals in the club's inaugural Football League match when they lost 6-3 to

Derby County and ended the season in which he was ever-present as the club's leading marksman with 13 goals. The following season he netted a hat-trick in the 13-0 defeat of Sheffield United in a second round FA Cup match. After losing his place to James Turner midway through the 1891-92 season, Brogan, who had scored 32 goals in 86 League and Cup matches, left the club and went to work in the shipyards where he remained until he was 85 years old!

1999　After drawing 1-1 at Darlington in a League Cup first round first leg tie, the Wanderers beat the Quakers 5-3 with five different players - Gudjohnsen, Gardner, Taylor, Frandsen and Johansen - getting on the scoresheet.

AUGUST 25th

1927　The new stand on the Burnden side of the ground was officially opened on the first day of the season for the visit of League Champions Everton. A crowd of 34,637 saw Dixie Dean score a hat-trick as the visitors won 3-2. George Gibson scored both the Wanderers' goals.

1987　After beating Wigan Athletic 3-2 at Springfield Park in a League Cup first round first leg tie, the Wanderers were confident of victory in the second leg, especially after John Thomas extended their aggregate lead. However, they reckoned without Northern Ireland international centre-forward Bobby Campbell, who scored a brilliant hat-trick to take the Latics through to the next round.

1998　Nathan Blake scored all Bolton's goals in a 3-0 League Cup first round second leg tie win at Hartlepool United.

AUGUST 26th

1995　Bolton secured their first-ever Premiership win

with a 2-1 defeat of local rivals Blackburn Rovers. Fabian de Freitas gave the Wanderers the lead but it was a goal ten minutes from time by Alan Stubbs that gave Bolton the points.

AUGUST 27th

1925 Birth of Nat Lofthouse *(right, holding the FA Cup aloft in 1958)*. His first game for the club was in March 1941, when at the age of 15 years 207 days, he scored twice as Bolton beat Bury 5-1 at Burnden Park in a Football League North game. The son of a Bolton coalman, he worked on the coalface during the war years, often going straight from the pit to assist the Wanderers in wartime games. He was on the field in March 1946 when 33 people lost their lives in the Burnden disaster.

Nat was recognised at international level in November 1950 when he was chosen to lead England's forward line at Highbury in the match against Yugoslavia. He fulfilled his promise by scoring both England goals in a 2-2 draw. In May 1952 he earned the tag of 'Lion of Vienna' after his heroic performances against Austria when he scored twice in England's 3-2 win. In September 1952 he scored six goals for the Football League against the Irish League at Molineux. He scored in every round of the 1952-53 FA Cup competition but injury-hit Bolton lost 4-3 to Blackpool in the final.

He was voted Footballer of the Year at the end of the season by the Football Writers' Association, whilst in 1955-56 he was the leading goalscorer in the First Division with 33 goals. In 1958 he captained Bolton to their FA Cup victory over Manchester United, scoring both goals in Wanderers' 2-0 win.

On 22 October 1958, Nat played his last game for England, scoring his side's final goal in the 90th minute of a 5-0 defeat of Russia. He won 33 caps and scored what was then a record 30 goals for his country.

A severely damaged ankle, incurred on Bolton's South African tour of 1959 threatened his career. But Nat the Lionheart refused to give up. He struggled to regain fitness and made several comeback attempts but in 1961, he finally accepted defeat. Bolton immediately appointed him assistant-manager and in 1968 he took over as manager.

He had two separate spells as team manager, in fact, before deciding to take a back seat. He returned to become executive club manager and later president to continue his devotion to Lancashire's oldest club.

Throughout his career, Nat Lofthouse, who scored 285 goals in 503 games gave total loyalty to Bolton Wanderers. His direct, yet stylish mode of play made him one of the world's greatest forwards of his age.

1966 Northern Ireland international centre-half John Napier scored a most unusual goal in the club's 3-1 win over Derby County. His upfield punt from inside his own half, floated not only over the heads of the Bolton forwards, but also over Derby's international keeper Reg Matthews, who had come out too far!

AUGUST 28th

1877 The footballers of Christ Church re-christened themselves Bolton Wanderers and established their headquarters in a pub!

1926 Bolton won their opening game of the season at Leeds United 5-2 with John Reid Smith netting a hat-trick.

1957 The Wanderers travelled to Molineux for their second game of the season, having lost 1-0 at Luton Town four days earlier.

It was nothing short of disaster, for after Nat Lofthouse had given Bolton the lead, Wolves hit back hard and ran out 6-1 winners!

AUGUST 29th

1925 During the close season, the offside law had been amended from requiring three opponents to only two between the attacker and the goal-line. In the opening game of the season against Newcastle United, Joe Smith and David Jack scored Bolton's goals in a 2-2 draw. Throughout the whole game there were only three offside decisions!

1942 Despite two goals by Harry Gee, the Wanderers lost 4-3 at Bury on the opening day of the Northern Section Wartime League.

AUGUST 30th

1919 Bolton went down 2-1 at home to Bradford Park Avenue in the first Football League game after the First World War. Both Joe Smith and Frank Roberts saw penalty shots saved by Scattergood, the Yorkshire club's keeper.

1941 The opening day of the Wartime League saw Bolton and Bury share eight goals. The 4-4 draw at Gigg Lane attracted a crowd of just 2,730.

1948 Willie Moir scored all four of the Wanderers' goals in a 4-2 win over Aston Villa at Villa Park. He ended the season as the First Division's leading scorer with 25 goals.

1961 The Wanderers had failed to win any of their opening three games but then beat Sheffield Wednesday 4-3 with Sheffield-born Freddie Hill scoring two of the goals.

AUGUST 31st

1946 In the first Football League game following the Second World War, the Wanderers travelled to Stamford Bridge for the First Division clash with Chelsea. A crowd of 62,850 saw a seven-goal thriller with the Pensioners winning 4-3.

Nat Lofthouse (2) and Ernie Forrest were Bolton's scorers.

1957 For Bolton's first home game of the season, Terry Allcock was brought into the side for the injured Nat Lofthouse. He responded by scoring two of the Wanderers' goals in a 3-0 defeat of Blackpool.

1968 Roy Greaves netted a hat-trick as the Wanderers beat Sheffield United 4-2.

SEPTEMBER 1st

1997 The opening game at the Reebok Stadium saw Bolton entertain Everton. The Goodison club had also been the Wanderers' first opponents at Burnden Park, 102 years earlier. Though millions on TV saw the sides play out a goalless draw, Gerry Taggart's second-half header was clearly over the line but the referee didn't have the benefit of a TV replay.

SEPTEMBER 2nd

1899 Laurie Bell scored Bolton's first-ever goal in the Second Division, following relegation in 1898-99, in a 3-2 win against Loughborough. The game though was played at Leicester because Loughborough's ground had been closed due to crowd disturbances.

1911 During the course of Bolton's opening League game at home to Newcastle United, the Manchester Road Stand caught fire. Fortunately though this was quickly extinguished with little damage. The cause of the fire was found to be a discarded cigarette.

1950 Though Wolves were one of the best teams in the Football League in the fifties, they ended this season in 14th place, five spots behind Bolton. Yet it didn't stop the Molineux club winning this home fixture 7-1!

1960 Birth of George Oghani. A late starter in professional football, he was a prolific scorer for Hyde United when Bolton manager John McGovern signed him for £3,000 in October 1983, with a further £2,000 when he completed 15 League games.

He made his Third Division debut in January 1984 but really made his impact the following season alongside Tony Caldwell when he scored 21 goals in all competitions.

Though he wasn't as prolific in 1985-86 he did collect four goals during Bolton's run to Wembley in the Freight Rover Trophy, which Bristol City won 3-0. During his time at Burnden Park, his disciplinary record began to catch up with him and in June 1987 after scoring 38 goals in 130 games, he was transferred to Burnley. He ended his first season at Turf Moor as the Clarets' leading scorer and helped them reach the final of the Sherpa Van Trophy that ended in defeat by Wolves at Wembley.

In April 1989 he was released by Burnley following a training ground incident and joined Stockport County. He later played for Hereford, Scarborough and Carlisle United having spent a season playing in Cyprus.

1964 Wyn 'the Leap' Davies netted all Bolton's goals in a 3-0 defeat of Southampton - his first hat-trick for the club.

SEPTEMBER 3rd

1923 John Reid Smith, who had received his marching orders in the earlier meeting with Sheffield United at Bramall Lane, gained some compensation in the return at Burnden Park, netting a hat-trick in a 4-2 win for the Wanderers.

1955 Nat Lofthouse scored three of Bolton's goals in a 4-1 home win over Arsenal who until this game were undefeated in the League.

SEPTEMBER 4th

1926 David Jack and John Reid Smith scored Bolton's goals in a 2-1 win over League leaders, and eventual First Division champions, Newcastle United.

1933 Bolton lost 4-0 at home to Grimsby Town. The Mariners, who had already beaten the Wanderers 3-2 at Blundell Park, went on to win the Second Division Championship. Bolton finished third, eight points adrift of Grimsby.

1984 George Oghani scored two of Bolton's goals in an exciting Football League Cup first round second leg tie against Oldham Athletic at Boundary Park. The Wanderers had won 2-1 at Burnden Park but this game had everything - the final score being 4-4 after extra-time, to give the Wanderers a 6-5 aggregate win.

SEPTEMBER 5th

1910 A Billy Hughes' hat-trick helped Bolton beat promotion favourites West Bromwich Albion 3-1. During the course of this game, Wanderers' captain Sam Greenhalgh was sent-off for kicking an Albion player and was subsequently suspended by the FA for 14 days.

1925 John Reid Smith and Joe Smith netted two goals each as Bolton beat Bury 5-0 at Gigg Lane. The Wanderers other scorer was David Jack. Though the Wanderers later completed the 'double' over the Shakers, it was Bury who finished the campaign in fourth place in Division One, with the Wanderers eighth.

SEPTEMBER 6th

1913 James Lillycrop, who ended the season with 24 goals in 37 games, opened his account with two in the club's 6-2 home win over Oldham Athletic.

1947 Birth of Bruce Rioch *(below)*. A Scottish international wing-half, he played for Luton Town, Aston Villa, Derby County, Everton, Birmingham City, Sheffield United and Torquay United, where he gained his first experience of management.

However, his first success came in February 1986 following his appointment by Middlesbrough. He guided the club from a dire financial position and lifted them from the Third to the First Division within two seasons. Rioch left Ayresome Park in March 1990 and in less than a month was in charge at Millwall.

In 1990-91 he led the London club to the Second Division play-offs but after their form slumped he left to join the Wanderers in March 1992. He achieved promotion in his first season at Burnden Park as the Wanderers finished runners-up in Division Two. That season, the Wanderers

beat Liverpool at Anfield before losing to Derby County in the fifth round of the FA Cup.

In 1993-94 he led Bolton to the sixth round of the FA Cup before taking the club to the League Cup Final and promotion to the Premiership via the play-offs the following season. In June 1995, Rioch left the Wanderers to manage Arsenal but after 15 months in charge, he was sacked and joined Queen's Park Rangers. He later managed Norwich City before taking charge of Wigan Athletic from whom he parted company in 2001.

1949 Birth of John Ritson *(right)*. Though he made his Bolton debut against Queen's Park Rangers in October 1967 in the No.7 shirt, it was at right-back that Ritson was to make a name for himself, appearing in 378 games in 11 seasons with the club. Though he only scored 13 goals for Bolton, he was renowned for unleashing virtually unstoppable blasts on goal and in 1977-78, his last season with the club, he scored vital goals in the club's 1-0 win at Mansfield Town and in the third round FA Cup replay against Spurs which Bolton won 2-1. He won a Third Division Championship medal in 1972-73 but after helping the Wanderers win the Second Division title in 1977-78, failed to make an appearance in the top flight, being sold to neighbours Bury for a fee of £25,000. After making 41 League appearances for the Shakers, he returned to Burnden Park as a non-contract player, but only played a handful of games in the club's Central League side.

1951 Birth of Alan Waldron. After captaining the Wanderers' youth team and appearing regularly in the club's Central League side, Alan Waldron made his first team debut against Orient in September 1970 as a replacement for Gareth Williams. One of a number of youngsters in the Bolton side that was relegated, he was also a member of the side that won the Third Division Championship in 1972-73. In August 1974, he broke a leg in the Wanderers' match at Blackpool and this kept him out of action for almost a year. After making a full recovery he found himself acting as cover to a successful Bolton midfield and in December 1977, after scoring nine goals in 170 games, he joined Blackpool. He made just 23 appearances for the Seasiders before joining Bury in the summer of 1979. He played in 34 games for the Shakers before leaving the first-class scene. Following a spell playing in Hong Kong, he returned to these shores to play briefly for Witton Albion.

SEPTEMBER 7th

1907 The offside rule had been changed in the close season, so that no player could be offside in his own half but it mattered little as Bury went in at the interval 4-1 up. Even though Albert Shepherd netted a hat-trick for Bolton, the Shakers ran out 6-3 winners.

1963 In their game against Arsenal at Highbury, the Wanderers held a half-time lead of 3-1 before the Gunners hit back to equalise with two early second-half goals. Wanderers' winger Brian Pilkington then missed a penalty and as Arsenal scored the winner in the last minute, Bolton keeper Eddie Hopkinson received a kidney injury that was to keep him out of action for eight weeks.

1966 Wyn Davies netted a hat-trick of headers as the Wanderers beat Carlisle United 3-0.

1968 Bolton lost 1-0 at Blackpool to a most controversial goal. The referee awarded an indirect free-kick but Alan Suddick placed the ball straight into the net without anyone touching it. Eddie Hopkinson made no attempt to save it and was booked for arguing whilst Gareth Williams received his marching orders.

1985 Steve Thompson and David Cross netted two goals apiece as the Wanderers beat Wolves 4-1 in a Third Division match.

SEPTEMBER 8th

1888 Bolton played their first game in the Football League, when Derby County were the visitors to Pikes Lane. Though the game was scheduled to kick-off at 3.15 pm, County arrived late and the game was delayed for half-an-hour. Bolton's first English international, Kenny Davenport opened the scoring after just two minutes play. He scored again a minute later and with James Brogan scoring shortly after, Bolton were 3-0 up with only five minutes played! Unfortunately for the Wanderers, the Rams came back to lead by a goal at half-time and as the final whistle went, they had extended their lead to finish the game 6-3 winners.

1906 Albert Shepherd began the new season in fine style, netting a hat-trick in the first game of the campaign at Burnden Park as the Wanderers beat Sheffield United 6-1.

1918 Birth of Bobby Langton. He played his early football for Southport League side Burscough Victoria before joining Blackburn Rovers in 1937. Quickly installed into the inside-left position, he scored 14 goals in 37 games during Rovers' promotion-winning season of 1938-39.
On his return to Ewood Park after the war, he won his first full cap for England but in August 1948 he was transferred to Preston North End for a fee of £16,000. After only 15 months at Deepdale, Langton was on his way to the Wanderers for a then club record fee of £20,000. He made his Bolton debut in a 3-0 home win over Manchester City and was a regular in the club's No.11 shirt until the end of the 1952-53 season when he was placed on the transfer list at his own request. He remained long enough to play in the 1953 FA Cup Final against Blackpool but having scored 18 goals in 132 League and Cup games, he returned to Ewood Park. In his second spell with Rovers, he took his total of goals to 57 in 212 League games before later playing for Ards, Kidderminster Harriers, Wisbech Town and Colwyn Bay. He then returned to the Southport area to manage Burscough Rangers.

1934 Jack Milsom and Ray Westwood scored two goals each as the Wanderers, who went on to win promotion to the First Division, beat Southampton 4-0.

SEPTEMBER 9th

1899 Bolton's first-ever Second Division game following their relegation the previous season, saw Laurie Bell score both the club's goals in a 2-1 home defeat of Newton Heath.

1902 Bolton played Manchester City in a benefit match for Dai Jones, the Wanderers' former captain. The 35-year-old Welshman fell on some glass whilst playing for City and tetanus set in.
He was still hugely popular in the town, having appeared in 255 League and Cup games, and large numbers of people paid their last respects at his funeral in Deane.

1911 The first Central League game was played at Burnden Park when the Wanderers drew 0-0 with Port Vale.

1931 Ray Westwood and Harold Blackmore both found the net twice in Bolton's 5-3 home win over Grimsby Town. The club's fifth goal was scored by George Gibson.

SEPTEMBER 10th

1960 Freddie Hill scored the only goal of the game as Bolton beat Blackpool 1-0 at Bloomfield Road in what was the first televised Football League game to be shown live.

1983 Tony Caldwell became the first Bolton player to score five goals in a Football League game when the Wanderers beat Walsall 8-1.
Bolton's other scorers were Ray Deakin, Simon Rudge and Peter Valentine and if Ally Robertson hadn't netted for the Saddlers in the last minute, the club's record League win would have been equalled.

SEPTEMBER 11th

1895 Football was first played at Burnden Park when the Wanderers took on Preston North End in a benefit match for full-back Di Jones, who had captained the club for the last six years. A crowd of just over 3,000 saw the visitors win 1-0.

1963 Birth of Wayne Foster. After some impressive displays for the club's Central League and Youth sides, Foster forced his way into the Wanderers' first team, making his debut as a substitute against Cambridge United in October 1981. That season, Foster's form led to him winning England youth honours and though over the next few seasons, he continued to make steady progress, he was playing in a struggling team. After the Whites had been relegated to the Third Division, competition for first team places became more intense and in May 1985 after scoring 17 goals in 120 first team outings, he signed for Preston North End. After a year at Deepdale, he was given a free transfer and tried his luck north of the border with Heart of Midlothian.
He became a regular in the Tynecastle side and playing wide on the right was instrumental in the club finishing as runners-up to Celtic in the 1987-88 Scottish League Championship.

1976 Paul Jones and Steve Taylor netted two goals a piece in Bolton's 5-1 home win over Hull City. The club's other scorer was Neil Whatmore, who ended the campaign as the Wanderers' leading scorer with 31 League and Cup goals.

SEPTEMBER 12th

1954 Birth of Barry Siddall *(right)*. Having appeared in the Wanderers' Central League side while still at school, the Ellesmere Port born goalkeeper went on to win England youth honours before making his league debut for Bolton against Walsall at Fellows Park in October 1972.

Following the retirement of Charlie Wright, Siddall made a great impact on the club's return to the Second Division and went on to appear in 133 consecutive League games. After appearing in 158 games for the Wanderers, Siddall joined Sunderland in September 1976 for a fee of £80,000.
He made his debut for the Wearsiders against Aston Villa and went on to appear in 103 consecutive League games immediately following his first appearance. He played in 189 League and Cup games for Sunderland and after a loan spell at Darlington, joined Port Vale.

Loan spells at Blackpool and Stoke City followed before he was transferred to the Potters for £20,000. He went on loan to Tranmere Rovers and Manchester City before signing for Blackpool in the summer of 1986 on a free transfer. He later played for Stockport County, Hartlepool United, Carlisle United, Chester City and Preston North End, eventually taking the total of League appearances for this much-travelled keeper to 613.

1964   Freddie Hill and Wyn Davies each found the net twice as Bolton beat Preston North End 5-1. The club's other scorer was Francis Lee, who was the Whites' leading scorer with 23 goals.

SEPTEMBER 13th

1892   At the Wanderers AGM, held at the public sales rooms on Bowkers Row, the issue of a new ground was raised, although Pikes Lane would still be available for two more seasons.

1914   Birth of George Eastham. After playing junior football in his home-town of Blackpool, George Eastham joined the Wanderers in the summer of 1932. He was 19 years old when he made his League debut for the Wanderers, coincidentally against Blackpool at Bloomfield Road. Despite Bolton's 3-1 win that day, they were relegated to the Second Division. Midway through the 1933-34 season, Eastham became a regular at inside-forward for the Wanderers, playing his part in the club winning promotion and reaching the FA Cup semi-finals in 1934-35. That season, Eastham won his only full international cap when he played for England against Holland. He had scored 17 goals in 131 games for Bolton when in May 1937 he left Burnden Park to join Brentford for a fee of £4,500. Just over a year later he returned to the north-west to play for Blackpool. During the Second World War, he 'guested' for the Wanderers before following the return to

peacetime football in 1946 he played for Swansea Town, Rochdale, Lincoln City and Hyde United before becoming player-manager of Irish League club, Ards. He later managed Accrington Stanley, Distillery and Ards again before coaching Stoke City and managing Hellenic in South Africa.

SEPTEMBER 14th

1895   A crowd of 15,000 attended Bolton's first-ever Football League game at Burnden Park where the visitors Everton were beaten 3-1.
The scorer of the club's first-ever League goal at the famous ground was James Martin.

1961   Birth of Mark Came. He joined the Wanderers from non-League Winsford United in April 1984 and made his first team debut five months later as a substitute in a 2-0 defeat at Doncaster Rovers. Over the next four seasons, Came missed very few games and in 1987-88 when the club won promotion, he was rated one of the best defenders in the Fourth Division. The following season he was appointed the club's captain but after leading the Wanderers to victory in the Lancashire Cup Final, he broke a leg in a League Cup tie at Chester and missed the rest of the season. Despite regaining full fitness, Came found it difficult to displace Mark Winstanley and Dean Crombie at the heart of the defence and though he stayed at Burnden Park until December 1992, his role tended to be that of understudy. He had scored 11 goals in 259 games when he joined Chester City for £10,000 and in 1993-94 helped them to runners-up spot in the Fourth Division. After appearing in 47 games for Chester he left to play for Exeter City, turning out in 70 games for the Grecians before returning to Winsford United as player-coach.

1983   Bolton travelled to Chester City for the second leg of the League Cup first round tie, having won the first meeting 3-0. They were beaten by the same scoreline, sending the game into a penalty shoot-out. Chester went through 2-0 after the Wanderers had missed four in succession!

SEPTEMBER 15th

1888 The visit of Burnley to Pikes Lane for Bolton's second game in the Football League, saw both sides take to the field in similar jerseys! The Wanderers had to change but it seemed to do them no harm as they took a three-goal lead. Then, as in the club's inaugural game in the competition, their opponents came from behind - the Clarets winning 4-3.

1920 Frank Roberts and Joc Smith both scored two goals as Aston Villa were beaten 5-0 at Burnden Park. The Wanderers other scorer was Tom Buchan, who showed his versatility by playing in five different numbered shirts during the course of the season.

1958 Birth of Steve Elliott. After serving his apprenticeship at Nottingham Forest under the watchful eye of Brian Clough, he appeared in just a handful games for the City Ground club before Preston North End paid a then club record fee of £95,000 to take him to Deepdale. In each of his four seasons with North End, he was the club's leading scorer but in June 1984 after scoring 70 goals in 208 League games for the Deepdale club, he joined Luton Town for another £95,000 fee. Unable to settle at Kenilworth Road, he moved on to Walsall in an exchange deal involving David Preece, and scored 21 goals in 69 games for the Saddlers before in July 1986 he joined Bolton for a tribunal set fee of £25,000. He found the net nine times in 40 games for the Whites in 1986-87 but it wasn't enough to prevent relegation to the Fourth Division. John Thomas and Trevor Morgan tended to be the club's strike force in the League's basement and after scoring 11 goals in 76 games he made the

short journey to Gigg Lane, joining Bury for £16,000. Two months after joining the Shakers he scored twice in a 4-2 win over the Wanderers and went on to score 11 goals in 31 games before ending his League career with Rochdale.

1978 Birth of Eidur Gudjohnsen *(below)*. Having started his career with Valur in his native Iceland, he moved to PSV Eindhoven in 1995, where he played in the same team as a young Ronaldo. A career-threatening broken ankle then put the brakes on a promising career.

His confidence was shattered and he went back to Iceland where he returned to first team action with KR Reykjavic.

When he joined the Wanderers in the summer of 1998, he was overweight and severely out of shape. He made his League debut for Bolton as a substitute in the home win over Birmingham City in September 1998 but then had to wait six months before making his first start.

The Icelandic international scored a number of important goals including one in the home win over promotion rivals Ipswich Town. In 1998-99, he produced some excellent performances and scored some sensational goals - the one against Wimbledon in the Worthington Cup where his mazy run took him past six or seven Dons players was proclaimed as one of the goals of the season. It was quite obvious that Eidur's talents were suited to a bigger stage and in June 2000 after scoring 27 goals in 73 games, he was transferred to Chelsea for £4 million.

After an indifferent start, he became Jimmy Floyd Hasselbaink's regular partner and had a superb first season in the Premiership. A great favourite with the Stamford Bridge crowd, he and Hasselbaink became the most parent pairing in the Premiership and in 2001-02 he scored 23 goals in all competitions.

Injuries and the form of Zola hampered his progress last season but the Icelandic international, who has played 24 times for his country, still took his total of goals for Chelsea to 46 in 128 games.

SEPTEMBER 16th

1889 Birth of Tom Buchan. Brother of the more famous Charles Buchan, he began his League career with Blackpool but in May 1914, he left the Seasiders to join the Wanderers. It was during the war years that he really came to the fore, missing only four games in a three-year spell between 1915-1918. Buchan played in every position apart from full-back, even turning out as a goalkeeper in a 4-2 defeat against Stockport County in November 1915 and against the same opposition in a 3-2 win two years later. In April 1917, he was one of nine players who took part in two games on the same day. When League football resumed in 1919-20 he was the only ever-present as the Wanderers finished sixth in Division One. After two more seasons, in which he took his total of goals to 14 in 117 games, he was allowed to leave and joined Tranmere Rovers, where he teamed up with another former Wanderer, Harold Hilton. Buchan later played non-League football for Atherton.

1992 Nat Lofthouse and Sir Stanley Matthews, who both played on the fateful day when 33 supporters lost their lives in the FA Cup sixth round match between Bolton and Stoke, unveiled a memorial plaque at the Embankment End.

SEPTEMBER 17th

1919 Joe Smith netted the club's first hat-trick following the resumption of League football as Bolton beat Middlesbrough 3-1.

1966 Francis Lee, who ended the season with 22 goals and Wyn Davies who netted 12 in 12 games before his move to Newcastle United, each scored twice in Bolton's 5-2 win over Cardiff City at Ninian Park. Bolton's fifth goal came courtesy of Bluebirds' centre-half Don Murray.

SEPTEMBER 18th

1963 Bolton beat Ipswich Town 6-0 at Burnden Park with Wyn Davies and midfielder Dave Lennard each scoring twice. The Wanderers' other scorers were Brian Pilkington and Gordon Taylor.

1995 The Wanderers received their highest incoming-fee of £4.5 million for the sale of Republic of Ireland international midfielder Jason McAteer to Liverpool.

SEPTEMBER 19th

1891 The first penalty-kick in a game involving the Wanderers came in the 4-3 home defeat of Sunderland. The Wearsiders' John Auld converted the spot-kick after Bolton keeper John Willie Sutcliffe had kicked John Hannah.

1931 Harold Blackmore scored three of the Wanderers' goals in a 4-2 home win over Middlesbrough.

1956 Birth of Gerry McElhinney *(below)*. He began his sporting life as a Gaelic footballer and heavyweight boxer before turning to football with Finn Harps and later Glasgow Celtic. McElhinney's time at Parkhead was brief and he soon returned to Ireland to play for Distillery. In September 1980, Bolton paid the Irish club £25,000 for his services and his impressive

displays for the Central League side led to him winning selection for the Northern Ireland squad before he had kicked a ball for the Wanderers' first team. Sadly, he missed out after breaking a bone in his foot. On recovering, he failed to find his earlier form and was loaned out to Rochdale but was soon recalled after an injury to Paul Jones. He then won the first of six Irish caps in November 1983 before Plymouth Argyle paid £32,500 to take the big Irishman to Home Park. McElhinney, who had scored just two goals in 127 games for the Wanderers, helped Argyle win promotion to Division Two before ending his first-class career with Peterborough United.

SEPTEMBER 20th

1890 The Wanderers entertained Everton, who went on to win that season's League Championship, and went down 5-0 at home. The Toffees completed the double the following month with a 2-0 victory at Goodison Park. Bolton did beat the Blues 6-0 though in that season's Lancashire Cup competition.

1919 Frank Roberts and Joe Smith each netted twice in Bolton's 6-2 home defeat of Manchester City. The Wanderers, who had already won 4-1 at Maine Road when Smith (2) and Roberts were again on the scoresheet, ended the season two points and one place above City in the First Division.

1956 Birth of Trevor Morgan. Known popularly as 'Sumo', Trevor Morgan was spotted playing non-League football for Leytonstone when he was signed by Bournemouth manager David Webb in 1981. He went on to score 13 goals in 53 games for the Cherries before joining Mansfield Town. Unable to settle at Field Mill, he rejoined the Dean Court club and helped them win promotion to the Third Division before signing for Bristol City.

He was only at Ashton Gate for eight months before he was on the move again this time to Exeter City.

Bristol Rovers were his next club and he scored the club's last-ever goal at Eastville in the defeat of the Wanderers. He later had another brief spell with Bristol City before joining Bolton for a fee of £30,000 in June 1987. Proving to be a perfect foil for strike partner John Thomas, he helped the Wanderers win promotion from the Fourth Division in 1987-88 before scoring one of the goals in Bolton's 4-1 Sherpa Van Trophy Final victory over Torquay United. This turned out to be the last of his 90 appearances - in which he scored 20 goals - for the Wanderers. After a spell with Shelbourne, he joined Colchester United before coaching both Exeter and Birmingham City. He later moved to Australia to take up another coaching post.

SEPTEMBER 21st

1935 Birth of Jimmy Armfield. Known as 'Gentleman Jim' he won fame as a player at Blackpool and as England's full-back. One of Bloomfield Road's greatest-ever servants, he appeared in 627 League and Cup games for the Seasiders before deciding to hang up his boots in 1971.

Armfield gained the first of his 43 full caps for England against Brazil in 1959 and won 37 of them in consecutive matches. Armfield *(right)* was appointed Bolton's manager in May 1971 and immediately set about restoring the club's confidence. The club's colours reverted from all-white to the traditional white shirts and navy blue shorts and by the end of his first season in charge, he had transformed things so much that only 41 goals were conceded, the club's best defensive performance since 1925. The foundations had been laid and in 1972-73 the benefits were reaped when the Whites secured the Third Division Championship with 61 points. Clearly recognisable by his tracksuit and pipe,

Armfield stood firm as the Wanderers blooded more youngsters alongside the shrewd signings of internationals Tony Dunne and Peter Thompson. In September 1974, Armfield finally gave way to an offer from Leeds United and took the Elland Road club to the 1975 European Cup Final, leaving three years later to become a full-time journalist.

SEPTEMBER 22nd

1934 Bolton's 3-0 win over Bradford City was their seventh consecutive victory since the season started - a new club record. Surprisingly, Jack Milsom was not amongst the scorers because he had found the net in each of the other six victories.

1962 The Wanderers lost 5-4 at West Bromwich Albion in a nine-goal thriller with Francis Lee netting a hat-trick. Two of the strikers' goals came from the penalty-spot.

1984 Despite being bottom of the Third Division, the Wanderers beat Plymouth Argyle 7-2 with Tony Caldwell hitting a hat-trick.

SEPTEMBER 23rd

1916 Previously unbeaten Stoke were beaten 9-2 in this wartime fixture with Joe Smith netting six of the Wanderers' goals. One of his goals was from the penalty-spot - the referee having to check if his shot had broken the net!

1981 Travelling to the Baseball Ground to play Derby County, the Wanderers turned out in a new away kit of all green! It obviously suited the club's Irish centre-half Gerry McElhinney who scored his first goal for the club in a 2-0 win.

1997 Alan Thompson scored the first-ever goal at the Reebok Stadium against Tottenham Hotspur. His spot-kick enabled the Wanderers to draw 1-1 with the North London club.

SEPTEMBER 24th

1892 James Cassidy netted three of Bolton's goals in a 5-2 home win over Aston Villa.

1904 Walter White scored a hat-trick including a penalty in Wanderers' 4-1 defeat of Grimsby Town.

1952 Nat Lofthouse hit a record six goals when playing for the Football League XI in a 7-1 win against the Irish League at Molineux.

SEPTEMBER 25th

1978 Birth of Ricardo Gardner *(below)*. The Jamaican international joined Bolton in August 1998 from Harbour View in Kingston Jamaica, having already made over 20 appearances for his country and shown his ability during the 1998 World Cup.

It took some time to sort out a work permit and he eventually made his debut as a substitute in a Worthington Cup victory over Hartlepool United. An exciting player who can light up a game with a flash of genius, he was having a superb 1999-2000 season, when it was cruelly short by damaged knee ligaments. Forced to miss the rest of that season plus the first two months of the 2000-01 campaign, he returned to the side to score some vital and spectacular goals including strikes in both rounds of the play-offs to help the Wanderers back into the Premiership.

Back in the top flight, he continued to be a real livewire on the left-hand side of midfield, scoring the all-important winner in the crunch match against West Ham United.

Having undergone knee surgery again last season, he returned to the side in a left wing-back role, a position he fulfils in the Jamaican side, for whom he has won 43 caps. However he still contributed some spectacular goals, perhaps none more so than the 30 yard free-kick in the Boxing Day victory over Newcastle United.

SEPTEMBER 26th

1886 Birth of Alf Bentley. After beginning his career with his home-town club of Alfreton Town, he joined Derby County in December 1906.
In 1909-10 he scored a club record 30 goals and was the Rams leading scorer for three consecutive seasons. He had scored 112 goals in 168 League and Cup games when in May 1911 the Wanderers paid £1,000 to bring him to Burnden Park. He scored four times in his first five games for the Wanderers but they soon dried up and he lost his place to Billy Hughes, the player who had made way for him. In 1912-13 Bentley was switched from centre-forward to inside-right for a number of games but in June 1913 after scoring 16 goals in 55 games, he was allowed to join West Bromwich Albion. He had some success at the Hawthorns scoring 46 goals

in 97 games. After the First World War he played non-League football for Burton Town before ending his career with Alfreton Town.

1964 Bolton beat Plymouth Argyle 6-2 with Freddie Hill and Wyn Davies both finding the net twice. The Wanderers' other goals were scored by Bromley and Taylor.

SEPTEMBER 27th

1884 The Wanderers tried out a new and startling kit for the home match with Sheffield Wednesday - "a loose white shirt with red spots" - this displaced the earlier salmon pink which figured in the FA Cup fourth round tie against Notts County in January 1884.

1919 Due to a railway strike, the Wanderers had to use private cars and taxis to get to their game at Derby County. The Wanderers won 2-1 with goals from Smith and Feebury. In goal for the Rams was James Kidd who until four days earlier, had been on Bolton's books!

1924 Bolton, who finished the season in third place in Division one, lost just once at home, going down 2-1 to Sunderland after the Wearsiders had netted two late goals.

SEPTEMBER 28th

1895 The first reserve game to be played on Burnden Park saw Burnley beaten 5-1 in a Lancashire Combination game. James Cassidy who had recently lost his first team place, netted a hat-trick - the first player to do so on this ground.

1930 Birth of Doug Holden. He signed as an amateur for the Wanderers in 1948 and appeared for the England youth side before completing his National Service. He made his League debut for the Wanderers in a 1-1 draw against Liverpool at

Anfield in November 1951, quickly proving that he possessed the temperament for the big occasion. Holden, in fact had only made 12 Central League appearances before his promotion to the first team. Though he played primarily on the left flank, it was on the opposite wing that he made a name for himself in the 1953 FA Cup Final. Five years later he reverted to the left-wing for the 1958 FA Cup Final against Manchester United - he and Nat Lofthouse being the only Bolton players to appear in both finals. In March 1959 he played for the Football League XI against the Irish League in Dublin. Impressing in that match, he was selected for the full England side against Scotland at Wembley. In November 1962, after scoring 44 goals in 463 League and Cup games for the Wanderers, he left to join Preston North End, for whom he appeared in the 1964 FA Cup Final against West Ham United. Holden later emigrated to Australia and played for the national side.

SEPTEMBER 29th

1888 The Wanderers, in their fourth game, recorded their first-ever victory in the Football League, beating Everton 6-2 with Kenny Davenport, Harry Tyrer and John Milne each scoring two goals.

1934 The Wanderers had won their first seven games of the season, scoring 21 goals (Jack Milsom 9) and conceding just two when they received their come uppance at Bramall Lane as Sheffield United ran out 6-2 winners.

SEPTEMBER 30th

1902 Birth of George Gibson. After beginning his career with Dundee, he joined Hamilton Academicals where his brother was on the board! In fact, it was his brother who was instrumental in the inside-forward joining the Wanderers for

£3,100 in February 1927. Gibson made his Bolton debut in a 1-1 draw against West Bromwich Albion and in the last ten games of the season, he netted nine goals, including his first hat-trick for the club in a 5-0 win over Everton. He remained a first team regular and in 1928-29 scored 20 League and Cup goals including another treble in a 3-1 home win over Sheffield United. Also that season, he was a member of the Bolton side that beat Portsmouth 2-0 in the FA Cup Final. His third hat-trick for the club came in February 1930 when Leeds United were beaten 4-2. Appointed club captain in 1931-32, he turned in some outstanding performances as the Wanderers struggled to avoid relegation to the Second Division. The following season the club were relegated, but Gibson, who played the last of his 255 games for Bolton in a 1-1 draw at Chelsea, where he scored the Wanderers goal - his 81st for the club - left Burnden Park in March 1933 to join the Stamford Bridge outfit.

OCTOBER 1st

1964 Birth of Tony Kelly. He started his apprenticeship at Anfield in September 1982, however, after failing to make the grade, he joined Derby County. Unable to make much headway with the Rams, he left the Baseball Ground and signed for Prescot Cables, before Harry McNally gave him his chance in League football with Wigan Athletic.
After moving to a midfield position, he became a regular in the Latics' side and played in 127 League and Cup games, scoring 22 goals including one in the club's Freight Rover Trophy success at Wembley.
He joined Stoke City for £80,000 but after just 45 games for the Potters, he moved to West Bromwich Albion. There followed loan spells with Chester City and Colchester United before Ian McNeill took him to Shrewsbury Town. He became captain at Gay Meadow and played in

120 games before joining the Wanderers in the summer of 1991. He made his debut in a 1-1 draw at home to Huddersfield Town and scored his first goals for the club on his return to Shrewsbury where the Wanderers won 3-1. He reached a career peak during the club's FA Cup run of 1993-94 when he was on song, giving the team a different dimension. Affectionately known as 'Zico', Tony Kelly went on to score eight goals in 142 League and Cup games before leaving to play for Port Vale.

OCTOBER 2nd

1915 This wartime game saw Stockport County beat the Wanderers 7-0 at Burnden Park. The visitors were captained by Jimmy Fay, who played for Bolton either side of the First World War.

1937 Bolton thrashed newly promoted Leicester City 6-1 with Ray Westwood netting a couple of the goals - the first being his 100th League goal.

1944 Birth of Willie Morgan *(right)*. He began his career with Burnley and made his League debut for the Clarets in a 1-0 win over Sheffield Wednesday in April 1963. He won a regular place on the Clarets' right-wing and quickly developed into one of the most feared wingers in the British game. Not surprisingly, his performances attracted the big city clubs and after making his international debut for Scotland against Northern Ireland in October 1967, he joined Manchester United for £117,000.

He soon settled in at Old Trafford alongside Best, Law and Charlton and in March 1969 netted a hat-trick in a 6-1 win over Queen's Park Rangers. After United had lost their First Division status, Willie Morgan helped them win promotion in 1974-75 before returning to Burnley. However, the move was not a success and he was soon on his way to Bolton.

He was instrumental in the Wanderers' success in the Second Division over the next few seasons, fourth in both 1976 and 1977 and Championship winners in 1978, when he missed just one game. While at Burnden Park, Morgan was able to enjoy summer loan periods in the NASL. After scoring 12 goals in 179 games, he moved to Blackpool where he ended his League career.

1997 Bolton paid a then club record £3.5 million for Wimbledon striker Dean Holdsworth.

OCTOBER 3rd

1981 Though the Wanderers lost 2-1 at Grimsby Town, John Thomas scored the club's 5000th League goal.

1986 Nat Lofthouse was made President of Bolton Wanderers – a fitting honour for the club's most respected player.

OCTOBER 4th

1922 Bolton's David Jack represented the Football League XI in their match against the Irish League at Burnden Park and scored two goals in a 5-1 win.

1931 Birth of Roy Hartle. Signed from non-League Bromsgrove Rovers, he made his Bolton debut in a 2-1 defeat at home to Charlton Athletic on New Year's Day, 1953. Despite the reversal, Hartle had impressed and kept his place in the side for the next 24 games which included seven matches in the club's run to the FA Cup Final at Wembley. He was devastated when he was dropped in favour of John Ball for the showpiece against Blackpool. However, after completing his National Service, he returned to win a regular place in the Bolton side and form with Tommy Banks, the most feared full-back pairing in the Football League! Hartle was a virtual ever-present in the Wanderers' side for the next 11 seasons, often captaining the side. He won an FA Cup winners' medal in 1958 and was considered unlucky not to gain full international recognition. He had played in 499 League and Cup games for the Wanderers when he left Burnden Park to end his playing career with non-League Buxton of the Cheshire League. Hartle, who served on the executive of the PFA, also spent a year coaching NASL side New York Generals before becoming chief scout at Bury.

1975 Neil Whatmore and John Byrom scored two goals apiece as the Wanderers beat Charlton Athletic 5-0. Bolton's other goal was scored by right-back John Ritson.

OCTOBER 5th

1894 It was decided on this day that Bolton Wanderers Football and Athletic Club should be incorporated under the company acts of 1862 and 1890, whereby the liability of each shareholder be limited to the amount of his shares.

1901 Laurie Bell and John Picken each netted twice for the Wanderers in a 4-0 home win over Grimsby Town.

1971 A crowd of 42,039 saw Garry Jones net a stunning hat-trick in a 3-0 third round League Cup tie defeat of First Division Manchester City. Included in the Maine Road club's side that evening were former Wanderers' stars, Wyn Davies, Freddie Hill and Francis Lee.

1976 Wanderers drew 2-2 with Fulham in a third round League Cup replay when defender Mike Walsh levelled the scores in the fifth minute of injury time! Three minutes later, the referee blew for full-time and was immediately surrounded by the Fulham players who were remonstrating about his time-keeping. The result was that former England captain Bobby Moore was sent-off and the Fulham players appeared to walk-off in support. The referee's ultimatum for them to return, saw them play out the extra-time which remained goalless. In the second replay at St Andrew's, Bolton won 2-1.

OCTOBER 6th

1934 The Wanderers' recorded their biggest home win in the Football League, beating Barnsley 8-0 in a Second Division match. Ray Westwood netted four of Bolton's goals as they went on to finish the season as runners-up to Brentford. Five of Bolton's goals came in the last six minutes of the match!

1952 Birth of Jim McDonagh. He joined the Wanderers from his home-town club of Rotherham United in August 1976, initially on loan.

His first game in goal for the Whites was in a 3-0 home defeat by Blackpool and after Barry Siddall's transfer to Sunderland, he kept his place in the side for the remainder of the season. He was an ever-present for the next three seasons and in 1977-78 helped the club win promotion to the First Division when he only let in 33 goals, the fewest-ever conceded by the Wanderers in a 42-match programme.

Jim McDonagh holds the club record for the most consecutive League appearances, having played in 161 games from his debut.

Following Bolton's relegation in 1980, he joined Everton for a fee of £250,000 and it was while on Merseyside that he won the first of 24 full international caps for the Republic of Ireland. Within a year he had returned to Burnden Park in the deal that saw Mike Walsh join the Blues. McDonagh *(right)*, who scored from a long-kick in the 3-0 defeat of Burnley in January 1983, played in 274 League and Cup games for Bolton before joining Notts County.

He later played for Birmingham City, Gillingham, Sunderland, Scarborough, Huddersfield Town and Charlton Athletic.

1958 The only FA Charity Shield game to be played at Burnden Park saw FA Cup holders Bolton Wanderers beat League Champions Wolves 4-1 in front of a crowd of 15,239.

1971 Birth of Alan Stubbs. A boyhood Everton fan, Alan Stubbs graduated through Bolton's junior ranks before making his League debut as a substitute in a 1-0 home defeat by Bradford City.

Three days later he scored on his full debut in a 2-1 League Cup win over Huddersfield Town. He seemed to spend most of that season on the bench, although he did play at Wembley in the play-off final against Tranmere Rovers.

Able to play in a number of positions, he made rapid strides over the next couple of seasons, establishing himself at the heart of the Bolton defence. Always dangerous when in the opposing

penalty area, he scored vital goals against Everton and Aston Villa in the club's run to the FA Cup quarter-finals in 1993-94. After that, he won international recognition when he was awarded a 'B' cap for England against Northern Ireland at Hillsborough.

He captained the Wanderers to play-off success against Reading and though he missed part of the club's campaign in the Premiership he returned to play his part in the club's fight against relegation. He had appeared in 256 games for the Whites when he left to join Celtic for £3.5 million in the summer of 1996, but was sent-off in his first League game for the Bhoys!

With the Scottish giants he won two Scottish Premier Division Championships and two Scottish League Cup Finals but in July 2001 after appearing in 130 games he joined his beloved Everton. Shortly after his arrival at Goodison Park he achieved a personal ambition when asked to captain the team at Tottenham Hotspur.

OCTOBER 7th

1939 As a depleted Bolton side lost 6-1 at Preston North End, the 53rd Royal (Bolton) Artillery with such stars as Stan Hanson, Harry Goslin, Albert Geldard, Jack Roberts and Ray Westwood amongst its number, beat Ashington in the north-east 5-1.

1950 Nat Lofthouse and Harry Webster each scored two of Bolton's goals in a 4-0 home defeat of high-flying Portsmouth.

OCTOBER 8th

1966 Wyn Davies scored a well-taken hat-trick in a 4-2 home win for Bolton over their Lancashire rivals, Preston North End. The Wanderers' other goal came courtesy of North End central defender Bill Cranston.

1984 The building of the £3.5 million Normid Superstore scheme was announced. It was the saviour of the Wanderers, giving the club a £500,000 windfall to help drag themselves back from the brink of extinction.

OCTOBER 9th

1886 Bolton Wanderers beat Wigan 14-0 in the first round of the Lancashire Cup.

1965 Roy Greaves, in only his second match for the Wanderers, scored both their goals in a 3-2 home defeat by Southampton. The match was the first time that the Wanderers used a substitute when Gordon Taylor replaced Irish international centre-half, John Napier.

OCTOBER 10th

1925 Ted Vizard netted his first hat-trick for the club in a 3-2 win against Arsenal at Highbury. The Welsh international's third goal, which proved to be the winner, came three minutes from time.

1936 Bolton's long-serving George T. Taylor was forced to miss the Wanderers' 3-1 home defeat at the hands of Derby County after playing in 290 consecutive first-class games for his first club, Notts County and the Wanderers.

1973 Bolton recorded their best away victory in the League Cup, beating Rochdale 4-0. Stuart Lee (2), Paul Jones and Alan Waldron were the Wanderers' scorers.

OCTOBER 11th

1924 Joe Smith and David Jack each netted twice for the Wanderers as Preston North End were beaten 6-1 at Burnden Park. Bolton's other goals were scored by Ted Vizard and Joe Cassidy.

1928 David Jack was transferred to Arsenal for a fee of £10,750 - the first five-figure fee paid for a player.

OCTOBER 12th

1889 Bolton fielded James McNee, a new signing from Scottish club Renton for the home match against Preston North End. The Wanderers who lost 6-2 were later fined £5 by the Football League for playing the Scotsman before he had served his proper qualification period.

1907 Scottish international forward Walter White scored all Bolton's goals in a 3-1 win over Chelsea at Stamford Bridge.

1993 Bolton's first Italian opponents in the Anglo-Italian Tournament were Ancona. A crowd of just 3,448 saw John McGinlay (2), Alan Thompson, Jason McAteer and Jimmy Phillips score the goals in a 5-0 win.

OCTOBER 13th

1928 Harold Blackmore scored three of Bolton's goals in a 4-2 home win over Portsmouth.

1945 Nat Lofthouse and Willie Moir each scored two goals and Don Howe and George Hunt one apiece as the Wanderers beat Leeds United 6-0 in a Football League (North) game.

1951 Ray Parry became Bolton Wanderers' youngest-ever player when at the age of 15 years 267 days he made his League debut in a 5-1 defeat by Wolverhampton Wanderers at Molineux.

OCTOBER 14th

1922 Wanderers' prolific marksman Frank Roberts was suspended indefinitely by the club for taking over the management of a licensed premises which

was completely against club policy. Roberts then left the Wanderers to join Manchester City and scored against Bolton the following month in a 2-0 win for City at Maine Road.

1957 The Burnden Park floodlights were officially opened when the Wanderers entertained Heart of Midlothian before a crowd of 21,058 who witnessed a 1-1 draw. The cost of erecting the lighting was put at £25,000 with the four pylons in each corner of the ground carrying 48 lights. They were switched on by the club Chairman Harry Warburton.

1978 The Wanderers led Chelsea 3-0 at Stamford Bridge with just a quarter-of-an-hour to go but the London club came back strongly to win 4-3 with a Sam Allardyce own goal giving them the points with what turned out to be the last kick of the game!

OCTOBER 15th

1892 James Dickenson netted a hat-trick for the Wanderers in a 4-4 home draw against Stoke.

1938 Wing-half John Roberts who joined the club from his home-town team of Swansea, was tried up front and responded with a second-half hat-trick in a 4-2 home win over Everton.

OCTOBER 16th

1880 One of Bolton's early defeats came when they lost 12-1 at Accrington!

1882 Birth of Jimmy Hogan. He had spells playing for his home-town team of Nelson, Rochdale, Burnley, Swindon and Fulham before signing for the Wanderers in October 1908. He made his League debut the following month, scoring both Bolton's goals in a 2-0 win at Chesterfield. He kept his place for the remainder of the season, scoring 11 goals in 24 games as the Wanderers won the Second Division Championship. His appearances in the top flight were spasmodic and he went to coach in the Netherlands for a year before returning to Burnden Park in readiness for the 1911-12 season. He went on to score 19 goals in 58 games before concentrating entirely on the coaching side of the game. He coached the Austrian national side before being interned in Budapest during the First World War and then coached Young Boys of Berne. In 1934 he returned to these shores to manage Fulham and then guided Austria to the 1936 Olympic Final before taking Aston Villa back to the top flight. After the Second World War he was involved with Celtic and Brentford finally acting as youth team coach for Aston Villa in 1953.

1961   Nat Lofthouse, who scored 285 goals in 503 first class appearances for the club, was awarded a testimonial match when a Bolton 1958 XI played an All Star side.

OCTOBER 17th

1903   Bolton Wanderers' centre-forward Sam Marsh netted a hat-trick as Gainsborough Trinity were beaten 5-0 at Burnden Park.

OCTOBER 18th

1970   Birth of Gerry Taggart. The Belfast-born defender had a season playing for Glenavon before Manchester City signed him as a trainee during the early part of the 1988-89 season. He made 11 appearances for City, helping them to runners-up spot in the Second Division before Barnsley paid £75,000 for his services in January 1990. Two months later, he won the first of his 51 full international caps for Northern Ireland when he played against Norway at Windsor Park. During his time at Oakwell, Barnsley were one place from taking part in the play-offs on two

occasions in 1991 and 1995. He went on to appear in 247 games for the Yorkshire club before signing for the Wanderers in August 1995. He suffered with injuries and a loss of form in his first season with the Whites but rediscovered his form in 1996-97 when the Wanderers won an immediate return to the Premiership. That season, he shared the captaincy with Gudni Bergsson and earned himself a little piece of Burnden history by scoring in the final game against Charlton Athletic, taking great delight in letting his team-mates know that it was down to his new red boots! He had one more season with the Wanderers, taking his total number of League and Cup appearances to 81 before joining Leicester City in the summer of 1998. Partnering Matt Elliott in the heart of the Foxes defence, he helped the club win the League Cup in 2000 and promotion to the Premiership in 2002-03 when he took his total number of appearances for Leicester to 133.

OCTOBER 19th

1954   Birth of Sam Allardyce. A product of the club's youth side, he made his Football League debut for the Wanderers against Notts County in November 1973. Following the departure of Don McAllister to Tottenham Hotspur, Allardyce won a regular place at the heart of the Bolton defence. During his time at Burnden Park, Allardyce scored a number of spectacular goals, perhaps none more so than the fearsome header from fully 18 yards against Second Division promotion rivals Sunderland in December 1975. Impressive in the air, he helped the Whites win the Second Division Championship in 1977-78 but after relegation two seasons later, Allardyce left to join Sunderland for a fee of £150,000. After just one season at Roker Park, he moved to Millwall followed by brief spells at both Coventry and Huddersfield before he rejoined the Wanderers. Sadly he was hampered by injuries and after appearing in 231 games in which he scored 24 goals he joined Preston North End. After helping the Lilywhites win promotion to the Third Division Allardyce *(below)* became the club's youth coach, before breaking into management with Blackpool. Surprisingly sacked after leading the Seasiders to the play-offs, he took charge of Notts County and led the Meadow Lane club to the Third Division Championship in 1997-98. Appointed Bolton manager in October 1999, his first season at the Reebok Stadium saw the Wanderers reach the semi-finals of both the Worthington Cup and FA Cup, the latter for the first time since winning the competition in 1958 and the First Division play-offs. In 2000-01, he led the club back into the Premiership with a 3-0 defeat of Preston North End in the play-off final

at the Millennium Stadium and with little money to spend in Premiership terms, has kept the club in the top flight for the last three seasons. He lead Wanderers to the final of the Carling Cup in 2004. Despite a valiant attempt, to recover a two goal deficit after seven minutes, Wanderers were defeated 2-1 by Middlesbrough.

1960 The first Football League Cup game to be staged at Burnden Park saw the Wanderers beat Hull City 5-1 in a first round replay. The scorer of the club's first goal in the competition was Northern Ireland international Billy McAdams. Bolton's other scorers were Freddie Hill (2), Brian Birch and Ralph Gubbins.

OCTOBER 20th

1888 Birth of Evan Jones. A bustling centre-forward, he was already a Welsh international when he joined the Wanderers from Oldham Athletic in the summer of 1912. Prior to playing for the Latics, he had appeared for both Aberdare Athletic and Chelsea. Wherever he had played, Jones had scored goals but on his arrival at Burnden Park, he was switched to inside-forward. He ended his first season with the club with 10 goals in 37 games and in the three seasons prior to the First World War scored 28 goals in 99 first team outings. Having appeared for the Wanderers in the 1915 FA Cup semi-final defeat by Sheffield United, he 'guested' for Newport during the First World War. On the resumption of League football in 1919, he turned down the chance of resuming his career with the Trotters, preferring to stay in South Wales with Swansea Town.

1906 Albert Shepherd, in only his sixth game of the season, netted his second hat-trick as Bolton beat Birmingham 4-2 at St Andrew's.

1928 The Wanderers won 5-3 at Villa Park. An enthralled crowd saw Harold Blackmore net his second hat-trick within the space of a week, with Billy Butler and George Gibson scoring Bolton's other goals.

1984 George Oghani in his first season of League football scored three of Bolton's goals in their 4-0 defeat of local rivals Preston North End.

OCTOBER 21st

2000 Ian Marshall scored twice for the Wanderers against lowly Stockport County at Edgeley Park, but the Hatters, who also took a point off the Whites at the Reebok, won 4-3 to inflict the club's first away defeat of the season.

OCTOBER 22nd

1881 Bolton drew their first-ever FA Cup game against local rivals Eagley 5-5 with the visitors contributing two own goals! The Wanderers won the replay 1-0 thanks to a Steel goal but lost 6-2 to Blackburn Rovers in the next round.

1958 Nat Lofthouse was recalled to the England team for the first time in two seasons and scored in the last minute of England's 5-0 win over the Soviet Union to equal the English scoring record of 30 goals held by Preston's Tom Finney.

1966 Birth of Mark Seagraves. He won England schoolboy and youth honours whilst with Liverpool and though he failed to make any League appearances during his time at Anfield. He appeared in two Cup games before following a loan spell with Norwich City, he joined Manchester City for a fee of £100,000 in September 1987. It was another two years before he won a regular place in the City side, but with the club heading for promotion, a knee injury curtailed his season.
In September 1990 the Wanderers paid £100,000 for his services and he and Alan Stubbs formed a formidable central defensive pairing that saw

Bolton reach the Third Division play-off final against Tranmere Rovers at Wembley. A regular member of the Bolton team that won promotion from Division Two in 1992-93, his most satisfying moment during that campaign was no doubt scoring against Liverpool in the third round FA Cup tie at Burnden Park. Injury then forced him to miss much of the 1994-95 season but he returned towards the end of the campaign and played in the Coca Cola Cup Final defeat against Liverpool. Seagraves had played in 195 games for the Wanderers when he left to join Swindon Town, helping the Robins win the Second Division title in his first season at the County Ground. On leaving the first-class game he went to play non-League football for Barrow.

OCTOBER 23rd

1860 Birth of John McNee. Beginning his career with Renton, he had helped them reach the Scottish Cup semi-finals in the season before he joined the Wanderers in 1889. He failed to show up for his first game with the club - a friendly against Sunderland - but turned up a week later after Alec Barbour had travelled north of the border to make sure McNee would keep his side of the bargain. He went straight into the Bolton side for the game against Preston North End but the Wanderers were subsequently fined £5 for playing him before the necessary qualification period had passed. In 1890 he helped the Wanderers reach the FA Cup semi-finals and a year later, was a member of the Bolton side that won the Lancashire Cup. At 5ft 4ins, he was one of the smallest players ever to turn out for the club, yet he was instrumental in the club finishing third and fifth in the First Division in successive seasons. He had scored 25 goals in 96 games before being transferred to Newcastle United where he ended his playing career after just one season with the Magpies.

OCTOBER 24th

1881 In the 'Football Field' published on this date, the Wanderers were called 'the reds'. Later that season they wore jerseys of 'scarlet and white quarters' which were decorated with an embroidery representing the coat of arms of the borough.

1942 Cliff Chadwick netted three of Bolton's goals in a 7-4 home win over Burnley in a Northern Section wartime game.

1950 Birth of Asa Hartford. He began his career with West Bromwich Albion, playing for the Baggies in the 1970 League Cup Final. He was soon thrilling the crowds with his skill and vision and it was only a matter of time before the inevitable big-money offer arrived. He will always be remembered as the player whose transfer to Leeds United was sensationally called off after a routine medical revealed a hole-in-the-heart condition. However in August 1974, he joined Manchester City and went on to play a major role in the club's glorious era of the late 70s, picking up a League Cup winners' medal with them in 1976.

In June 1979 he joined Nottingham Forest but after just three games he was on his way to Everton. After two seasons on Merseyside, the Scottish international who won 50 caps for his country, rejoined Manchester City. Following a spell in the NASL with Fort Lauderdale Sun, he helped Norwich City win the 1985 League Cup Final when his shot was deflected into the net for the only goal of the game. He joined the Wanderers in the close season and was ever-present in 1985-86, captaining the club to the Freight Rover Trophy Final at Wembley. Despite his experience, the Wanderers were relegated to the Fourth Division the following season and after scoring 10 goals in 101 games he joined Stockport County as player-manager.

He later managed Shrewsbury Town before coaching at Blackburn, Stoke and Manchester City.

OCTOBER 25th

1931 Birth of Jimmy McIlroy. As a player, he was a marvellously gifted inside-forward who won League Championship and FA Cup runners-up medals with Burnley, where he made over 400 appearances.

Winning 55 full international caps for Northern Ireland, 34 in consecutive matches, he formed an amazing understanding with Danny Blanchflower. In March 1963 he joined Stoke City, helping the Potters win the Second Division Championship. When his playing days were over, McIlroy became manager of Oldham Athletic, before returning to the Victoria Ground as Stoke's chief coach. On 4th November 1970 he was officially appointed Bolton team manager. His first game in charge was a 1-0 defeat at Norwich City which was followed by a 2-0 reversal at Millwall. Unbelievably on 22nd November and after only 18 days in charge, the popular Irishman parted company with the club. He had refused to sell players as directed by the board because if they had left it would undoubtedly have weakened the team and it was obvious that he could not work within those constraints.

1971 Birth of Simon Charlton *(right)*. The Huddersfield-born defender began his career with his home-town club, making 157 appearances before Southampton paid £250,000 for his services in the summer of 1993.

A natural left-footer he brought a good measure of stability to that side of the Saints' defence before a spate of injuries restricted his first team appearances. The possessor of a long throw, an added weapon which was used to place the ball in the opponent's danger area during the south

coast club's annual fight against relegation. He went on to play in 136 games for Southampton before moving to Birmingham City for the same amount of money the Saints had paid out four and a half years earlier. Regarded as a bargain buy, the strong tackling defender unfortunately suffered more than his fair share of injuries at St Andrew's and in July 2000, joined the Wanderers. Despite an early season hamstring injury, he proved a revelation at left-back, impressing with his accurate distribution, crossing ability and skill on the ball. In 2001-02 he deservedly won one of Bolton's 'Player of the Year' awards as his foraging runs down the flank, brought him quite a few goal assists. In 2002-03 he continued to give a series of consistent performances whether at left-back, central defence or in midfield, to take his total number of appearances to 97.

OCTOBER 26th

1894 A general meeting of the club was called with the object of raising funds. It was decided at this meeting to turn the club into a limited liability company and issue 4,000 shares at £1 each.

1895 The first fatality at Burnden Park was recorded when, during a 3-1 defeat of Stoke, a spectator on the railway embankment, climbing for a better view, fell in front of an oncoming train.

1960 Nat Lofthouse netted a hat-trick for the Wanderers in a 6-2 League Cup second round victory over Grimsby Town.

OCTOBER 27th

1914 Birth of Jack Hurst. After playing his early football for local club Lever Bridge, he joined the Wanderers in 1934 and made his debut at centre-half as a replacement for the injured Jack Atkinson in the match at Hull City. In his first two seasons with the club, he was restricted to just eight appearances but got his chance for an extended run in the 1936-37 season. Unfortunately he suffered a bad knee injury in the match against Middlesbrough and when he did return to action, it was as an understudy although he did play centre-forward in the FA Cup game against West Ham United. The Second World War deprived the Wanderers of Hurst's best years and though he played in the side that reached the 1945 FA Cup semi-final, he only made a handful of appearances after the hostilities to take his total of first team games to 72 before joining Oldham Athletic. He later played non-League football for Chelmsford City.

1928 Sheffield United were beaten 3-0 with Scottish born forward George Gibson netting all the Wanderers' goals.

1930 Birth of Bryan Edwards. He made his Bolton debut in a 3-3 draw at Liverpool in September 1950 and later that season became a regular in the Wanderers' side. Two years later he was called up for National Service and this not only prevented him from playing on a regular basis and cost him his place in the 1953 Cup Final team but also prevented him from beating the Trotters' appearance record then held by Alex Finney. He regained his first team spot from Eric Bell at the start of the 1954-55 season and over the next five seasons missed just six games, culminating in him collecting an FA Cup winners' medal in 1958 when Bolton beat Manchester United 2-0. It was Edwards' pass that was deflected into the path of Nat Lofthouse to open the scoring after two minutes. Edwards, whose experience in the latter years of his Bolton career proved invaluable to young wing-halves Warwick Rimmer and Graham Stanley, appeared in 518 League and Cup games.
After leaving Burnden Park, he coached at Blackpool, Preston and Plymouth, then managed Bradford City before serving Huddersfield Town,

Leeds United and Bradford City again in a variety of roles including physiotherapist.

1990 A goal from the club's leading scorer Tony Philliskirk was enough to beat Swansea City 1-0 and so give Bolton their 1000th home League victory.

OCTOBER 28th

1899 A South African touring team known as the Kaffirs were beaten 13-3 and even the Wanderers' keeper John Sutcliffe got on the scoresheet!

1916 The Wanderers won 6-0 at Rochdale with Joe Smith scoring four of the goals.

1949 Birth of John McGovern *(left)*. As a player, he followed Brian Clough around from club to club and captained Nottingham Forest to European Cup Final success. He had made his Football League debut as a 16-year-old for Hartlepool United and after helping Derby County into the First Division in 1969. He was the youngest player to have appeared in all four divisions. In all he made 545 League appearances for Hartlepool United, Derby County, Leeds United and Nottingham Forest. He joined Bolton Wanderers as player-manager in June 1982 and had little success and a lot of bad luck during his time in charge. At the end of his first season with the club, the Whites lost their Second Division status and with no money available to strengthen the squad, McGovern took a drop in wages, ran in a fund-raising marathon and organised supporters' evenings. During 1983-84 an influx of younger players such as Warren Joyce, Neil Redfearn and Steve Thompson brought some good results and positive play but the following season with the Wanderers sixth from bottom of the Third Division, he parted company with the club. Sadly for the Bolton fans, he had made just 16 League appearances in two-and-a-half years as player-manager.

1963 Birth of Simon Farnworth *(right)*. Originally on the books of Manchester United, the England schoolboy international goalkeeper joined the Wanderers and under the watchful eye of coach Charlie Wright, he made good progress. Following the departure of Jim McDonagh and Bolton's relegation to the Third Division in 1983, Farnworth grabbed his chance, making his League debut against Wimbledon on the opening day of the 1983-84 season. An ever-present in 1984-85, he lost confidence the following season and was replaced by loan signing Dave Felgate. However, he was between the posts when Bolton faced Bristol City in the Freight Rover Trophy Final at Wembley because Felgate's loan had expired.

He went on to make 139 League and Cup appearances for Bolton before following loan spells with Tranmere Rovers and Stockport County, he joined Bury. He soon replaced Phil Hughes as the Shakers first-choice keeper before later ending his career with Wigan Athletic, for whom he later worked as a physiotherapist.

1967 John Byrom and Gareth Williams each scored two goals as the Wanderers beat Derby County 5-3. The Whites' other scorer was Roy Greaves in a game watched by a crowd of 12,631.

145

OCTOBER 29th

1932 The Wanderers went down 7-4 at Sunderland in an incredible game.
The Wearsiders were 5-0 up after half-an-hour and though Gibson and Butler each scored two goals to put Bolton back in the game, the home side scored two late goals to extend their lead.

1935 Birth of Eddie Hopkinson *(below)*. The holder of the club's appearance record with 578 first team outings between 1956 and 1969, he remains possibly the best goalkeeper the Wanderers have ever had. He signed as an amateur for Oldham

Athletic and was only 16 years of age when he played in three Third Division (North) games in 1951-52. At the end of that season, the Latics overlooked him to Bolton's lasting satisfaction and after joining the Wanderers in August 1952, turned professional the following November. His meteoric rise began in 1956 when Bolton's regular keeper Ken Grieves couldn't be released from his cricketing duties with Lancashire as they were chasing Championship honours. Hopkinson got his chance in the senior side against Blackpool, a match the Wanderers won 4-1 and went through a brilliant first season without missing a game. In the summer of 1957 he was awarded the first of six England Under 23 caps on a tour behind the Iron Curtain and in October of that year he made his first full international appearance against Northern Ireland, going on to win 14 caps. In 1958 he kept a clean sheet to win an FA Cup winners' medal as the Wanderers beat Manchester United 2-0 at Wembley. At Norwich City in January 1969, he broke Bolton's long-standing appearance record set by Alex Finney and but for an injury which kept him out of the side for most of the 1958-59 season and another which put him out of action for a 10-match spell in 1963-64, he would have passed Finney's record much earlier. An injury forced his retirement and he became assistant-trainer at Burnden Park before joining Stockport County as assistant-manager. He later rejoined the Wanderers as goalkeeping coach but eventually left the game to become a representative for a chemical company.

1955 Nat Lofthouse and Doug Holden scored two goals apiece as Bolton defeated Luton Town 4-0.

OCTOBER 30th

1920 Joe Smith netted a hat-trick as the Wanderers beat Middlesbrough 6-2. Frank Roberts (2) and Tom Buchan were Bolton's other scorers.

1937 Despite being without regular centre-forward Jack Milsom, the Wanderers found the net five times in a remarkable 10-goal thriller against Chelsea, which ended all-square at 5-5 after the Stamford Bridge club equalised with the last kick of the game. Bolton's hero was Ray Westwood who scored three of Bolton's goals.

1941 Birth of Gareth Williams. Though he was born in Wembley, his family returned to South Wales, where the Welsh-speaking Williams began his career with Cardiff City. He was a virtual ever-present in the Bluebirds' midfield for five seasons, appearing in 161 League games before in October 1967 joining the Wanderers for a fee of £45,000.

Despite being appointed club captain, he suffered a loss of form which was not helped by a poor disciplinary record. In November 1969 he was suspended by the Bolton board for refusing to train, whilst claiming that he was being made the scapegoat for the club's poor results. Sadly, Williams never really fulfilled his promise at Burnden Park and after scoring 12 goals in 117 games, joined neighbours Bury for a fee of £5,000. He made 42 League appearances for the Shakers before retiring to join the prison service. He later ran a Fylde coast hotel before moving to Gran Canaria where he ran a bar.

1943 Birth of Dave Hatton. He made his Wanderers' debut in a 1-1 draw at Leicester City in April 1962. The strong-tackling half-back then had a run in the side at left-back in 1962-63 in place of the injured Syd Farrimond before establishing himself the following season. Hatton missed very few games over the next six seasons and had appeared in 259 League and Cup games when in September 1969 he joined Blackpool for a fee of £40,000. He was badly missed by the Wanderers but helped the Seasiders win promotion to the First Division in his first season with the Bloomfield Road club. After Blackpool were relegated, Dave Hatton continued to be a regular member of the side that was constantly pushing for promotion to the top flight. He had played in 274 games for the Seasiders before joining Bury as player-manager but after the Gigg Lane club narrowly avoided relegation to the Fourth Division in 1978-79, he was sacked.

1984 Bolton were 6-0 down at half-time in the League Cup third round tie at Notts County with five of the Meadow Lane club's goals coming in a five-minute spell. For the record, Wayne Foster scored for the Wanderers but County ran out 6-1 winners.

OCTOBER 31st

1891 Four different forwards - McNee, Turner, Cassidy and Munro - scored Bolton's goals in a 4-2 victory over local rivals Blackburn Rovers.

1995 Though the Wanderers finished the season at the foot of the Premiership, a John McGinlay goal gave them the points in their home match against high-flying Arsenal. The Gunners got their revenge on the final day of the season with a 2-1 win.

NOVEMBER 1st

1924 In the game against Arsenal at Burnden Park, which the Wanderers won 4-1, one of the linesmen was late in turning up, so Joe Cassidy, whose place had gone to John Reid Smith, took over the role!

1980 Brian Kidd netted his second hat-trick for the club in a 6-1 defeat of Cambridge United.

NOVEMBER 2nd

1964 Birth of Steve Thompson. The dynamic midfielder impressed in a strong Bolton youth side before making his first team debut in a goalless draw at Derby County in November

1982. But it wasn't until the following season that he began to make his mark and over the next eight seasons, he was a virtual ever-present. He appeared for the Wanderers in the Freight Rover Trophy Final at Wembley in 1986 when the Whites lost 3-0 to Bristol City, but was successful on his second visit to the Twin Towers in 1989 when Bolton beat Torquay United 4-1 to lift the Sherpa Van Trophy. His performances helped the Wanderers reach the play-offs in seasons 1989-90 and 1990-91 but after scoring 57 goals in 422 games, he left the club to join Luton Town in a £220,000 deal. After less than two months at Kenilworth Road, he was on the move again, this time to Leicester City. He helped the then Filbert Street club to the First Division play-offs in seasons 1991-92 and 1992-93 and then again the following season when he made a substitute appearance as they eventually won a place in the top flight. Leaving Leicester in 1995, he returned to the north-west with Burnley before joining Rotherham United and later ending his career with Halifax Town. Having appeared in 796 first team games for his six clubs, he then entered non-League football with Leigh RMI.

NOVEMBER 3rd

1917 Bolton recorded one of their best wartime results with an 8-0 home defeat of Burnley.

1956 John Higgins, the son of a Buxton baker became the first Bolton player since the Second World War to be sent-off in a League game. He received his marching orders in the match against Sheffield Wednesday at Hillsborough, which the 10-men Wanderers won 2-1.

NOVEMBER 4th

1882 Bob Struthers scored five of Bolton's goals in a 6-1 FA Cup victory over Bootle.

1905 Derby County were beaten 5-0 at Burnden Park with Sam Marsh netting a quickfire hat-trick.

1957 Bolton's second game under the new floodlights saw renowned opponents in the Russian Army side CDSA. A crowd of 34,139 turned up to see the Wanderers win 3-0.

NOVEMBER 5th

1888 Bolton beat FA Cup holders West Bromwich Albion 5-1 at the Hawthorns. The game was stopped in the 87th minute after crowd disturbances which started when Seddons, who was making his Wanderers' debut and West Brom's Hendry were fighting. Both players were suspended and Seddons didn't play for the club again.

1904 Walter White and Sam Marsh scored two goals apiece as the Wanderers beat Gainsborough Trinity 5-1. Bolton's other scorer was Sam Greenhalgh.

1927 Bolton beat Burnley 7-1 with Harold Blackmore scoring four of the goals including a first-half hat-trick whilst David Jack also netted a hat-trick - all of his goals being headers. However, it has to be said that the Clarets were handicapped. Their goalkeeper Somerville was carried off with a broken collar bone and two other outfield players were tried between the posts in an effort to stem the tide!

1949 Field Marshall the Viscount Montgomery of Alamein was introduced to the teams prior to Bolton's home match with Newcastle United which ended all-square at 2-2.

1967 Birth of David Lee *(right)*. The flying winger began his career with Bury, whom he helped to two Division Three play-offs, losing the second of them to the Wanderers. He appeared in 249 first team games for the Shakers, scoring 40 goals before moving into the top flight with Southampton who paid £350,000 for his services in the summer of 1991.

Unable to settle on the south coast, he returned to the north-west in November 1992 when he joined Bolton on loan. His first match for the Wanderers was in a 3-1 win at Exeter City and after impressing in all of his loan games, he joined the club on a permanent basis for a fee of £300,000. He played in every game for the rest of that season as the club won promotion to the Second Division as runners-up to Stoke City.

He continued to torment the opposition defences in 1993-94 and Nigel Winterburn ragged in the FA Cup replay at Highbury when Bolton beat the Gunners 3-1. Lee's goals were quite often spectacular, probably the best being his solo effort against Norwich City in the 1994-95 League Cup.

A broken ankle and a loss of confidence then limited his opportunities and after 199 appearances for the Wanderers, he joined Wigan Athletic. He proceeded to be a great favourite with the Latics' supporters before following a loan spell with Blackpool, he ended his first-class career with Carlisle United.

NOVEMBER 6th

1937 John Calder signed from Morton, scored a hat-trick in only his third game of the season as the Wanderers won 4-2 at West Bromwich Albion.

1948 Moved into the forward line for the first time this season, Malcolm Barrass netted four of the Wanderers' goals in a 5-1 home win over Manchester City.

NOVEMBER 7th

1896 Fog and mist from the River Croal was an eternal problem for Burnden Park and the First Division encounter with Everton had to be abandoned after an hour's play with neither side having found the net.

1953 Harold Hassall, who had just been called up into the England squad for their game with Ireland at Goodison Park, celebrated with a well-taken hat-trick in Wanderers' 6-1 home defeat of Portsmouth.

NOVEMBER 8th

1968 Birth of Dean Holdsworth *(right)*. Along with his twin brother David, he joined Watford as an associated schoolboy in the summer of 1984 and after progressing to the Hornets' professional ranks, made his League debut against Luton Town in December 1987.

There followed loan spells at Carlisle United, Port Vale, Swansea City and Brentford before he joined the Bees on a permanent basis in September 1989.

He was an immediate success at Griffin Park and after helping the club win the Third Division Championship in 1991-92, Holdsworth, who had scored 75 goals in 137 games, joined Wimbledon for a fee of £750,000. Despite a series of injuries, including a hernia operation, he was the third top scorer in the Premier League with 19 goals. He was Wimbledon's leading scorer for the next four seasons, but in October 1997 after netting 76 goals in 208 games, he became the Wanderers' most expensive signing when he joined the club for £3.5 million. Though Bolton fans expected great things from him, a series of niggling injuries made life difficult for him. He scored the winner in his third match against Chelsea but ended the campaign with just three goals in 20 League games. Over the next couple of seasons, he popped up with some vital goals and his wholehearted displays gradually won over the Bolton fans.

Though he missed a sitter in the FA Cup semi-final against Aston Villa at Wembley, he scored the goal that beat Norwich City to ensure Bolton a place in the play-offs.

The following season he netted the 200th senior goal of his career and proved that there was much more to his game than just hitting the back of the net. In 2001-02 he was Bolton's super-sub but early the following term after scoring 49 goals in 186 first team outings, he joined Coventry City, later playing for Rushden and Diamonds.

1971 After holding First Division Chelsea to a 1-1 draw at Stamford Bridge, the Wanderers suffered their heaviest home defeat in the League Cup fourth round replay, going down 6-0 at Burnden Park.

NOVEMBER 9th

1897 Birth of Harry Nuttall. His father Jack, who served the Wanderers both as a trainer and groundsman, lived in a cottage at the corner of the railway embankment at Burnden Park. After spells with local club St Mark's and then Fleetwood, Harry Nuttall joined the Wanderers in December 1920. Playing at half-back, he made his League debut for Bolton against Tottenham Hotspur in September 1921, going on to form a famous half-back line with Seddon and Jennings. Nuttall won three FA Cup winners' medals in the 1920s and made three full international appearances for England. In May 1932 after scoring six goals in 326 League and Cup games he was allowed to join Rochdale, for whom he played for a season. He then joined Nelson as coach before in 1935 returning to Burnden Park as the club's second team trainer. He remained with the Wanderers until his retirement and in his later years was responsible for the kit and the dressing-rooms.

1909 Birth of Harry Goslin. One of the game's true gentlemen, he was also a great leader. He joined the Wanderers in the summer of 1930 for a £25 donation to Nottingham club Boots Athletic. He made his Bolton debut in a 7-2 defeat at Liverpool but kept his place in the side for the remainder of the season. After that he missed very few games and was ever-present in 1934-35 when the Wanderers won promotion to the First Division and 1938-39.
When Alex Finney left the club, Goslin was appointed captain, a position he held up to the outbreak of the Second World War when he had

scored 23 goals in 334 games.
During the hostilities he 'guested' for Chelsea and Norwich City and won selection for England's wartime team. He was killed in the Italian campaign on 18th December 1943 when serving with the 53rd Field Regiment RA (Bolton Artillery) with which he had also fought in Africa and France.

NOVEMBER 10th

1883 Bob Struthers netted a hat-trick in the Wanderers 9-0 defeat of Bolton Olympic in an FA Cup first round match.

1888 James Turner remains Bolton's only player to have scored a hat-trick on his first team playing debut for the club - in a 9-0 FA Cup second round replay victory over West Manchester. He had been selected for the previous rounds' match away at Hurst, but the Wanderers' opponents scratched from the competition.

1923 David Jack, who ended the season as the club's top scorer with 24 goals in 39 League games, netted a hat-trick for the Wanderers in a 4-0 home win over Chelsea.

1929 Birth of Tommy Banks. The Farnworth-born defender was one of the 'hard men' of the Bolton side during the 1950s. Tales of opposition wingers who were deposited on the cinder track at Burnden Park being only part of the story of this England international. On his arrival at Burnden Park, he found his first team opportunities limited by his older brother Ralph, who occupied one of the full-back berths. Despite making his League debut in a 1-0 defeat at Wolves in April 1948, it was to be the 1953-54 season before he won a regular place in the Bolton side, Banks making just 12 appearances in his first five seasons with the club! It was towards the end of his Bolton career that Banks reached his peak. After winning an FA Cup winners' medal against Manchester United in May 1958, he won the first of six England caps when he played against the Soviet Union in Moscow.

He later played in the World Cup Finals in Sweden. Banks, who was the subject of an inquiry by Manchester United during their rebuilding after the Munich air disaster, played in 265 games for the Wanderers before leaving to join non-League Altrincham in 1961. He later left the game to concentrate on the building trade.

NOVEMBER 11th

1899 Burnden Park hosted its first representative game when the English League beat the Irish League 3-1. Of interest to the Bolton fans was the presence of John Fitchett, the Wanderers' right-half who had an outstanding game.

1931 Bolton beat Liverpool 8-1 in a Lancashire Cup third round replay with winger Billy Butler netting four of the Wanderers' goals.

NOVEMBER 12th

1910 Birth of Harry Hubbick. On leaving school, he worked down the mines and played for Blyth Spartans and Spennymoor United before joining Burnley in March 1935. After two years at Turf Moor, Hubbick joined the Wanderers as a replacement for the recently retired Alex Finney. He was a virtual ever-present in the Bolton side leading up to the outbreak of the Second World War and though during the hostilities he returned to the pits, he still managed to turn out for the Wanderers.

In six wartime seasons, he missed just one game. He also 'guested' for Blackpool when they won the League North War Cup and the North v South Final. In 1945 he captained Bolton to success in the same cup competitions.

At the end of the first season of peacetime football, Hubbick, who had appeared in 144 League and Cup games, joined Port Vale. After two years with the Valiants, he signed for Rochdale before becoming a fully qualified FA coach. He was then appointed trainer-coach of Accrington Stanley and with the exception of a brief spell as Bury trainer, he remained at Peel Park until Accrington withdrew from the League in 1962. He later became trainer at Halifax Town and finally Preston North End.

NOVEMBER 13th

1899 Birth of Harold Hilton. After beginning his career with his local club Tranmere Rovers, he joined the Wanderers in March 1910. Though he was to spend 11 years at Burnden Park, his career was hampered both by injuries and then the outbreak of the First World War. Unable to prevent the Wanderers from being relegated in 1910, he then proceeded to have his best season for the club, scoring 13 goals in 31 games as they returned to the top flight at the first time of asking.

Following a bad knee injury at Notts County in December 1911, he was out of the game for 15 months and after an aborted comeback, did not appear for the club's first team again until November 1914.

Though he scored after half-a-minute of his comeback game as Bolton beat Spurs 4-2 and found the net in the club's 7-1 win over Aston Villa at Villa Park, he was again soon incapacitated. He had scored 24 goals in 65 games when he returned to play for Tranmere Rovers in May 1921.

1961 In the Manchester Cup Final, held over from the previous season, after the initial game had been postponed due to a waterlogged pitch, the Wanderers beat Manchester United 1-0 at Old Trafford.

NOVEMBER 14th

1908 Jimmy Hogan scored both Bolton's goals in a 2-0 win at Chesterfield. The Wanderers, who completed the 'double' over the Spireites, won the Second Division Championship, whilst the Saltergate club finished bottom of the table.

1914 Joe Smith scored twice from the penalty-spot but the Wanderers went down 5-3 at home to Bradford City.

NOVEMBER 15th

1932 Birth of John Higgins. In his early days with the Wanderers, he was a full-back but while doing his National Service, he developed into a fine centre-half. Though he made his debut for the injured Malcolm Barrass in a 1-0 win at Burnley in March 1953, it wasn't until midway through the 1956-57 season that he established himself as a first team regular. He was at his best in 1957-58 when he was the club's vice-captain and the only ever-present in a season when the Wanderers won the FA Cup. In fact, he captained the side in the absence of Nat Lofthouse in the FA Cup semi-final when the Wanderers beat Blackburn Rovers 2-1 at Maine Road. Standing over 6ft and weighing 15st, Higgins' strength was an important factor in the Wanderers twice finishing in the top six of the First Division during his time with the club. In February 1960 he became the first Bolton player to be dismissed in a Football League game since the war when he received his marching orders at Hillsborough in a 1-0 defeat by Sheffield Wednesday. He went on to appear in 202 games for the Wanderers before joining non-League Wigan Athletic and later becoming general manager of Stockport County.

1969 Bolton goalkeeper Eddie Hopkinson produced a fantastic last-minute save to earn the Wanderers a vital point in a goalless draw against Sheffield United. Having previously taken a knock, it turned out to be the last of his record 519 League appearances.

NOVEMBER 16th

1895 The first postponement at Burnden Park saw Bolton's game against Small Heath called off as the ground was under six inches of water, due to poor drainage.

1918 Peacetime football returned to Burnden Park as the Wanderers beat Southport Vulcan 3-2. Joe Thomas of the Guards had the distinction of being the first Bolton player to return from the hostilities to take his place in the team.

1994 Bolton drew 1-1 in Pisa in the Anglo-Italian Cup. Around 500 Wanderers' fans made the trip to Italy, making up half the attendance!

NOVEMBER 17th

1888 Linfield Athletic of Belfast were the first non-League club to put the Wanderers out of the FA Cup. Bolton, however, did have some excuse for going down 4-0. They had to send their reserves to play the tie in Ireland as the first team were involved in a Football League game against West Bromwich Albion on the same day. For the record, the Wanderers lost 2-1.

NOVEMBER 18th

1893 The club's lowest-ever League gate of 700 saw Bolton go down 1-0 to Aston Villa. The game was not expected to take place and really should have been abandoned with a storm of hail and wind lashing across the waterlogged pitch.

1905 Albert Shepherd scored four of the Wanderers' goals as they beat Nottingham Forest 6-0.

1959 Ray Parry, inside left for Wanderers, netted England's winner on his full international debut as England beat Northern Ireland 2-1 at Wembley.

NOVEMBER 19th

1889 The Wanderers took part in an early floodlit game against Sheffield United at Bramall Lane, running out 2-0 winners.

1904 Both Sam Marsh and Walter White netted hat tricks as Bolton completely outplayed Burton United to win 7-1.

1967 Birth of David Reeves *(right)*. Though he joined Sheffield Wednesday in the summer of 1986, he made his League debut while on loan with Scunthorpe United, scoring twice in a 3-1 win over Exeter City. In October 1987 he returned to the Irons for a second loan spell and in his first game netted a hat-trick in a 3-2 defeat of Hereford United.

The following month he joined Burnley on loan and in his first game scored for the Clarets in a 2-1 win over the Wanderers! He eventually made his League debut for the Owls but after 17 games, he was signed by Bolton for a tribunal-set fee of £80,000. His only hat-trick for the Wanderers came in a 4-1 Autoglass Trophy win over Rochdale in December 1991. Reeves missed very few games in his first three seasons with the club, but his opportunities for first team football were restricted following the signing of Andy Walker. Forming a prolific goalscoring partnership with Tony Philliskirk, he had scored 42 goals in 173 games before leaving Bolton to join Notts County. Later he played for Carlisle United and helped the Brunton Park club win the Third Division Championship. After a brief spell with Preston North End, he joined Chesterfield and though he later had a spell with Oldham Athletic, he returned to Saltergate and has now scored 64 goals in 238 games for the Spireites.

NOVEMBER 20th

1969 Wanderers' wing-half Gareth Williams was suspended for refusing to train whilst claiming that he was being made the scapegoat for the club's poor results. The Welsh-speaking Williams never really fulfilled his promise at Burnden Park and joined neighbours Bury for a fee of £5,000.

NOVEMBER 21st

1970 The recalled Roger Hunt, who had been out of the Bolton side for almost two months, hit a hat-trick in Wanderers' 3-0 home win over Birmingham City.

1990 The Wanderers met Swindon Town in the third round of the League Cup. This marathon tie was eventually settled at the fourth attempt - after seven-and-a-half hours of football, with the Wiltshire club winning 2-1.

NOVEMBER 22nd

1908 Birth of Tom Grosvenor. Having played his early football with Birmingham, it was whilst with the Blues that he made his three full international appearances for England. He had scored 18 goals in 116 games for the St Andrew's club when in 1936 he left to play for Sheffield Wednesday. He left the Owls after just one season following their relegation to the Second Division, signing for the Wanderers as a replacement for George Eastham. In his first season with the club, 1937-38, Grosvenor missed just one League game but in the last season before the Second World War, he had to share the inside-forward duties with Jack Roberts and Tom Sinclair. Though he played in a number of wartime games for the Wanderers, it was during the hostilities that he decided to retire, having scored seven goals in 56 games.

1919 Bolton drew 3-3 at Everton with goals from Buchan, Stokes and Herbert. David Stokes, who was 39 years old, remains the oldest outfield player to have appeared for the club in the Football League.

1950 Nat Lofthouse scored both England's goals on his full international debut in a 2-2 draw with Yugoslavia at Highbury.

NOVEMBER 23rd

1946 Willie Moir and Nat Lofthouse each scored two goals in Bolton's 5-1 home win over Derby County. The Wanderers other goalscorer was Tom Woodward. Bolton, who ended the season four places behind the Rams, also won 3-1 at the Baseball Ground.

1948 Birth of Frank Worthington. He was a very talented footballer and an extrovert character who became a footballing hero at Burnden Park in what was a relatively short career there.
He began his career with Huddersfield Town and after helping them to win the Second Division Championship in 1970, the chance came for him to join Liverpool. A fee of £150,000 had been agreed but a medical examination revealed that he had high blood pressure; Leicester City seized their chance and a cut-price Worthington moved to Filbert Street for £80,000.
His elegant, effective centre-forward play was rewarded with an England call-up and he went on to make eight appearances at full international level. He had scored 72 goals in 210 games for the Foxes when he joined Bolton on loan, as Ian Greaves was searching for that extra quality to lift the Wanderers into the First Division after two near misses. He scored on his debut against Stoke City and was signed permanently for £80,000. He soon rediscovered the style which had made him one of the best strikers in the game and in 1977-78 he helped the Wanderers win the

Second Division title. The following season Worthington *(left)* proved his class as a target man and a finisher.

Although Bolton struggled against relegation, Worthington ended the season with 24 League goals to top the First Division goalscoring charts. His televised goal against Ipswich Town won the Goal of the Season competition.

He had scored 38 goals in 93 games when he moved on to Birmingham City for £150,000. He later had spells with Leeds United, Sunderland, Southampton, Brighton, Tranmere, Preston and Stockport County. One of the game's most gifted and colourful strikers, he made 757 League appearances in a career that saw him approaching his 40th birthday before he left the first-class game.

NOVEMBER 24th

1928 Harold Blackmore netted twice for the Wanderers in a 4-1 home win over West Ham United. Blackmore ended the season as the club's leading scorer with 30 goals in 35 League games.

1995 The club's own web site was founded. The Wanderers were one of the first clubs in England to have their own official site. The ever-growing user base spans right across the world with fans regularly viewing from Canada, the United States, Australia, Japan, South Africa and Scandinavia. The pages contain up-to-the-minute news, latest ticket details, match reports and a host of other information relating to the football club.

NOVEMBER 25th

1916 Joe Smith scored four of Bolton's goals in a 6-2 wartime win over Preston North End.

1933 League leaders Port Vale were beaten 3-0 by the Wanderers with centre-forward Jack Milsom netting all their goals, his last from the penalty-spot.

1950 Bolton beat Sheffield Wednesday 4-3 at Hillsborough with Nat Lofthouse and Harry Webster scoring two goals apiece.

1961 Birth of Paul Comstive. The midfielder began his career with Blackburn Rovers but after just a handful of appearances, he had a loan spell with Rochdale, prior to joining Wigan Athletic. He made 35 League appearances for the Latics before a free transfer took him to Wrexham. He helped them to success in the Welsh Cup in 1986 and was in their European Cup Winners' Cup side that lost to Real Zaragoza the following season. In the summer of 1987 he joined Burnley and it was while at Turf Moor that he produced his best form. Two years later, Phil Neal paid £37,500 to bring him to Burnden Park. One of the club's most versatile players, on New Year's Day 1991 he netted two goals in the 4-1 win over Bournemouth - both of them coming direct from corner-kicks!

Later that year he made a Wembley appearance in the play-off final against Tranmere Rovers but in November 1991 after scoring five goals in 67 games, he joined Chester City.

Though he scored against the Wanderers in 1992-93 he couldn't prevent Chester from being relegated. On leaving the Cestrians, he played non-League football for a number of clubs including Southport, Morecambe and Chorley.

1972 The Wanderers beat Rotherham United 2-1 with a bizarre second goal.

Jim McDonagh, later to make 274 appearances in two spells with Bolton, placed the ball for what he thought was a goal-kick, but the referee shouted play on and Garry Jones ran in to put the ball into the empty net!

1997 The store at the Reebok Stadium opened with an official opening two days later by the Mayor of Bolton and the players. A town centre store on Newport Street opened a week later. In conjunction with the retail outlets, a mail order service was available with a catalogue on request from the Stadium.

NOVEMBER 26th

1917 Birth of Don Howe. He spent his entire League career - which spanned the Second World War - with the Wanderers. He was employed on the groundstaff at Burnden Park until he became old enough to sign professional forms. He made his Bolton debut in October 1936, taking over from Jack Rimmer in a goalless draw at Liverpool. Even when Rimmer returned to the side, a place was found for Howe, who in that 1936-37 season, played in every forward position. Though the arrival of Tom Grosvenor curtailed his league appearances, he later proved his versatility by playing in a variety of positions before settling at wing-half after the war. Howe was also appointed club captain. He went on to score 35 goals in 286 League and Cup games before hanging up his boots. A qualified FA coach, he could have stayed in the game after his retirement and was offered the chance to run the Bolton 'B' side but opted to sever his ties with the game and joined a local firm of paper merchants.

1957 Birth of Tony Henry *(right)*. Beginning his career with Manchester City, he spent three seasons in the club's Central League side before winning a regular midfield spot at Maine Road in 1978. Henry then began to demonstrate his versatility, playing at full-back and in the forward line as well as his preferred midfield. He appeared as a substitute for City in the 1981 FA Cup Final against Spurs but in the close season he moved to Bolton Wanderers, who paid £120,000 for his services. In 1981-82, his first season at Burnden Park, Henry was the club's leading scorer with 13 goals.

He continued in the same vein the following season when he again finished as top scorer with

11 goals, this in spite of leaving a relegation-bound Bolton team in March 1983.

Being short of cash, the Wanderers sold Henry to Oldham Athletic for meagre £20,000. At Boundary Park, he made 190 Second Division appearances before joining Stoke City.

NOVEMBER 27th

1929 Birth of Eric Bell. He began his career with Manchester United in 1949, but his spell at Old Trafford only lasted a month as the Wanderers who had spotted him playing for the RAF, secured his services. When he joined Bolton, Bell was an inside-forward and it was in this position that he made his League debut. Eventually, he was converted to wing-half and midway through the 1952-53 season, won a regular place in the Bolton side. In that season's FA Cup Final against Blackpool he was struck by an injury after only 18 minutes and was dispatched to outside-left from where he managed to score Bolton's third goal. The following season was his most consistent as Bolton finished fifth in Division One. Selected for the England 'B' side against Scotland and for the Football League against the Scottish League, his only goal in Bolton colours came in February 1955 as the Wanderers beat Wolves 6-1. He went on to play in 118 games for the Wanderers before losing his place to Bryan Edwards.

1942 Birth of Peter Thompson *(below)*. After beginning his Football League career with Preston North End, Peter Thompson joined Liverpool for £35,000 in August 1963. There were few more exciting sights in the Football League than to see Peter Thompson running at defenders with the ball at his feet.

In nine seasons at Anfield, he played in just over 400 games, scoring 54 goals. In his first season with the Reds, he won four England Under 23 caps and also played his first full international. He was eventually capped 16 times by England while at Anfield, collecting League and FA Cup honours as well. After losing his place to Steve Heighway, he joined Bolton on loan in December 1973 and made his debut in a 1-0 home win over Sunderland. A month later he signed on a permanent basis, giving the Wanderers an exciting new attacking dimension. A great crowd favourite, he helped the club through one of its most exciting periods but at the end of the club's Second Division Championship-winning season of 1977-78 after which he had played in 132 games, he left the game to run a hotel in the Lake District.

1965 Birth of Scott Sellars. A regular in the Leeds United following his debut in 1983, Scott Sellars had appeared in 76 games for the Elland Road club when Blackburn paid £20,000 for his services in July 1986.

He missed very few games in his six seasons at Ewood Park, making a Wembley appearance as Rovers beat Charlton Athletic in the final of the Full Members Cup. Rovers suffered a number of near misses in the Second Division play-offs before making it into the top flight in 1992. However, that summer he rejoined Leeds United for a fee of £800,000 and shortly afterwards was on his way to Newcastle United.

After helping the Magpies win the First Division Championship, he found his chances in the Premiership limited and in December 1995 he

joined the Wanderers for £750,000. He was on the scoresheet in only his second game for the Wanderers, a spectacular goal though it was 1996-97 when the Bolton supporters saw the best of Scott Sellars *(left)*.

He scored the goal that secured the First Division Championship at Manchester City. Occasionally wearing the captain's armband, injuries hampered his progress during the latter stages of his Bolton career. He had scored 16 goals in 126 games when in July 1999 he joined Huddersfield Town. He later had brief spells with Port Vale and Mansfield Town.

1996 Bolton recorded their best victory in the League Cup when a John McGinlay hat-trick helped them beat Tottenham Hotspur 6-1. The Wanderers' other scorers in a tie watched by a crowd of 18,621 were Gerry Taggert, Nathan Blake and Scott Taylor.

NOVEMBER 28th

1914 Two penalties by Joe Smith helped the Wanderers to a 4-2 home win over bottom of the table Tottenham Hotspur. Despite their lowly position, Spurs won the return match at White Hart Lane by the same scoreline.

1964 Francis Lee and Wyn Davies, both of whom later went on to play for Manchester City, scored two goals apiece in the Wanderers' 4-2 win at Maine Road. Davies scored another brace against the Maine Road club later in the season as the Wanderers completed the 'double' with a 4-0 win.

1998 Neighbours Bury were beaten 4-0 at the Reebok with Icelandic striker Arnar Gunnlaugsson netting twice.

NOVEMBER 29th

1924 John Reid Smith, who had recently been placed on the transfer list after losing his place to Joe Cassidy, netted a hat-trick in the space of 13 minutes as Bolton beat West Ham United 5-0. For the record, Joe Cassidy scored the Wanderers' other two goals!

1969 There were goals galore on a frosty Burnden Park. Queen's Park Rangers took the lead after only 45 seconds but the Wanderers bounced back to win a ten-goal thriller 6-4.

NOVEMBER 30th

1881 Bolton recorded one of their best-ever pre-League results with a 13-1 defeat of Liverpool!

1889 James Cassidy scored four of Bolton's goals in a 7-1 home defeat of Derby County.

1933 Birth of Dennis Stevens. A cousin of the great Duncan Edwards, he made his Bolton debut in a 3-1 defeat at Preston North End in September 1953 though it was the 1955-56 season before he became a regular following the retirement of Harold Hassall.
He continued to make steady progress and won selection for both the Football League and England Under 23s, though a full cap continued to elude him, despite being called into Walter Winterbottom's squad in 1957
A year later, Stevens won an FA Cup winners' medal when the Wanderers beat Manchester United 2-0 at Wembley. His best season for Bolton in terms of goals scored was 1959-60 when Nat Lofthouse was injured, Stevens finding the net 15 times. He had scored 101 goals in 310 games when in March 1962 he was allowed to join Everton for £35,000. Playing in a much deeper role, he helped the Blues win the League Championship in 1962-63 but after scoring 21

goals in 130 games, joined Oldham Athletic before ending his first-class career with Tranmere Rovers.

DECEMBER 1st

1962 Bolton travelled to Villa Park to take on fellow strugglers Aston Villa. Though a close game was anticipated, the Wanderers were beaten 5-0 and if Eddie Hopkinson in the Bolton goal hadn't performed heroics, the defeat could have been much worse. The Wanderers did get their revenge later in the season with Wyn Davies scoring twice in a 4-1 win.

DECEMBER 2nd

1905 Walter White scored two of Bolton's goals in a 4-0 home win over near neighbours Bury. The Wanderers striker also scored the winner in the return at Gigg Lane.

1950 Arsenal, with one of the best away records in the First Division visited Burnden Park. A crowd of 43,684 saw the Wanderers emerge easy winners, 3-0. Bobby Langton (2) and Willie Moir were the Bolton scorers.

DECEMBER 3rd

1910 Billy Hughes, who ended the season as the club's top-scorer with 21 goals in 28 games, netted all Bolton's goals in a 3-1 home win over Huddersfield Town.

1921 Joe Smith was sent-off in Bolton's 3-2 win over Manchester City.
He received his marching orders in the 84th minute following a skirmish with City's Horace Barnes. The Bolton forward was later acquitted from suspension by the FA.

DECEMBER 4th

1890 Birth of Alex Donaldson. He began his career with Ripley Athletic where his exciting performances on the left-wing attracted interest from a number of clubs. After an unsuccessful trial with Sheffield United, he signed for the Wanderers in December 1911. Unable to break into the Bolton side in his first season with the club, he shared the outside-left spot with David Stokes in the years leading up to the First World War. In April 1914 he almost became the first Scotsman to play for England when he was invited to the North v South England trial. Unknown to the FA, Donaldson was born in Barrhead and not in Leicestershire where his family moved to when he was a few months old! During the hostilities, he worked in a munitions factory but when League football resumed in 1919 he began to be dogged by injury including a fractured kneecap in the match against Preston North End in February 1921. On regaining full fitness, he found his place had been taken by Billy Butler and after having scored six goals in 146 games, he left to play for Sunderland. A year later he returned to the north-west with Manchester City before finishing his career with Chorley.

1948 James Bradley and Willie Moir netted two goals each in Bolton's 5-3 win over Preston North End at Burnden Park. The Wanderers' other scorer was Malcolm Barrass.

1978 Birth of Michael Ricketts *(right)*. Beginning his career with Walsall, the well-built striker had a penchant for getting into goalscoring positions and ended the 1999-2000 season as the Saddlers leading goalscorer.
He became unsettled at the Bescot Stadium and in July 2000, Bolton paid £500,000 for his services. He scored on his debut against Preston North End and continued to find the net with

some regularity for the remainder of the 2000-01 season. Though his early chances were mostly limited to substitute appearances, he went on to finish the season as the Wanderers' leading scorer with 24 goals in all competitions. The

following season he exploded onto the Premiership scoring 11 goals by the beginning of December. Though the goals did dry up after the turn of the year, he did score some fantastic goals, the most memorable being a wonderfully executed strike against Arsenal at Highbury. This form led to him being selected by England for the match against Holland.

In 2002-03, he struggled to find his form and it came as no surprise that after having scored 46 goals in 112 games, he joined Middlesbrough for £2.2 million. His only goal in nine outings for Boro came on the final day of the season against the Wanderers, a match Bolton won 2-1 to retain their Premiership status.

DECEMBER 5th

1885 Bolton beat the once mighty Blackburn Olympic 11-2 in a third round Lancashire Cup tie.

1973 Due to the power strike, the Wanderers entertained FA Cup holders Sunderland on a midweek afternoon. A crowd of just 8,425, the lowest of the season - saw Neil Whatmore score the only goal of the game to give the Wanderers two valuable points.

DECEMBER 6th

1947 Nat Lofthouse married his bride Alma at 11 o'clock in the morning - four hours later he was trotting out at Burnden Park for a First Division match against Wolverhampton Wanderers which Bolton won 3-2 with Nat scoring two of the goals!

1952 Harold Hassall had just been placed on the transfer list at his own request but it didn't stop him scoring two of Bolton's goals in a 4-2 home win over Newcastle United. Wanderers' other scorers were Willie Moir and Nat Lofthouse.

DECEMBER 7th

1886 Birth of George Lillycrop. After playing his early football in his native north-east with South Shields Albion and North Shields Athletic, he joined Barnsley. He was the Oakwell club's leading scorer in each of his five seasons with the club and a member of the team that reached the FA Cup Final in 1910. Two years later he did win an FA Cup winners' medal and in 1912-13 he scored 22 goals for the Tykes. In August 1913, the Wanderers paid a club record fee of £1,300 to bring him to Burnden Park. He missed just one game in his first season with the Whites and scored 25 goals in 40 games to top the club's scoring charts. The following season, he began by scoring six goals in seven games but then lost his place through injury to Frank Roberts. Sadly the war intervened and Lillycrop, who had scored 32 goals in 55 games returned to play for South Shields once the hostilities had ended. In 1922 he became their trainer and then had spells in a similar capacity with Gateshead and Crewe.

1889 Davie Weir and Kenny Davenport scored two goals apiece as the Wanderers beat West Bromwich Albion 7-0. The club's other scorers were Brogan, Bullough and Cassidy. The win was sweet revenge for the Wanderers who had lost 6-3 at the Hawthorns the previous month.

1907 Albert Shepherd scored all of Bolton's goals in a 3-1 home defeat of Woolwich Arsenal.

DECEMBER 8th

1917 Birth of Tom Woodward. The Horwich-born winger was playing local football for Westhoughton club, White Horse Temperance, when the Wanderers signed him in January 1935. After a year playing in the club's reserve team, the 18-year-old Woodward made his League debut for the Wanderers in a 2-1 defeat by Stoke but it was then another two years before he appeared in the club's first team again.

In the years leading up to the Second World War, he shared the right-wing duties with Albert Geldard but in 1944-45 was ever-present as Bolton won the Football League (North) Cup and the North v South Final. When League football resumed in 1946, Woodward was the club's first-choice right-winger, going on to score 19 goals in 169 League and Cup games before a £7,500 transfer took him to Middlesbrough. His first game for his new club was against the Wanderers at Burnden Park and he scored one of Middlesbrough's goals in a 2-1 win for the north-east club. He later returned to the north-west to play for Wigan Athletic.

DECEMBER 9th

1885 Birth of Marshall McEwan. The Scottish winger began his first-class career with Blackpool and had made 45 appearances for the Bloomfield Road club when Bolton signed him in February 1905.

His only appearance for the Wanderers in their promotion-winning season of 1904-05 came in a 2-0 home win over Bradford City.

However, after just one game of the following season, McEwan found himself in favour and over the next five campaigns, missed very few matches. Though he wasn't a prolific scorer, netting just 15 goals in 164 League and Cup games, his wing-play created many goalscoring opportunities for the likes of Albert Shepherd and Walter White. After helping the Wanderers win promotion to the First Division in 1908-09, McEwan joined Chelsea midway through the club's first season back in the top flight as Bolton's finances necessitated such a sale. On leaving Stamford Bridge, McEwan played for Irish club Linfield before ending his career with non-League Fleetwood.

1916 The Wanderers beat Manchester United 5-1 in a wartime league fixture with Tom Buchan and Joe Smith netting two goals apiece.

1922 David Jack scored all Bolton's goals in a 3-0 home win over West Bromwich Albion.

DECEMBER 10th

1898 Birth of Fred Kean. He made his name with his home-town club, Sheffield Wednesday, having previously spent a short time with Portsmouth. He joined the Owls in the summer of 1920, playing initially as an inside-forward before switching to his more familiar wing-half position. He spent six seasons in the Hillsborough club's Second Division side before they won the title in 1925-26. Though he was the club captain, he soon lost his position once the club were in the top flight and in September 1928, Bolton paid £5,600 to bring the England international to Burnden Park. Whilst with the Wanderers, he won a further two caps to take his total to nine and was a member of the Bolton side that beat Portsmouth in the 1929 FA Cup Final.

He went on to appear in 89 games, his only goal for the club coming in a 4-1 defeat of West Ham United in November 1928. On leaving the Wanderers, he joined Luton Town before ending his playing days with non-League Sutton Town.

1904 Walter White netted his third hat-trick of the season in just his 13th appearance as Bolton beat Doncaster Rovers 4-0 at Belle Vue.

1921 Frank Roberts and David Jack both netted twice in Wanderers' 5-0 defeat of Manchester City. Joe Smith completed the rout for the rampant Whites.

1955 Despite Birmingham City sitting three places above the Wanderers in the League, Bolton ran out winners 6-0 with Nat Lofthouse netting four of the club's goals.

1991 Bolton's lowest attendance for a first-class game, 1,507, turned out to watch the Autoglass Trophy game with Rochdale. The Wanderers won 4-1 with David Reeves netting a hat-trick.

DECEMBER 11th

1938 Birth of Charlie Wright. The Glasgow-born goalkeeper began his career with Rangers, but unable to make the break through into the first team, joined Workington. In 1960 he gained three international caps for Hong Kong while on National Service and in the match against Peru he saved a penalty. Later he was voted Hong Kong Player of the Year. When he returned to these shores, he played for Grimsby Town and Charlton Athletic before in the summer of 1971, joining the Wanderers. After making his debut in a 2-2 draw at Oldham Athletic, he went on to be ever-present, helping Bolton register their best goals against record since 1925. Wright had a great sense of humour and continually chatted to spectators behind the goal. In 1972-73 he won a Third Division Championship medal with the Whites, but had to retire a year later through a persistent back injury after appearing in 109 games. After managing York City, he returned to Burnden Park, initially as reserve team coach before following John McGovern's departure he was put in temporary charge of the team. Within three weeks he had led the Trotters to five consecutive victories. In February 1985 he was named as the Wanderers' new manager but incredibly the club only won one of their next 10 games. Though they eventually avoided relegation, he left the club by mutual consent in December 1985, ending his Bolton career in exactly the opposite way to which it had started with five consecutive defeats!

1950 Birth of Garry Jones. He turned down offers from both Manchester City and Manchester United before joining the Wanderers. His first game in

Bolton colours was in a 3-0 defeat at Huddersfield Town in March 1969, although it was the 1970-71 season before he began to establish himself in the Wanderers' side. On 5th October 1971, Garry Jones *(below)* hit the headlines when he scored a hat-trick in a 3-0 League Cup win over Manchester City. The following season, he helped Bolton win the Third Division Championship when he netted 20 League and Cup goals, his best season in terms of goals scored. After these he suffered with a spate of niggling injuries and a loss of form but after a loan spell with Sheffield United, he returned to

Burnden Park to be the club's joint-top scorer in 1974-75 with 13 goals.

Following the signing of Frank Worthington, Jones, who had scored 55 goals in 247 League and Cup matches, joined Blackpool before ending his League career with Hereford United.

1971 The Wanderers were drawn away to local non-League side Rossendale United, who because their ground lacked the necessary facilities to host the second round FA Cup game, switched the tie to Gigg Lane.

The minnows took a shock lead but a Roy Greaves' hat-trick helped Bolton to a 4-1 win.

2001 A patched-up Bolton side travelled to White Hart Lane for a fifth round League Cup tie against Tottenham Hotspur. The home side won 6-0 to inflict Wanderers' equal heaviest League Cup defeat and their highest away from home.

DECEMBER 12th

1885 Birth of Albert Shepherd. The Bolton-born forward made his debut in November 1904 for his home-town club in a 5-1 home win over Gainsborough Trinity. He went on to score 15 goals in 24 League games as the Wanderers won promotion to the First Division. In 1905-06, Shepherd was the club's top scorer with 26 goals in 31 games including four against Nottingham Forest (Home 6-0) and Sunderland (Home 6-2). That form earned him international recognition and in April 1906 he scored England's goal in a 2-1 defeat by Scotland.

He was Bolton's leading scorer again in 1906-07 with 19 goals including a hat-trick in a 6-1 home win over Sheffield United.

Though the Wanderers were relegated in 1907-08, Shepherd continued to find the net, scoring 25 goals in 29 League games including hat-tricks against Bury (Home 3-6), Woolwich Arsenal (Home 3-1) and Newcastle United (Home 4-0).

The Magpies were the club that Shepherd joined after the Wanderers had made a poor start to the 1908-09 season. He had scored 90 goals in 123 games for Bolton and continued his prolific scoring for Newcastle, topping their charts for the next three seasons and scoring both goals in their 1910 FA Cup Final victory over Barnsley.

1907 Birth of George T. Taylor. Known to Bolton fans of the 1930s as 'GT' so as not to confuse him with the other George Taylor, he began his League career with First Division Notts County. The Meadow Lane club were relegated in 1926 but Taylor remained with them even though they suffered another relegation four seasons later. He helped County win promotion back to the Second Division in 1932 but in December 1933, after 265 League appearances for County, he joined the Wanderers for a fee of £3,500. He went straight into the Bolton side in his usual right-wing role, helping the club win promotion to the First Division and to the 1935 FA Cup semi-finals. In October 1936, Taylor ended a run of 290 first-class games (of which 158 were for Notts County and 132 for Bolton) when he was injured. He had scored 29 goals in 170 games when he left Burnden Park to play for Coventry City where he later ended his career.

1925 Joe and John Reid Smith were at it again, both scoring twice in a 6-1 home win over Huddersfield Town - the eventual League Champions! The club's other scorers were Billy Butler and David Jack.

1948 Birth of Colin Todd *(right)*. An elegant and poised player, he developed a great partnership with Roy McFarland at the heart of the Derby County defence which was later transferred into the England team.

Todd won two League Championship medals with the Rams and in 1974-75 was voted PFA Footballer of the Year. He later helped

Birmingham City win promotion to the First Division and Oxford United to the Third Division Championship. After managing Whitley Bay, he became Bruce Rioch's assistant at Middlesbrough before succeeding him as manager. After resigning he teamed up with Rioch again, this time at Bolton Wanderers. He played an important role in the club's promotion to the Premier League and the Wanderers' Cup exploits which culminated in them reaching the 1995 League Cup Final at Wembley.

When Rioch left for Arsenal, Todd stayed as assistant to newly appointed boss Roy McFarland, but when he was dismissed in January 1996, Todd took over the reins. Though he couldn't prevent the Whites from being relegated, he turned things round the following season. The 1996-97 campaign saw the Wanderers run away with the First Division Championship but the Premiership proved just too much the following season when Bolton were relegated on the final day, on goal difference. Todd took the Whites to the play-offs in 1998-99 only to lose in the final to Watford. The start of the following term saw them struggle at the wrong end of the table and in September 1999 he parted company with the club. After spells managing Swindon Town and Derby County, he is now at Bradford City as new manager Bryan Robson's assistant.

DECEMBER 13th

1890 Alec Barbour netted a hat-trick in Bolton's 6-0 home defeat of Accrington.

1911 The Wanderers won the Lancashire Cup beating Burnley 4-1 in the final played at Turf Moor.

DECEMBER 14th

1881 The Wanderers recorded another high-scoring victory in their pre-League days with a 12-0 defeat of Macclesfield.

1929 Willie Cook scored his first hat-trick for the Wanderers in the 4-1 home win over West Ham United.

DECEMBER 15th

1888 Sunderland visited Pikes Lane for a friendly match but were beaten 10-0 with James Brogan netting five of the Wanderers' goals.

1894 James Henderson scored three of Bolton's goals in a 6-0 defeat of Wolverhampton Wanderers.

1923 Joe Smith and David Jack netted two goals apiece as the Wanderers beat Notts County 7-1.

1924 Birth of Malcolm Barrass. The son of a former professional, his father Matt Barrass having played for Blackpool, Sheffield Wednesday and Manchester City. Having turned down an approach from Wolves, he signed for Bolton in November 1944 and during the wartime competition, played for the Wanderers at centre-forward, scoring 30 goals in 68 games. His performances led to him playing for England in the Victory international against Wales at the Hawthorns. When League football resumed in 1946, he showed his versatility by playing in a number of positions and in one game against Manchester City in November 1948 he wore the No. 9 shirt and scored four goals in a 5-1 win. Eventually he reverted to centre-half and that was the position in which he appeared against Blackpool in the 1953 FA Cup Final. After 12 years with the Wanderers in which he scored 27 goals in 357 League and Cup games, he left Burnden Park to play for Sheffield United in September 1956. Barrass later became player-manager of then non-league Wigan Athletic. He eventually ended his playing days in the Southern League with Nuneaton Borough.

DECEMBER 16th

1939 The Wanderers entertained the Royal (Bolton) Artillery in front of a Burnden Park crowd of 1,509. It was virtually a current Bolton XI v Old Bolton XI and the fans certainly got their money's worth as the teams fought out a 3-3 draw.

DECEMBER 17th

1932 Sheffield Wednesday suffered only their second defeat of the season when Jack Milsom scored all Bolton's goals in a 3-0 win for the Trotters.

1955 Nat Lofthouse scored a second successive hat-trick in a 4-0 home win over Chelsea.

DECEMBER 18th

1909 Herbert Baverstock converted two penalties for the Wanderers in a 3-1 home win over local rivals Preston North End - Bolton's other scorer was Billy Hughes.

DECEMBER 19th

1936 Bolton beat the league leaders Charlton Athletic 2-1 with Jack Milsom and Ray Westwood the scorers. Jack Milsom also had the misfortune to miss a penalty in each half!

DECEMBER 20th

1913 Birth of Jack Atkinson. Spotted by the Wanderers whilst playing for his local club Washington Colliery, he graduated through the club's Lancashire Combination and Central League sides before making his first team debut in a 2-2 home draw against West Bromwich Albion in April 1933. Over the six seasons leading up to the Second World War, the powerful centre-half was the defensive kingpin of the Bolton side and was unlucky not to win international honours. Sadly, many of his best years were lost to the war, during which he 'guested' for Blackpool and Everton as well as the Wanderers. After the hostilities had ended, Atkinson managed only one full season of League football before losing his place at the heart of the defence to Lol Hamlett. Atkinson, who had scored five goals in 263 games joined New Brighton as player-manager.

1960 Birth of Brian Borrows. He began his career with Everton and after replacing Gary Stevens, held his place in the Blues' side until a 5-0 defeat in the Merseyside derby, a game which turned out to be his last appearance for the Goodison club. In March 1983 he joined Bolton, initially on loan and took up a midfield position in the club's desperate and sadly unsuccessful bid to remain in Division Two. A £6,000 fee was eventually agreed with Everton and the following season, he made the right-back spot his own. He became a model of consistency and during the 1984-85 season he was easily Bolton's best player as they struggled to avoid relegation to the League's basement. In June 1985 having appeared in 110 games for the Wanderers, he returned to the top flight with Coventry City, who paid £80,000 for the full-backs services. Though he had to sit out the 1987 FA Cup Final when the Sky Blues beat Spurs 3-2, because of injury, he gave the Highfield Road club great service. He went on to appear in 488 League and Cup games before ending his long first-class career with Swindon Town.

DECEMBER 21st

1889 Having beaten Blackburn Rovers 3-2 at home just a couple of weeks earlier, the Wanderers travelled to Leamington Street expecting a close game. Rovers though were outstanding and ran out winners 7-1 with James Cassidy, recently signed from Glasgow Hibernians scoring Bolton's goal.

1918 The Wanderers suffered an identical scoreline defeat at Stoke - the Potters, who were pushing hard for the final wartime Championship, scored the majority of their goals in the last ten minutes of the game.

DECEMBER 22nd

1888 Davie Weir netted Bolton's first hat-trick in the Football League as the Wanderers beat Accrington 4-1.

1973 Birth of Alan Thompson *(below)*. He began his career with Newcastle United but it was almost nipped in the bud when he broke his neck in a car crash, an injury which sidelined him for nearly 12 months before he courageously recovered. He appeared in 20 first team games for the Magpies before joining the Wanderers for a fee of £250,000 in the summer of 1993. He made his Bolton debut in a goalless draw at Grimsby Town and scored his first goal for the club in the televised 4-3 victory over Nottingham Forest.

Thompson scored a number of memorable goals during the 1994-95 season, none more so than the strike in the Coca Cola Cup Final against Liverpool at Wembley. On the opening day of the following season, Thompson scored the Wanderers' first Premiership goal in a 3-2 defeat at Wimbledon, though it was to be his only League goal of a campaign in which he suffered a loss of form. He also scored the first goal at the Reebok Stadium- netting a penalty for Bolton against Spurs in September 1997. He had scored 42 goals in 198 games for the Wanderers when his all-action displays prompted Aston Villa to pay £4.5 million for his services in the summer of 1998. He had made 58 appearances for the Midlands club when in September 2000 he was sold to Martin O'Neill's Celtic for £2.7 million. A dead-ball expert of some repute, he has helped the Bhoys win numerous Scottish Cup and League Championship honours and having won England Under 21 honours, can't be far away from winning full international honours.

1994 Bolton's last game in the group stages of the Anglo-Italian Cup saw them draw 1-1 at Ascoli with Mark Seagraves scoring the Wanderers' goal. The club were undefeated, winning three and drawing three of their six games, but it was Notts County who went through to the final.

DECEMBER 23rd

1899 Top-of-the-table Bolton travelled to Burton Swifts and Laurie Bell, who was to net four goals against the Swifts on the final day of the season to secure promotion, netted twice in a 5-2 win for the Wanderers.

2001 Despite taking the lead against Chelsea at Stamford Bridge after only three minutes through Kevin Nolan, the Wanderers went down 5-1 - their heaviest defeat of the season.

DECEMBER 24th

1910 Birmingham City were beaten 5-1 with Wanderers' prolific marksman Billy Hughes netting his third hat-trick of the campaign.

1927 A special train with ten coaches was laid on for Bolton fans to travel to Bramall Lane for the match with Sheffield United but unfortunately only 13 people decided to make the journey. They missed a seven-goal thriller - David Jack netting a hat-trick in a 4-3 defeat for the Wanderers.

DECEMBER 25th

1893 The club played its first-ever Christmas Day League game against Sheffield Wednesday with James Cassidy scoring Bolton's goal in a 1-1 draw.

1899 Birth of Billy Wright. The son of Jocky Wright, he worked his way up through the ranks before making his Bolton debut in a 2-0 defeat at Manchester City in November 1922. He then spent the next four seasons in which the Wanderers won the FA Cup twice, in the reserves when he appeared to have made his breakthrough against Huddersfield Town on the final day of the 1926-27 season - Wright netted a hat-trick in a 4-0 win. Though he did play more often in the first team the following season, all his appearances were at half-back!
Though he began to appear more regularly, the Wanderers were now a struggling team and in May 1933 after 11 seasons with the club, Wright, who had scored 22 goals in 159 games, was allowed to join Reading. Here he served under Joe Smith and Billy Butler, both former Wanderers' leading Reading close to promotion from the Third Division (South) on a number of occasions.

1903 Sam Marsh netted his second hat-trick of the season as the Wanderers defeated Barnsley 5-1.

1919 Local rivals Preston North End were beaten 4-1 with the versatile Tom Buchan scoring a hat-trick.

1920 Joe Smith scored four of Bolton's goals in a 6-2 win over Sunderland. This took his tally to 22 and a place at the head of the First Division's scoring charts.

1926 Billy Butler completed his hat-trick in the final minute of Bolton's 3-1 win over Derby County from the penalty-spot.

1952 The Wanderers fought back well in the 6-4 home defeat at the hands of Arsenal. With just five minutes left, they trailed 6-2 but two late goals reduced the arrears before Bobby Langton had a penalty saved by the Gunners', Welsh international keeper, Jack Kelsey!

DECEMBER 26th

1882 In the club's pre-League days with the Wanderers losing 3-1 to Nottingham Forest, the referee gave some indifferent decisions which resulted in the Forest players leaving the field and refusing to return!

1899 Jimmy Hanson netted three of Bolton's goals in a 6-1 home win over Barnsley.

1914 Bolton recorded their biggest-ever away win in the Football League, beating Aston Villa 7-1 at Villa Park. Joe Smith netted four of the Wanderers' goals with Frank Roberts (2) and Harold Hilton the other scorers.

1923 Bolton completed the 'double' over West Bromwich Albion, having beaten them 2-0 at Burnden Park, they came away from the Hawthorns with a 5-0 victory - David Jack netting his second hat-trick of the season.

1924 In the game against Nottingham Forest at the City Ground, the home side were awarded a penalty. But no Forest player wanted to take the spot-kick, so the game was held up for over five minutes. Forest's normal penalty-taker Harold Martin had left the field injured and he returned to take the kick, which he converted, sending Pym the wrong way to produce a 1-1 draw.

1928 Harold Blackmore netted his third hat-trick of the season - he went on to score 30 goals in 35 games - as Bolton beat Birmingham 6-2.

DECEMBER 27th

1915 Birth of Stan Hanson. Famed for his long-distance kicking, he had amateur experience with both Liverpool and Southport before turning down overtures from Aston Villa and signing for the Wanderers. He made is Bolton debut in a 2-0 defeat at Huddersfield Town in September 1936 but it wasn't until the 1938-39 season that he established himself as the club's first-choice custodian. During the Second World War he appeared for the Eighth Army in their 4-2 win over Yugoslavia. When League football resumed in 1946-47, Hanson was ever-present and missed very few games over the next nine seasons, being ever-present in 1950-51 and 1952-53. His consistency was rewarded when in 1950 he toured Canada with an FA party.
Hanson was in the Bolton goal in the 'Matthews Final' in 1953 when the Wanderers lost 4-3 to Blackpool. He stayed with the Wanderers until 1955, his 40th year, when after 423 appearances, he was given a free transfer. He then played part-time for Rhyl before running the Burnden Post Office opposite the ground.

1948 Willie Moir netted his second four-goal haul of the season as Bolton beat Sheffield United 6-1 in front of a Burnden Park crowd of 42,630.

1975 One of the best goals ever scored by a Bolton player. Sam Allardyce's headed equaliser against league leaders Sunderland was a classic. He rose between Joe Bolton and Jack Ashurst to power the ball past Jim Montgomery. This spurred the Wanderers on and John Byrom netted the winner in what was his first game back after injury.

DECEMBER 28th

1889 The Wanderers beat Burnley 6-3 at Pikes Lane. Both sides had protested to the referee over the rock hard ground, but he insisted the game went ahead. The official later reported the club's disapproval of the conditions and the Football League ordered the game to be replayed at the end of the season. For the record, the replayed game ended all-square at 2-2.

1929 Harold Blackmore netted four of Bolton's goals in a 5-0 demolition of Everton, who ended the season bottom of Division One and were relegated.

1931 Birth of Derek Hennin. Having previously played for Prescot Cables, the England youth international made his debut for the Wanderers in March 1954 as a replacement for the injured Johnny Wheeler in a 3-2 defeat at Tottenham Hotspur. He held his place in the Bolton side for the remaining 11 games of the season as the Whites ended the campaign in fifth place in Division One. Hennin then returned to the reserves and helped them win the Central League title in 1954-55.
It wasn't until Wheeler left to join Liverpool in 1957 that Hennin established himself as a first team regular and over the next five seasons, appeared in 183 games for the club. In April

1958, the versatile Hennin turned out as an emergency centre-forward for the Wanderers' game at home to Aston Villa. He scored a hat-trick in a 4-0 win for Bolton with one of his goals coming from the penalty-spot. He picked up an FA Cup winners' medal in 1958 but after losing his first team place to Graham Stanley, he left Burnden Park in 1962 to join Chester. He later played non-League football for Wigan Athletic.

1944 Birth of Gordon Taylor. Now Chief Executive of the PFA, he joined the Wanderers on amateur forms, turning professional in January 1962 after six months as an apprentice at Burnden Park. He made his League debut in a 4-0 defeat against Wolverhampton Wanderers at Molineux in March 1963, though it was midway through the following season before he won a regular place in the side. Though he made his name on the left-wing, Taylor *(below)* was also able to play on either flank.

An ever-present in 1964-65 when the club finished third in Division Two, Taylor went on to score 46 goals in 286 games before joining Birmingham City for a fee of £18,000 in December 1970. He helped the Blues win promotion from Division Two in 1971-72 and was a member of the side in two FA Cup semi-finals in 1972 and 1975. In March 1976 after having scored 10 goals in 203 games, he returned to the north-west to play for Blackburn Rovers. He spent just over two years at Ewood Park, a season with the Vancouver Whitecaps in the NASL and then two full seasons with Bury before taking a job with the PFA on a full-time basis after serving on the committee during his playing days at Gigg Lane.

1959   The Wanderers became the first team to win under the Molineux floodlights. Wolves, who had beaten a number of Europe's top teams, went down 1-0 to a Brian Birch goal.

DECEMBER 29th

1883   Irwell Springs were beaten 8-1 in an FA Cup game with Davenport, Fallon and Steel all netting two goals apiece. The prolific Bob Struthers and an own goal made up Wanderers' eight goals.

1890   James McNee netted a hat-trick as Bolton beat Wolverhampton Wanderers 6-0. The Molineux club finished the season in fourth place, one ahead of the Wanderers.

1969   Bolton went a goal down after just 45 seconds of their home game against Queen's Park Rangers but in a 10-goal thriller, they fought back to win 6-4 with goals from John Manning (2), John Byrom (2), Gordon Taylor and Terry Wharton.

2001   Down to nine men for over two-thirds of the game after the dismissal of Dean Holdsworth and Paul Warhurst, the Wanderers fought back from

2-0 down to draw 2-2 with Leicester City - Michael Ricketts scoring a last minute equaliser.

DECEMBER 30th

1899   Laurie Bell scored three of the Wanderers' goals in a 7-0 beating of Loughborough Town.

1933   Bolton beat West Ham United 5-1 with Jack Milsom netting four of their goals. Wanderers' other scorer was Ray Westwood.

DECEMBER 31st

1910   Leicester Fosse, who had beaten the Wanderers 5-0 earlier in the season were on the receiving end of a 6-2 drubbing as centre-forward Billy Hughes netted his fourth hat-trick of the season.

1944   Birth of Dave Lennard. He made his Bolton debut in April 1963 in a 2-2 draw at Birmingham City and remained in the side for a seven-game spell for the injured Graham Stanley. In 1963-64, Lennard won the right-half position outright but he along with a number of other youngsters in the Bolton side, was unable to prevent their relegation to Division Two. He then lost his place to Dave Hatton but found a way back into the side at inside-left following an injury to Freddie Hill. Though he was a good squad member, his first team appearances became few and far between and in July 1969 after scoring three goals in 126 games, he joined Halifax Town. He was ever-present for the Shaymen in 1971-72 when they just missed out on promotion to Division Two. Leaving to join Blackpool, he never really established himself with the Seasiders and was soon on the move again, this time to Cambridge United who were experiencing their first season of Third Division football. He later had spells with Chester and Stockport County before ending his first-class career with Bournemouth.

2001 PLAY-OFF FINAL
Nat Lofthouse and Sam Allardyce celebrate promotion to the Premiership.